To Amanda Urban,
the good shepherd

BY THE

PEOPLE

BY THE
PEOPLE

Rebuilding Liberty
Without Permission

CHARLES
MURRAY

CROWN
FORUM
NEW YORK

Copyright © 2015 by Cox and Murray, Inc.

All rights reserved.
Published in the United States by Crown Forum,
an imprint of the Crown Publishing Group,
a division of Penguin Random House LLC, New York.
www.crownpublishing.com

CROWN FORUM with colophon is a registered trademark
of Penguin Random House LLC.

Originally published in hardcover in the United States by Crown Forum,
an imprint of the Crown Publishing Group, a division of
Penguin Random House LLC, New York, in 2015.

Library of Congress Cataloging-in-Publication data is available upon request.

ISBN 978-0-385-34653-5
eBook ISBN 978-0-385-34652-8

Illustrations by Joe LeMonnier
Cover design by M80

First Paperback Edition

Contents

I think that the species of oppression by which democratic nations are menaced is unlike anything that ever before existed in the world. . . .

The supreme power then extends its arm over the whole community. It covers the surface of society with a network of small, complicated rules, minute and uniform, through which the most original minds and the most energetic characters cannot penetrate to rise above the crowd. The will of man is not shattered, but softened, bent, and guided; men are seldom forced by it to act, but they are constantly restrained from acting. Such a power does not destroy, but it prevents existence; it does not tyrannize, but it compresses, enervates, extinguishes, and stupefies a people, till each nation is reduced to be nothing better than a flock of timid and industrious animals, of which the government is the shepherd.

—ALEXIS DE TOCQUEVILLE, *Democracy in America*

The power which a multiple millionaire, who may be my neighbour and perhaps my employer, has over me is very much less than that which the smallest functionaire possesses who wields the coercive power of the state, and on whose discretion it depends whether and how I am to be allowed to live or to work.

—FRIEDRICH VON HAYEK, *The Road to Serfdom*

A Note on Presentation

By the People takes on topics that are esoteric in some cases and in all cases have been the subject of extensive and contentious scholarship. How does one deal with the complexities and still present the material in a way that an intelligent but not obsessive reader can be asked to follow? I use my three favorite measures: For those who want to dig deeper, I give short reading lists of the books I have found most useful. Boxed text introduces related issues that are of interest but not essential. Endnotes expand upon points that are stated briefly in the main text. You can identify which endnotes contain additional material by the brackets flanking their superscripted call-out numbers.

Regarding singular third-person pronouns, I continue to think that "his or her" and "he or she" are stylistically barbaric, and that for male authors to default to "her" and "she" is too precious by half. So I continue to promote a solution I have advocated for many years: Unless there is an obvious reason not to, use the gender of the author or, in a co-written text, the gender of the principal author. I use the masculine third-person singular throughout.

Introduction

The twin propositions of this book are that we are at the end of the American project as the founders intended it, but that opportunities are opening for preserving the best qualities of the American project in a new incarnation.

By *the American project* I mean the continuing effort, begun with the founding, to demonstrate that human beings can be left free as individuals, families, and communities to live their lives as they see fit as long as they accord the same freedom to everyone else, with government safeguarding a peaceful setting for those endeavors but otherwise standing aside.

When I say that we are at the end of the American project as the founders intended it, I mean that only remnants remain, and they are reserved for a lucky few. The largest remnant is that able, industrious people can still get ahead in today's America regardless of their origins. That's good, but the people who become successful as measured by the metrics of money, power, and celebrity make up a small minority of the whole: an elite.

That's exactly what the American project was *not* supposed to be. America at its founding broke with history. Liberty and the pursuit of happiness were no longer to be privileges for a few but the unalienable rights of all. All Americans, high and low, were to be left free to live their lives as they saw fit.

That was the essence of the American promise. For the first century and a half, the nation kept that promise for white Americans. For the last seventy-five of those years, the nation began to make good on it for black Americans. Then the promise was intermingled with other priorities and other agendas. What made America unique first blurred, then faded, and is now almost gone. Part I describes how it happened and my reasons for concluding that the normal political process will not rescue us.

The second proposition of *By the People* is that opportunities are opening for preserving the best qualities of the American project in a new incarnation. This hopeful proposition takes two forms. The center of my attention in Part II is how to restore important aspects of American freedom based on this truth: The federal government is genuinely powerful, as it should be, when it comes to tasks such as defending the nation. But when it comes to micromanaging the lives of more than 300 million people, government is the Wizard of Oz: fearsome when its booming voice is directed against any single target, but, when the curtain is pulled aside, revealed as impotent to impose its will in the face of widespread refusal to comply with its rules. Part II describes practical strategies for taking advantage of this weakness, using the resources of the private sector to nullify rules that arbitrarily and capriciously interfere with ordinary people trying to live their lives as they see fit.

Part III takes up a more indefinite but potentially transforming set of possibilities. We are at a peculiarly propitious moment for reshaping the polity. The reasons range from cultural to demographic to fiscal. I believe the openings created by these conditions have the potential to break today's political logjam, opening the way for reforms that are impossible now.

By the People is written for people who are devoted to limited government. In today's terminology, that includes classical liberals, libertarians, and many conservatives.

As I got into the book, I discovered that I had to find a label less cumbersome than "people who are devoted to limited government" yet one that almost all of us can live with. My first impulse was to call us *Jeffersonians*, but Jefferson was well to the libertarian side of the spectrum, and I wanted to include advocates of limited government who think of themselves as conservatives. I settled on *Madisonians* instead. It was Madison who, more than any other individual, midwifed the Constitution and the Bill of Rights. It was his Constitution that preserved limited government for the first century and a half of America's existence. Classical liberals, libertarians, and conservatives who love limited government disagree on many things, but not, I think, on this: If we could restore limited government as Madison understood it, all of our agendas would be largely fulfilled.

Because Madisonians are my primary audience, I assume that my readers do not need to be persuaded of the rightness of our cause. Shelves of books have made the theoretical and empirical cases for liberty. *By the People* focuses on how to rebuild liberty, not on why.

Everyone else is invited to listen in. Progressives who hope America will become like Europe won't like *By the People*—I'm highly critical of Wilsonian progressivism. But millions of others who think of themselves as moderate liberals are as attached to America's heritage as Madisonians are—holding different policy preferences, of course, but ones that fall within our common vision of what has made America exceptional. I assure such readers that they will find here no cheap shots about their points of view. I hope they will enjoy observing a different way of looking at the world. I dare to think they will find a lot to agree with in my description of the problems, and maybe even in some of my solutions.

CHARLES MURRAY
Burkittsville, Maryland
December 16, 2014

THE PARADOX

In the United States at this time Liberalism is not only the dominant but even the sole intellectual tradition. For it is the plain fact that nowadays there are no conservative or reactionary ideas in general circulation. . . . The conservative impulse and the reactionary impulse do not, with some isolated and some ecclesiastical exceptions, express themselves in ideas but only in action or in irritable mental gestures which seek to resemble ideas.

—LIONEL TRILLING, *The Liberal Imagination* (1950)

AT THE MIDDLE of the twentieth century, the concept of limited government seemed moribund. Americans still called their nation the "land of the free," but hardly anything was said about the dream of the founders, in which "the sum of good government," as Thomas Jefferson expressed it in his first inaugural address, is one that "shall restrain men from injuring one another [and] shall leave them otherwise free to regulate their own pursuits of industry and improvement." As of 1950, hardly anyone was talking about Madisonian ideals in academia, the broadcast media, newspapers, popular or intellectual magazines, or the halls of Congress.

For the next decade, liberalism expanded its influence even among Republicans. Dwight Eisenhower, who didn't identify himself as a Republican until the late 1940s and never identified himself as a conservative, won the White House as a "modern Republican," which he defined as "conservative when it comes to money and liberal when it comes to human beings."[1] By the 1960 election, Arthur Krock could write in the *New York Times* that "when the national platforms and candidates of 1960 have been chosen, the American voters will find it difficult to detect a major ideological difference between the two major parties."[2]

Another *New York Times* journalist, Charles Frankel, captured the spirit of 1960 in an article entitled "A Liberal Is a Liberal Is a Liberal—": "The word [liberal]," he wrote, "apparently designates an attitude of mind and an outlook on the world which relatively few Americans are willing to say unequivocally that they do not share." He pointed out that Herbert Hoover, Dwight Eisenhower, and Richard Nixon had each "had kind words to say about 'liberalism' and . . . would bridle if he were called 'anti-liberal.' "[3]

The Resurgence of Madisonian Thought

Just four years later, the Republican Party nominated Barry Goldwater, a full-fledged Madisonian, for president of the United States. Beneath the radar screen of the *New York Times* and the rest of the mainstream media, Madisonian thought had been making a comeback.

It began in the 1930s, even as the New Deal was triumphant in the United States, with Ludwig von Mises and Friedrich Hayek, leaders of the Austrian School of economics. Their ideas entered the public conversation in 1944 with Hayek's brilliant polemic *The Road to Serfdom*. In 1947, two young economists, Milton Friedman and George Stigler, were part of a conference organized by Hayek that led to the formation of the Mont Pelerin Society. In 1951, William F. Buckley Jr. published *God and Man at Yale*. In 1955, Buckley founded the *National Review*.[4] In 1957, Ayn Rand published *Atlas Shrugged*. In 1960, Sen. Barry Goldwater published *Conscience of a Conservative*. In 1962, Milton Friedman published *Capitalism and Freedom*.

These events were outcroppings of a larger movement by which an older generation of Republicans rediscovered the founders' vision of a free society and the new generation encountered it for the first time. They believed passionately, labored tirelessly, and turned out the Goldwater vote in the primaries. And so to the dismay of the Republican establishment, Barry Goldwater defeated the quintessential modern Republican, Nelson Rockefeller, for the 1964 presidential nomination.

Goldwater then lost to Lyndon Johnson by a landslide. It was no surprise. The mood of the country after John F. Kennedy's assassination would have produced a Johnson landslide against any Republican candidate. Apart from that, the ideas of limited government attracted the support of just one segment of the Republican Party, never mind the electorate as a whole. But Goldwater's candidacy signaled that the Madisonian political legacy had been resuscitated. The capstone of the 1964 election campaign was provided not by Goldwater himself but by Ronald Reagan, in a nationally broadcast speech delivered the week before the election. It was a full-throated evocation of Madisonian ideals that catapulted a second-tier movie star to national attention as a political figure. Reagan captured the California governorship two years later.

The Republican establishment reasserted itself in 1968, nominating Richard Nixon, but the new generation of Madisonians did not think of themselves as Republicans first. Some saw themselves as conservatives, others as libertarians, but they all channeled their energies into spreading the cause of limited government. Their cause blossomed.

In the 1970s, wealthy men provided the money for Madisonians to compete with an elite culture that had become monolithically liberal, and the result was a network of energetic think tanks of the right. The venerable American Enterprise Institute, Hoover Institution, and Foundation for Economic Education were joined by the Heritage Foundation in 1973 (Joseph Coors provided the seed money), the Cato Institute in 1976 (marking Charles Koch's entry into the policy world), the Manhattan Institute in 1978 (Antony Fisher and William Casey), and the Pacific Research Institute in 1979 (Antony Fisher and James North). They were followed in the 1980s and 1990s by many more.[5] Together, they changed the policy conversation.

The public intellectuals of the Madisonian right were recognized in unlikely places. The Nobel Prize in economics was awarded to Friedrich Hayek in 1974 and to Milton Friedman in 1976. Robert Nozick's dazzling philosophical treatise on limited government, *Anarchy, State, and Utopia*, won the National Book Award for 1975. The right even became cool in some circles. Libertarians, with their laissez-faire policies toward sex, drugs, and the rest of the counterculture, were most naturally cool. But in the public-policy arena, the neoconservatives were even cooler. Irving Kristol's *The Public Interest* and Norman Podhoretz's *Commentary* became must-reads for everyone, including serious policy wonks of the left, who wanted to be up to speed on new ideas in public policy.

The continued resurgence of Madisonian thought during the 1970s was fueled by the failures of liberalism. The idealism that had accompanied the passage of the 1964 Civil Rights Act was gone within a few years, replaced by antiwar bitterness and disillusionment over what Johnson's domestic policies had wrought. Welfare rolls had tripled in the decade after Johnson came to office. Unprecedented crime rates had made living in a major city a daily exercise in self-protection. Aggressive affirmative action had outraged the members of the white working class who were most directly affected. School busing had enraged parents—a rage that burned even hotter as high-profile liberals such as Teddy Kennedy piously praised the public schools while sending their own children to private schools. The poverty rate, which had been dropping rapidly from the end of World War II through the first half of the 1960s, had leveled off in the late 1960s and had stopped going down altogether by the early 1970s. The central cities of America's great metropolises were scarred with blocks of burned-out and abandoned buildings. The homeless had become a new and painfully visible American subculture.

Meanwhile, the intellectual wing of liberalism was digging itself into the humorless and impossibly abstruse schools of postmodernism and semiotics, explaining every conceivable topic with the new holy trinity of the left: race, class, and gender. By the mid-1970s, nobody in the public-policy world paid much attention to thinkers on the left—all the interesting action was coming from the right. Democratic politicians became as reluctant to call themselves liberals as Republican politicians had been to call themselves conservatives in the 1950s.

In terms of excitement and optimism, the Reagan years from 1981 through 1988 saw the apogee of the limited-government movement. But even after Reagan left office, political representation of principled Madisonians in Congress increased. In the 1994 election, the GOP won both houses of Congress for the first time since the 1940s, pledged to a "contract with America" that had several limited-government components. In 2000, Republicans added the presidency to their control of Congress—the first time the GOP had controlled the White House and both houses of Congress since the Hoover administration. In 2009, the political appeal of Madisonian thought saw a fresh manifestation in the Tea Party, which in its initial stage was focused single-mindedly on restoring limited government.

The progress made since the end of World War II remains dramatic.

Today, rigorous Madisonian policy analysis is prominent in almost any important policy debate. The nation's leading law faculties include Madisonian constitutional scholars. Free-market economists are represented in the economics departments of the nation's elite universities. In the popular culture, talk radio and the Fox television network abound in spokespersons for Madisonian ideas. By objective measures, the last fifty years have seen Madisonian thought emerge from obscurity to prominence and influence.

And Yet Government Metastasized

T he resurgence of Madisonian thought also coincided with unprecedented—actually, previously unimaginable—growth in the size and reach of government.

Lyndon Johnson's accession marked the beginning of sixteen years of explosive growth in federal authority. In 1963, the number of pages in the *Code of Federal Regulations* was about the same as it had been at the end of World War II. From 1963 through 1968, the code increased by an average of 5,537 pages per year.[6] In addition to the flood of new regulations, Lyndon Johnson's administration saw the advent of covert regulation through federal largesse. Thus the Elementary and Secondary Education Act of 1965 began to provide large-scale financial support to K–12 schools, but only if those schools adopted federal guidelines on how the money was to be used. Of course, the schools did take the money, and everybody had to comply with Washington's preferences.

It was a strategy that the federal government employed for a variety of programs. By the time Lyndon Johnson left office at the beginning of 1969, the federal government had acquired major roles in local education and law enforcement. The policy environment surrounding the formation of families had been radically altered. The federal government was watching over employers' shoulders about employment decisions, how products were designed, how they were marketed, and how services were provided. Directly and indirectly, federal rules about permissible conduct reached down to the neighborhood and into the home.

The Nixon years brought no relief. On the contrary, Richard Nixon presided over a regulatory revolution from 1970 to 1974 that included the creation of two of the most visible regulatory agencies, the Occupational Safety and Health Administration (OSHA) and the Environmental Protection Agency (EPA). The Supreme Court's decision in *Griggs v. Duke Power* in 1971 followed by congressional legislation in 1972 gave the Equal Employment Opportunity Commission (EEOC) expanded authority to oversee employers' employment practices. Combined, OSHA, the EPA, and the EEOC affected virtually every workplace. It was also during the Nixon years that the slope of federal spending on social and economic programs turned sharply upward.[7]

By the time Ronald Reagan was inaugurated, the expansion of the federal government had a life of its own. Reagan slowed that expansion during the 1980s, but he could not stop it, let alone reverse it. Entitlements were going to grow no matter what, mandated by laws that Congress was not about to change. Regulations were going to proliferate no matter what, because regulatory agencies have legal authority to go on making up regulations without additional instruction from Congress or approval from the White House.

It is hard to find metrics to convey how much the federal government's scope and power grew during the same fifty years when Madisonian thought was resurgent. I can give you the dollar figures (from a federal budget of $679 billion in 1960 to $3.4 trillion in 2012, in constant 2010 dollars).[8] Or the increase in pages in the *Code of Federal Regulations* (from 22,877 pages in 1960 to 174,545 pages in 2012).[9] I can tell you that the number of federal independent agencies grew from thirteen to seventy.[10]

But such numbers are too abstract. They don't capture the reality of the Leviathan that the federal government has become. Thinking that perhaps a specific example would help, I went to the website for the Department of Energy (you may replicate the exercise with any cabinet department you prefer) and pulled up its organization chart.[11] As of 2013, three undersecretaries reported to the Office of the Secretary of Energy. Combined, those three undersecretaries ran twenty-nine separate offices, most of them headed by a deputy administrator or associate administrator. In addition, the heads of fifteen other offices reported directly to the Office of the Secretary. That's forty-four entities that reported either to the Secretary of Energy or to one of his three undersecretaries.

While examining this chart, I clicked randomly on one of those forty-four entities, the Office of Health, Safety and Security, and found that up to that point I had reached only the lobby of the bureaucratic maze. The Office of Health, Safety and Security had five divisions reporting to the chief. The heads of those divisions had a total of thirty-seven offices reporting to them. And lest you think that by the time you get this deep into the organization chart, "office" means literally a single office with just one person in it, all of these offices had directors and staffs of unknown size. We're looking at hundreds—I didn't try to count them all—of entities within the Department of Energy alone. Throughout the exercise, as I read gobbledygook office titles and incomprehensible mission statements, the question echoing in my head was, "What do these people *do* every day?"[12]

That's one cabinet department out of fifteen, not to mention seventy independent agencies that are not part of any cabinet department. Let that sink in for a moment. And then realize that all of those people in all of those offices are just a fraction of those who *actually* are part of the federal Leviathan. Consider:

- Federal funds account for about a quarter of state and local revenues. Some large proportion of state and local employees are, for practical purposes, federal employees. The number of state and local employees increased from 7.2 million in 1963 to 19.3 million in 2012.[13]
- The federal government now spends more than $500 billion a year on contracts with for-profit firms, many of which depend on the federal government for most or all of their income. As of 2012, businesses getting federal contracts accounted for about 22 percent of the American workforce.[14]
- The subset of nonprofit organizations that filed reports with the IRS had about $2 trillion in revenues, of which about one-third comes from government. Nonprofits employ about 11 percent of the American workforce.[15]
- Government spending at all levels now averages about 40 percent of GDP, with the federal government accounting for 24 percent.[16]

Under Republicans and Democrats alike, the federal government went from nearly invisible in the daily life of ordinary Americans in the 1950s to an omnipresent backdrop today.

The Paradox in Perspective

The government's continuing expansion doesn't mean that the resurgence in Madisonian thought had no effects. On the contrary, the resurgence made a big difference in terms of discrete policy issues. Crime is no longer a national issue, as it was during the 1970s and 1980s, in large part because of scholars and activists on the right whose work revolutionized policing and imprisonment policy. Such scholars and activists were instrumental in producing the welfare reform act of 1996 and the large drop in the welfare rolls that followed. Scholars and activists on the right energized the school-choice and deregulatory movements. Free-market economists have over the last half century established the superiority of capitalism in generating wealth, with immeasurable effects on sustaining capitalism (which had been losing ground before the Madisonian resurgence) and reducing poverty throughout the world. Similar observations could be made about the positive effects of efforts from the right that dealt with taxes, housing, land use, and many other policy matters.

So let it be clear that I think the resurgence in Madisonian thought has won battles and done good. This book is not intended to belittle those accomplishments or to discourage us from continuing our efforts. But we need to rethink our larger strategy. We have won battles, but we are losing the war. It's time to open a new front.

PART I

COMING TO TERMS WITH WHERE WE STAND

Prudence, indeed, will dictate that governments long established should not be changed for light and transient causes.

—Declaration of Independence

This book calls for such an adversarial stance toward the federal government that, as the Declaration of Independence instructs me, a decent respect for the opinions of my readers requires that I should declare the causes that impel me to this position. Those causes are most assuredly not "light and transient." America's political system has been transmuted into something bearing only a structural resemblance to the one that the founders created. The substance is nearly gone. The purpose of Part I is to convince you, as I have found myself convinced, of these truths:

The founders' Constitution has been discarded and cannot be restored, for reasons that are inextricably embedded in constitutional jurisprudence.

Aspects of America's legal system have become lawless, for reasons that are inextricably embedded in the use of law for social agendas.

Congress and the administrative state have become systemically corrupt, for reasons that are inextricably embedded in the market for government favors.

The federal government is in a state of advanced sclerosis for reasons that are inextricably embedded in the nature of advanced democracies.

Inextricably embedded means that solutions are beyond the reach of the electoral process and legislative process. The citizenry must create new counterweights.

Strong claims. The next five chapters attempt to justify them.

CHAPTER 1

A BROKEN CONSTITUTION

In which I argue that the Constitution that once sustained limited government is broken, and cannot be fixed by a Madisonian majority on the Supreme Court.

MANY MADISONIANS, INCLUDING me until recently, have thought that progress toward restoring limited government was possible if we could place five or more Madisonian justices on the Supreme Court. I still think that doing so would be a major victory. A Madisonian majority would do much to block further spread of the government's reach. But could it significantly roll back the federal government's power? No Supreme Court can do that without a change in the zeitgeist. To understand my reasons for that pessimistic conclusion, it is essential to understand the enormity of what happened to the Constitution over the six years from 1937 through 1942. That in turn requires us to take a look at how the Constitution had evolved—and how much had remained unchanged—between the founding and the New Deal.

1789–1932

Until the 1930s, the federal government remained tiny. The federal budget of 1928 totaled $38.0 billion, expressed in 2010 dollars. Today, when the media routinely express the federal budget in trillions of dollars rounded to one decimal place, $38 billion is literally rounding error. Of that total budget in 1928, $9.4 billion went to defense. Of nondefense spending, another $9.4 billion went to repayment of the national debt and $9.0 billion went to pensions and the Veterans Bureau.[1] That left $10.2 billion for everything else—all the expenses associated with the White House, the federal judiciary, Congress, and the Departments of State, Treasury, Justice, Commerce, Interior, Labor, the Post Office, and all the independent agencies of the federal government. Expressed as per-capita spending in constant dollars, that $10.2 billion amounted to 1.0 percent of comparable per-capita federal spending in 2013. Think about it: one one-hundredth.

There's no mystery why government was still so small when FDR came into office. The Madisonian Constitution restricting the powers of the federal government was still nearly intact. The Supreme Court had been guilty of bad constitutional reasoning in the nineteenth century—in *Scott v. Sandford*, *The Slaughter-House Cases*, and *Plessy v. Ferguson*, among others—but the basis of federal authority was still tightly constrained by the provisions of the Constitution.[2] In some ways, Americans' freedoms were better protected in 1932 than they had been when the Constitution went into effect in 1789. The Thirteenth Amendment had rid America of slavery, the original sin that had always compromised the Constitution's moral authority, and the Fourteenth Amendment was almost as important. Under the first eight amendments of the Bill of Rights, Americans' constitutional rights had been protected only against infringement by the federal government. The Fourteenth Amendment extended that protection to infringement by state and local governments, and its Due Process Clause protected a range of rights not specifically listed in the Bill of Rights (although the Supreme Court took many decades to recognize the full extent of the change).

But if constitutional jurisprudence and the federal government itself were still largely Madisonian in 1932, the prevailing constitutional theory among intellectuals was not. The progressives had been making war on the founders' vision for more than thirty years.

The story of the "Progressive Era" that I learned in American history textbooks focused on the fight against political bosses, the muckrakers who exposed scandalous behavior among meatpackers and the Trusts, the establishment of greater direct democracy through ballot initiatives and referendums, and the campaign for women's suffrage—a sort of "Good Government" movement. It was partly that, and it was these aspects of the Progressive Era that gave rise to twentieth-century liberalism. But philosophically, the progressive movement had roots in German philosophy (Hegel and Nietzsche were big favorites) and German public administration (Woodrow Wilson's open reverence for Bismarck was typical among progressives). To simplify, progressive intellectuals were passionate advocates of rule by disinterested experts led by a strong, unifying leader. They were in favor of using the state to mold social institutions in the interests of the collective. They thought that individualism and the Constitution were both outmoded. That's not a description that Woodrow Wilson or the other leading progressive intellectuals would have argued with. They openly said it themselves.[3]

Three intellectual themes of progressivism would be implemented, not through the ballot box but through the judicial system. They ultimately transformed the nation. Two of these involved regulation and legal liability, and are discussed in the next two chapters. The one that applies here is the progressives' belief that modernity had made the Constitution obsolete.

From the end of the nineteenth century onward, prominent progressives had been saying that the America of 1787 was irrelevant to the urban, industrial, scientifically advanced nation that America had become. Frank Goodnow, a leading progressive theorist, deplored the "reverence" that amounted to "superstition" for the founders' outdated creation.[4] "Under present circumstances," he wrote, the principles of the Constitution "are working harm rather than good."[5] The young Roscoe Pound wrote treatises arguing that "mechanical" jurisprudence (applying the text of the Constitution to the case at hand) must be jettisoned in favor of a "sociological" jurisprudence (one that would adapt the Constitution to the realities of modern America).[6]

Woodrow Wilson, a passionate progressive from the beginning of the movement, joined this school of thought, thereby becoming the first president who was critical of the Constitution. In a famous speech delivered during the 1912 presidential campaign, later published under the title "On Progress," he said to the electorate some of the same things he had been saying in his written work since the 1890s. The founders were Newtonians, Wilson said, and made a mechanical government with its three separate branches and checks and balances. But since then, science had progressed. Blessed with the superior knowledge of Wilson's era, it was now understood that government is not a machine, but a living thing. It falls, not under the theory of the universe, but under the theory of organic life. It is accountable to Darwin, not to Newton. It is modified by its environment, necessitated by its tasks, shaped to its functions by the sheer pressure of life. No living thing can have its organs offset against each other, as checks, and live. On the contrary, its life is dependent upon their quick co-operation, their ready response to the commands of instinct or intelligence, their amicable community of purpose. . . . All that progressives ask or desire is permission—in an era when "development," "evolution," is the scientific word—to interpret the Constitution according to the Darwinian principle.[7]

This view was not limited to presidents and professors. Louis Brandeis was already sitting on the Supreme Court when in 1917 he expressed his contempt for the founders' vision:

Political as well as economic and social science noticed these revolutionary changes [in America's economy and society]. But legal science—the unwritten or judge-made laws as distinguished from legislation—was largely deaf and blind to them. Courts continued to ignore newly arisen social needs. They applied complacently eighteenth century conceptions of the liberty of the individual and of the sacredness of private property.[8]

All Brandeis needed was four other justices who thought the same way.

1933–1936

By the time FDR was inaugurated in 1933, Brandeis had been joined on the Supreme Court by two other progressives, Harlan Stone and Benjamin Cardozo, appointed by Calvin Coolidge and Herbert Hoover, respectively. They were known to the press as the Three Musketeers. Arrayed against them were four Madisonian justices: Pierce Butler, James McReynolds, George Sutherland, and Willis Van Devanter, known as the Four Horsemen (of the Apocalypse). The two swing votes were Owen Roberts and Chief Justice Charles Evans Hughes.

Some erosion in constitutional protections occurred during Roosevelt's first term. Two cases gutted the clause in Article 1, Section 10, that forbids the states from passing any "law impairing the obligation of contracts," known as the Contracts Clause.[9] Another case, *Nebbia v. New York*, foreshadowed the revolution to come (more on *Nebbia* presently). But a breach in the Contracts Clause did not touch on the Constitution's central restraints, and *Nebbia* was about a state's right to regulate business, not the federal government's right to do so. In two cases that did touch on the central restraints on the federal government, the Supreme Court held the line, striking down the legislation that implemented Roosevelt's two most ambitious programs, the National Industrial Recovery Act (NIRA) and the Agricultural Adjustment Administration (AAA). The Court also directly confronted the argument that the extraordinary conditions of the Great Depression warranted extraordinary measures. In the 1935 opinion that voided NIRA, Chief Justice Hughes, writing for the majority, was eloquent:

> We are told that the provision of the statute authorizing the adoption of codes must be viewed in the light of the grave national crisis with which Congress was confronted. Undoubtedly, the conditions to which power is addressed are always to be considered when the exercise of power is challenged. Extraordinary conditions may call for extraordinary remedies. But the argument necessarily stops short of an attempt to justify action which lies outside the sphere of constitutional authority. *Extraordinary conditions do not create or enlarge constitutional power. The Constitution established a national government with powers deemed to be adequate, as they have proved to be both in war and peace, but these powers of the national government are limited by the constitutional grants. Those who act under these grants are not at liberty to transcend the imposed limits because they believe that more or different power is necessary.* Such assertions of extra-constitutional authority were anticipated and precluded by the explicit terms of the Tenth Amendment—"The powers not delegated to the United States by the Constitution, nor prohibited by it to the States, are reserved to the States respectively, or to the people."[10]

That paragraph turned out to be the last hurrah for the Supreme Court's traditional understanding of the Constitution.

What happened next is still disputed. The best-known narrative is that pressure on the Supreme Court to back down was becoming irresistible by the end of Roosevelt's first term.[11] The unemployment rate was still around 20 percent when the NIRA and AAA decisions were handed down, and Americans suffering from the Great Depression weren't interested in constitutional limits on what the federal government could do. After his reelection, Roosevelt took advantage of this mood to try to pack the Supreme Court with more favorable justices. That attempt failed, but the message was clear: if the Supreme Court continued to void New Deal legislation, public opposition could jeopardize the legitimacy of the institution.

In his book *Rethinking the New Deal Court*, Barry Cushman offers a revisionist history.[12] The Court directly responded neither to FDR's court-packing plan nor even to more general political pressures, Cushman argues. If there had been a pivotal switch, it really (though subtly) surfaced in *Nebbia* in 1934. But getting into the details would take us far afield. This much is undisputed: In 1937, Charles Evans Hughes and Owen Roberts permanently joined the Three Musketeers. The result was a series of judicial hammer blows that removed the barriers to federal power that the founders had put in place.

1937–1942

Dismantling Limits on the Federal Government's Spending Authority (*Helvering v. Davis*, 1937)

On August 14, 1935, Franklin Roosevelt signed the act that created Social Security. The purpose of Social Security had nothing to do with any of the enumerated powers. A constitutional challenge was inevitable, and it came in the form of *Helvering v. Davis*, brought by a shareholder in the Edison Electric Illuminating Company who wanted the courts to restrain the company from making the payments and deductions required by the Social Security Act. The Supreme Court handed down its ruling on May 24, 1937, holding that the Social Security Act was constitutional by explicitly reversing a judicial consensus about the meaning of a key phrase in the Constitution. The Court thereby destroyed the limits on

The Great Depression as a Cause of the Constitutional Revolution

The popular explanation for the Great Depression—a stock-market crash caused by too little regulation of financial markets—offered a justification for more government regulation. Keynesian economics, formulated during the Great Depression, offered an economic justification for discarding the enumerated powers and allowing the federal government to spend freely.[13] There's no question that the Great Depression served as a rationale for abandoning the Madisonian Constitution. But was it a valid rationale?

The United States had experienced financial panics, the bursting of speculative stock bubbles, and deep recessions many times before 1929. The economy had usually shrugged off their effects quickly—within months or a few years at most.[14] The Crash of 1929 was accompanied by a series of public-policy errors—government errors, not failures of free markets—that are now widely accepted to have exacerbated the effects of the stock market's fall and changed a familiar economic event into a catastrophe. One mistake was the largest peacetime tax increase in American history, devastating to consumer spending and business investment. Another was the passage of the Smoot-Hawley Tariff Act, devastating to international trade. But the most important government failures are attributable to the Federal Reserve, as documented by Milton Friedman and Anna Schwartz in their seminal 1963 work, *A Monetary History of the United States, 1867–1960*. Disputes remain about precisely what the policy implications should be, but the explanatory power of their analysis is now consensually acknowledged within the economics profession. And so it came to pass at Friedman's ninetieth birthday party in 2002 that Ben Bernanke, then a Federal Reserve governor and an expert on the Great Depression in his own right, said in his tribute, "I would like to say to Milton and Anna: Regarding the Great Depression, you're right. We did it. We're very sorry."[15] Just six years later, Bernanke helped stave off another depression by doing just the opposite of what the Federal Reserve had done in 1929: immediately pumping massive liquidity into the banking system.

the federal government's spending authority. It was the most far-reaching decision since 1803, when the Court asserted its right of judicial review in *Marbury v. Madison.*

The history behind *Helvering* goes all the way back to the ratification debates of 1788. Among the potential loopholes that worried the Anti-Federalists was one that consisted of just two words, *general welfare*, used in the opening of Article 1, Section 8.[16] Here is the exact wording of the relevant portion: "The Congress shall have power to lay and collect taxes, duties, imposts, and excises, to pay the debts and provide for the common defense and general welfare of the United States." After this preamble come seventeen enumerated powers separated by semicolons.

The Anti-Federalists fixated on the phrase "general welfare," worrying that it could be interpreted to mean anything. When James Madison wrote *Federalist #41*, he answered that charge as definitively as anyone could—he being the man who had sat through every session of the Constitutional Convention and taken exhaustive notes on all of them. The plain sense of the text, said Madison, was to proclaim the federal government's power to tax and spend, and the rest of that opening clause of Article 1, Section 8, was a quick way to summarize what the taxes could be used for. "Nothing is more natural nor common than first to use a general phrase, and then to explain and qualify it by a recital of particulars," Madison wrote. "The idea of an enumeration of particulars which neither explain nor qualify the general meaning, and can have no other effect than to confound and mislead, is an absurdity. . . . For what purpose could the enumeration of particulars be inserted, if these and all others were meant to be included in the preceding general power?"[17] For Madison, along with the other Federalists who defended the Constitution in the state ratifying conventions, the whole point of enumerating the powers of the federal government was to limit them to those enumerated powers.

Let me emphasize that the debate was exclusively between the Anti-Federalists, who feared that *general welfare* would be interpreted as conferring a plenary power on Congress, and the Federalists, who said categorically that those fears were groundless. None of the leading Federalists in any of the ratifying conventions defended the notion that *general welfare* should be interpreted as conferring authority for Congress to do anything that advanced the general welfare. Not even Alexander Hamilton.[18]

How can this be, since Hamilton is constantly cited as evidence that some founders wanted a powerful federal government? Because when he wrote his own defense of the Constitution in *The Federalist*, Hamilton knew that to come out openly in favor of a broad interpretation of the General Welfare Clause would jeopardize ratification. He had openly acknowledged during the Constitutional Convention that "no man's ideas were more remote from the plan [of the Constitution] than his were known to be," but he could not afford to say so during the ratification debates; hence the absence in *The Federalist* of any hint of his own wish that *general welfare* should be broadly interpreted.[19]

It was only in 1791, two years after the Constitution was safely ratified, that Hamilton introduced his *Report on the Subject of Manufactures*, which publicly expressed his position. If Hamilton had said in *The Federalist* what he said in 1791, Madison would have disassociated himself from Hamilton and made his case for the Constitution independently. The other founders also would have dissociated themselves from Hamilton. Among the major voices in the long process of ratification, Hamilton's view was unique.

It is in that context that the Supreme Court ruled on the constitutionality of the Social Security Act in *Helvering v. Davis*. Justice Benjamin Cardozo, writing for a 7–2 majority, was conscious that the Court was making history. He wrote with stunning bluntness:

> Congress may spend money in aid of the "general welfare." There have been great statesmen in our history who have stood for other views. We will not resurrect the contest. It is now settled by decision. The conception of the spending power advocated by Hamilton and strongly reinforced by Story has prevailed over that of Madison, which has not been lacking in adherents.[20]

It was over. Hamilton, whose opinions were the most extreme in the Constitutional Convention, who had not dared voice his true opinion about the General Welfare Clause during the ratification debates because it was so unpopular, and whose exposition of an expansive interpretation of the General Welfare Clause postdated the ratification of the Constitution by two years, had been declared the right and true interpreter of what the founders had in mind.

The Talmudic Morass of
Constitutional Jurisprudence

The scholarship that has grown up around the interpretation of the words of the Constitution is dazzling if seen as demonstrations of intellectual agility, but depressing in terms of the sophistry that accompanies much of it. Not being a constitutional scholar myself, I have drawn my description of the key Supreme Court decisions and their historical context in this chapter from the work of Randy Barnett, Richard Epstein, Michael Greve, Gary Lawson, and other eminent scholars whose analysis of constitutional jurisprudence proceeds from a Madisonian perspective. Richard Epstein's magisterial *The Classical Liberal Constitution* (2014) is the most complete exposition. Shorter works that will help you dig into the topic are Epstein's *How Progressives Rewrote the Constitution* (2006) and Randy Barnett's *Restoring the Lost Constitution* (2004). Robert Levy and William Mellor's *The Dirty Dozen* (2008) is an accessible discussion of twelve key Supreme Court decisions that deformed the Madisonian Constitution.

Even lacking expert standing, I will venture a response to those who find support for an expansive federal government in the writings of the founders: The Constitution wouldn't have had a snowball's chance in hell of being ratified if the Federalists had defended the interpretations of the General Welfare Clause and the Commerce Clause that revolutionized the Constitution in the twentieth century. The Constitution was ratified *only* because all of the leading Federalists vigorously rejected those interpretations during the debate over ratification—earnestly in the case of advocates such as Madison, disingenuously in the case of Hamilton.[21]

The Court, having trashed the enumerated powers, then managed to make matters worse. Cardozo acknowledged that defining what constitutes *general welfare* is a matter of discretion. "The discretion, however, is not confided to the courts," he continued. "The discretion belongs to Congress, unless the choice is clearly wrong, a display of arbitrary power, not an exercise of judgment." Congress could spend on pretty much whatever it wished that it deemed to be for the *general welfare* as long as it wasn't completely outlandish. As subsequent years were to prove, even completely outlandish could be okay.

And so the accepted interpretation of *general welfare* was overturned in a stroke, without apology, and even with a sort of flippancy about the enormity of the reinterpretation that seven individuals had imposed on the nation's founding document. Or such is my personal reaction to Cardozo's litotes that Madison's position "has not been lacking in adherents."

Gutting the Ninth Amendment and More (*United States v. Carolene Products Co.*, 1938)

United States v. Carolene Products Co. was almost as far-reaching in its expansion of federal power as *Helvering*. It had three effects, overlapping but distinct. First, it effectively did what the Ninth Amendment had been intended to prevent—it limited the rights of the American people to those that were explicitly named in the text of the Constitution and its amendments. Second, it effectively wiped out protection of economic rights. Third, it gave the Court latitude to decide which rights were fundamental and which were not—and thereby cut the legs from under the Court's protection even of rights that *are* spelled out in the Constitution.

Let's start with the Ninth Amendment. The original motivation for the Ninth Amendment and its intended purpose could hardly be more explicit. On June 8, 1789, the first United States Congress was considering the amendments to the Constitution that would make good on the Federalists' promise of a bill of rights. James Madison rose to speak. He referred to what he called "one of the most plausible arguments I have ever heard urged against a bill of rights," to wit:

> It has been objected also against a bill of rights, that, by enumerating particular exceptions to the grant of power, it would disparage those rights which were not placed in that enumeration; and it might follow by implication that those rights which were not singled out were intended to be assigned into the hands of the General Government, and were consequently insecure.

But, Madison continued, he thought that the danger could be guarded against. "I have attempted it, as gentlemen may see by turning to the last

clause of the fourth resolution."[22] Madison was referring to the draft
of what would become the Ninth Amendment, which in its final form
reads, "The enumeration in the Constitution of certain rights shall not be
construed to deny or disparage others retained by the people."23

During the first century and a half of America's history, when federal
restrictions on liberty were so few, there was seldom a need to invoke the
Ninth Amendment. Only two Supreme Court cases from 1789 until the
New Deal even mention it.24 But starting in the late nineteenth century,
a competing approach, the Presumption of Constitutionality Doctrine,
was gaining supporters. The seminal statement on the subject was written by Harvard legal scholar James Thayer in 1893, arguing that courts
at all levels should presume legislative acts were constitutional, putting
the burden of proof on those who would argue otherwise.25 This would
become the standard progressive position as well, explicated in later years
by Louis Brandeis.

It was a wonderful resource for those who wished to pass progressive
social legislation. At the time Thayer wrote, the Supreme Court still held
that economic freedoms, especially freedom of contract, were constitutionally protected, even though they were not expressly included among
the first eight amendments in the Bill of Rights. Numerous lower court
and Supreme Court decisions had voided state laws because they violated
economic freedoms, most famously in *Lochner v. New York* (1905).[26] If
the Presumption of Constitutionality Doctrine prevailed, the logic behind those decisions could be repudiated.[27]

The ascendancy of the Presumption of Constitutionality Doctrine
had been signaled in 1931 in *O'Gorman & Young, Inc. v. Hartford Fire
Insurance Co.*, when Justice Brandeis wrote that "the presumption of
constitutionality must prevail in the absence of some factual foundation
of record for overthrowing the statute."28 It was given an even stronger
boost in 1934 in *Nebbia v. New York*, when the Court upheld a New
York law that fixed the price at which milk could be sold, saying that
"if the laws passed are seen to have a reasonable relationship to a proper
legislative purpose, and are neither arbitrary nor discriminatory, the requirements of due process are satisfied."[29] In 1938, the Supreme Court's
ruling in *United States v. Carolene Products* made explicit what *Nebbia* had
left implicit, and extended it to federal laws as well as state laws.[30] It

proclaimed a principle that came to be known as rational-basis scrutiny. It was the Presumption of Constitutionality Doctrine on steroids. In the words of Justice Stone, who wrote the Court's opinion,

> Regulatory legislation affecting ordinary commercial transactions is not to be pronounced unconstitutional unless, in the light of the facts made known or generally assumed, it is of such a character as to *preclude the assumption that it rests upon some rational basis* within the knowledge and experience of the legislators.[31]

Robert Levy and William Mellor have translated the legalese for lay readers: "Unless a challenger can demonstrate that a challenged regulation is wholly irrational—that there is no possible justification, no matter how attenuated, for the government's action—the regulation will be upheld."[32] The slender reed protecting economic freedoms left by *Carolene Products*—that at least a regulation could be challenged "in the light of the facts made known"—was subsequently dispatched by the Warren Court in 1955.[33]

Rational-basis scrutiny raised an obvious question: If any rational basis made a piece of legislation constitutional, what was left of Constitutional protections for *any* rights that might be intertwined with "commercial transactions"? The Court gave a vague answer in a footnote, known to law students ever since as Footnote Four. Exceptions to rational-basis scrutiny *may* be justified (the Court wouldn't even commit itself to language stronger than *may*) for rights that meet certain conditions. One such condition is that "legislation appears on its face to be within a specific prohibition of the Constitution, such as those of the first ten amendments."[34] A second is that the Court might (but, who knows, might not) take an interest in—subject to "more exacting judicial scrutiny"—legislation that was manifestly corrupt, rigging the political process.[35] The third possible exception might be legislation that reflects "prejudice against discrete and insular minorities," specifically "religious or national or racial minorities."[36]

The Federalists had been reluctant to include a bill of rights because they had worried that to enumerate some rights would eventually give an opening for government to take away protection of rights that had not been enumerated. That's precisely what *Carolene* did—with the added insult of making the Court the arbiter of which rights are worth protecting and which are not.

Removing Limits on What the Government Can Regulate
(*National Labor Relations Board v. Jones & Laughlin Steel Corp.*, 1937, and *Wickard v. Filburn*, 1942)

The debate over the meaning of *general welfare* was about the things on which Congress could spend money. The debate over the Commerce Clause, meanwhile, was about the ways in which the federal government could regulate Americans' behavior.

It sounds simple. The Commerce Clause says that "Congress shall have power . . . to regulate commerce with foreign nations, and among the several states, and with the Indian tribes." The meaning is obvious, isn't it? The states of the new Union couldn't be permitted to set themselves up as independent economies, with, say, Pennsylvania charging tariffs on rice "imported" from South Carolina. That's the kind of chaos that had happened in the bad old days under the Articles of Confederation, and the Constitution allowed the federal government to prevent it.

More formally, *commerce* as used at the time of the founding referred to "buying, selling, or bartering, as well as transporting for those purposes."[37] It did not refer to manufacturing or agriculture, let alone to any broader definition of *commerce* as "gainful activity." Constitutional scholar Randy Barnett has documented that all known uses of the word *commerce* in the Constitutional Convention, the ratification debates, and *The Federalist*—literally 100 percent of them—applied the narrow meaning of the word.[38] The phrase *among the several states* surely meant (follow me closely here) that more than one state had to be involved.

Throughout the nineteenth century, the Supreme Court's decisions involving the Commerce Clause, summarized in the note, were broadly consistent with a commonsense understanding of what the founders had in mind.[39] From the turn of the century to the New Deal, the progressives made inroads on the prevailing understanding of the Commerce Clause in a series of cases that broadened its interpretation to include railroads that operated within a single state under certain circumstances.[40] But railroads were a special case—front and center in the conduct of interstate commerce, and more likely to have monopolistic power in the marketplace than other modes of transportation. An observer at the outset of FDR's administration could reasonably think that the Commerce Clause still meant more or less what it had always meant.[41]

In 1937, within six weeks of *Helvering*, the Court ruled that the National Labor Relations Act was constitutional. The challenge to it had come from Jones & Laughlin Steel Corp., which was being fined because it had fired employees who were trying to form a union. The Court ruled that manufacturing fell within the purview of the Commerce Clause, and that the definition of *interstate* was broad. Activities that occurred within a single state could be regulated by federal law if they had a "close and substantial" relationship to interstate commerce.[42] This represented a huge expansion of the meaning of the Necessary and Proper Clause ("The Congress shall have Power . . . To make all Laws which shall be necessary and proper . . .") as it related to the Commerce Clause, gathering all forms of manufacturing into its embrace along with anything that had indirect effects on interstate commerce.

It was left until 1942, in *Wickard v. Filburn*, for the Supreme Court to complete its redefinition of the Commerce Clause. Roscoe Filburn was a small farmer in Ohio. He had been fined by the Department of Agriculture because he produced 239 more bushels of wheat than the Agricultural Adjustment Act said he was supposed to produce. None of Filburn's wheat was sold outside Ohio. In fact, hardly any of it was sold at all—he used most of it for feeding his family and for feeding livestock, which he subsequently sold as meat. But the Supreme Court ruled that the provisions of the Agricultural Adjustment Act were constitutional under the Commerce Clause anyway. After all, if Filburn had not used his own wheat, he would have had to buy it. If enough farmers like him had to buy their own wheat, it would have an effect on the price of wheat. And the price of a commodity has an effect on interstate trade. So it's constitutional for the federal government to tell a farmer what he may grow on his own land for his own use.

In effect, the Supreme Court announced to the nation that the federal government could regulate just about any economic activity of any sort that it felt like regulating—indeed, as subsequent decades were to reveal, it could regulate even non-economic activities that had potential effects on economic activities that had potential effects on interstate commerce.

Bullies and Little Guys in the Key Cases

A common justification for the regulation of economic liberties is that it prevents powerful employers from browbeating employees or cheating the public. In that light, a look at the parties in the key cases of the New Deal is bemusing. One of them fits the evil-capitalist narrative: *Jones & Laughlin Steel,* in which a corporation fired employees for trying to unionize. But in *Nebbia,* Leo Nebbia was a shopkeeper who had been convicted of selling two quarts of milk and a five-cent loaf of bread for eighteen cents, when New York's Milk Control Board had set the price of milk at nine cents a quart. He was guilty of giving his customers a good deal, cutting into his own profit margin. In *Carolene Products,* the losing party was a manufacturer of "filled milk," a combination of condensed milk and coconut oil that cost only seven cents a can compared to ten cents for standard condensed milk. The dairy lobby, in a classic example of collusive capitalism, used the United States Congress to write legislation that eliminated Carolene Products' ability to get its product to market, based on false claims about the unhealthiness of filled milk. In *Wickard,* the government went after a small farmer who grew his own wheat on his own land; what little he sold went to people in a nearby town. The big corporation lost in *Jones & Laughlin Steel.* The little guy lost in *Nebbia, Carolene Products,* and *Wickard.*

And so, as federal judge Alex Kozinski has put it, the Commerce Clause became the "Hey, You Can Do Anything You Feel Like" Clause.[43]

Why We Can't Go Home Again

The Constitution needed to change as the United States evolved from the agrarian society of the eighteenth century to the post-industrial society of today, and some of those changes would have permitted wholly new areas of government activity. If in the 1930s FDR had mounted a campaign for an amendment permitting government spending for Social Security, there is good reason to think that it would have succeeded—

just as earlier in the twentieth century, the Constitution was changed to allow the income tax and women's suffrage (and, less happily, prohibition). If in the 1960s, LBJ had mounted a campaign for passage of an amendment permitting the government to spend money on protecting the environment, he would have been seeking permission for the government to engage in an activity that meets all the classic tests of a public good. Environmentalism was one of the most popular movements of the last half of the twentieth century. The amendment would undoubtedly have passed. The constitutional revolution of 1937–1942 took the nation on a different route, lifting the requirement that new government powers needed to be constitutionally ratified, and instead letting Congress unilaterally authorize whatever new powers it wanted.

Why do I say so dogmatically that the Constitution's power to limit government cannot be restored? After all, the Supreme Court has overturned precedent in the past. *Brown v. Board of Education* reversed the separate-but-equal doctrine established by *Plessy v. Ferguson*, for example. In more recent decisions, the Court has acted to shore up the Second Amendment and the right to bear arms, the First Amendment and freedom of speech, and has stated that the Commerce Clause is no longer going to be treated as the "Hey, You Can Do Anything You Feel Like" Clause.[44] Furthermore, I will argue in Part II that a few key Supreme Court decisions could result in a de facto rollback of the regulatory state.

These are, or would be, significant improvements. The Constitution is not altogether dead, and the Supreme Court can still make a big difference in national life. But it's one thing to circumscribe the continued expansion of the power of the federal government and quite another to reduce the legal limits of that power; one thing to make regulatory agencies more cautious about using their regulatory power and quite another to remove their power to make those regulations.

In a phrase, the difference is between one of the *operations* of the federal government, which can be affected, and *limits* on the federal government. Limits on the federal government have been broken in ways that cannot be mended.

To illustrate, let's return to *Brown v. Board of Education* in 1954. It had huge effects—but nothing remotely as huge as the effects of reversing *Helvering, Carolene Products,* or *Wickard.* The decision in *Brown* said that state-enforced racial segregation in the schools had to end. This affected one specific institution, public schools, in twenty-one states that required or permitted school segregation.[45] The remaining twenty-seven states and the territories of Hawaii and Alaska were unaffected. The elimination of school segregation enjoyed support among a broad cross-section of Americans in the north and west, not to mention among African Americans in the twenty-one affected states. *Brown* had convulsive effects in the states of the Deep South, but they were tolerable for the polity as a whole.

Now suppose that the Supreme Court were to reverse *Helvering*, ruling that Congress is not permitted to spend money for the "general welfare" and instead may spend only on the enumerated powers. If so, the federal government would be required to end Social Security, Medicaid, Medicare, all welfare programs, all spending on K–12 education . . . and that's just the beginning. Hardly any of the domestic spending of today's federal government is associated with one of the enumerated powers. To reverse *Helvering*, and have that reversal enforced by the executive branch, would throw the country into chaos. Even in the unimaginable event that five justices would be willing to accept that chaos, they wouldn't vote to reverse *Helvering* anyway, because they could be sure that no president would be willing to enforce the decision. In reversing *Helvering*, they would be signing the Supreme Court's death warrant. *Helvering* is not going to be reversed, no matter who is on the Supreme Court or in the White House. As constitutional scholar Gary Lawson has put it, "In this day and age, discussing the doctrine of enumerated powers is like discussing the redemption of Imperial Chinese bonds."[46] And as long as *Helvering*'s interpretation of the General Welfare Clause remains in force, there are no constitutional ways to restrain Congress from spending money on whatever it wishes to spend money on. It is only fractionally easier to imagine a reversal of *Carolene Products, Jones & Laughlin Steel*, or *Wickard*. The consequences of reversals in those cases would also be so drastic that no president would try to enforce them.

Thus my reasons for asking you to accept that a restoration of limited government is not going to happen by winning presidential elections and getting the right people appointed to the Supreme Court. A Madisonian majority on the Supreme Court would help significantly at the margins. But the revolution in constitutional jurisprudence has gone too far, with too many consequences that are now part of the warp and woof of the nation's economy and society, to be reversed. The landmark Supreme Court decisions from 1937 to 1942 irreversibly increased the range of legislation that Congress could pass and the activities in which the executive branch could engage.

It was an outcome that would not have surprised the founders. The members of the Constitutional Convention in the summer of 1787 had systematically studied previous attempts at republican government. They tried their best to construct a Constitution that would survive the forces that had destroyed other republics. But they were realists. Their letters, essays, and public pronouncements are sprinkled with warnings of how things could go wrong.

Thomas Jefferson said it most succinctly: "The natural progress of things is for liberty to yield and government to gain ground."[47] In *Federalist #51*, Madison put that ancient truth about humans and their governments alongside the task that faced the founders. Here is the most famous passage from *Federalist #51*, and one of the most acute passages in all the literature of the founding era:

> It may be a reflection on human nature that such devices should be necessary to control the abuses of government. But what is government itself, but the greatest of all reflections on human nature? If men were angels, no government would be necessary. If angels were to govern men, neither external nor internal controls on government would be necessary. In framing a government which is to be administered by men over men, the great difficulty lies in this: you must first enable the government to control the governed; and in the next place oblige it to control itself.[48]

From 1937 through 1942, for what were believed to be greater goods, we stopped obliging the American government to control itself.

CHAPTER 2

A LAWLESS LEGAL SYSTEM

In which I argue that the American legal system increasingly functions in ways indistinguishable from lawlessness, for reasons that are authorized by judges and Congress.

"WHEREVER LAW ENDS, tyranny begins," wrote John Locke, encapsulating in five words the intimate relationship between liberty and the rule of law.[1] In the United States as of the second decade of the twenty-first century, law has ended in some ways and tyranny has made some beginnings.

Such a strong statement seems overwrought. Aspects of the American legal and criminal-justice systems are better than they have ever been. Compared to a century ago, attorneys and judges have more formal training in the law. Police investigative techniques and technology are incomparably better than they were a century ago. Police are better trained and police forces are (in general) better administered. Most prisons are more humanely designed than they were a hundred years ago. Prison guards are better trained and prisons are (in general) better administered.

The American legal system is also more "ruleful" than it has ever been. What is and is not permissible in the investigative process, within the courtroom, and during the appeals process is spelled out in intricate detail, and violation of these elaborate protocols can lead to the overturn of a judicial decision.

When I indict the government for lawlessness, I have things other than equipment, training, and rulefulness in mind.

The Manifestations of Lawlessness

First, let's talk about the legal system not as it looks from thirty thousand feet to law professors, where everything can be fit together and rationalized, but how it looks at ground level to ordinary law-abiding citizens, of whom I count myself one. I am reminded of science-fiction author Arthur C. Clarke's famous observation that "any sufficiently advanced technology is indistinguishable from magic."[2] From ground level, our encounters with today's legal system as it actually functions are often indistinguishable from lawlessness.[3]

When the legal process is more costly than you can afford, it is indistinguishable from lawlessness.

If you are engaged in a business and are prudent, you have acquired liability insurance that covers the costs of legal defense against a lawsuit. If you work for a corporation, you are shielded from legal liability under most (though not all) circumstances. But if you are an ordinary private citizen of ordinary means, you usually cannot afford to pursue a legal defense against an allegation that will take you to court.[4] In the case of a criminal charge, you can hope for the best from a public defender. But in a civil case, you face a tough choice, *even if you are certain that you have done nothing wrong and that the courts would eventually vindicate you.* You know that you will be unable to recoup your legal costs, and that those costs will probably run well into five figures, or more, not to mention the weeks, months, or years in which the litigation hangs over your life. Citizens of average net worth usually cannot afford their day in court. So if the accuser, be it the government or a plaintiff in a lawsuit, gives you the option of giving in at a price you can afford, you give in. When defending yourself against a wrongful allegation is not financially feasible, in what sense are you protected by the rule of law?

Criminal law that is sufficiently removed from the concept of *mens rea* is indistinguishable from lawlessness.

For centuries, common law recognized two requirements for a criminal act: a guilty act and a guilty mind. The legal terms are *actus reus* and *mens rea*.[5] You not only had to do something wrong, you had to be aware you were doing something wrong. But the law also held that ignorance of the law is no defense. How could these two principles be reconciled? Because there weren't many laws. Most of the laws that did exist prohibited acts that were obviously wrong in themselves (*malum in se*), such as murder, rape, and theft. Other laws prohibited things the state decided to prohibit (*malum prohibitum*) that were not wrong in themselves (for example, sumptuary laws), but these were of a manageable number and were part of daily life.

Today, we often haven't the least idea whether we have broken a law. Setting aside state and municipal law, which add hugely to the problem, so many things have become federal crimes that it is impossible to keep track of them. Through the first half of the nineteenth century, virtually all criminal law was defined and prosecuted by the states, with fewer than a score of crimes defined by the federal government (for example, treason or bribery of federal officials).[6] By World War I, the number of federal laws had reached the 500s. As of the most recent count, in 2007, the federal code numbered about 4,450 crimes. We have seen an increase of about 50 percent just since 1980.

To see the implications for the requirement of having a guilty mind, take a moment to list all the acts you can think of that qualify as *malum in se*. I doubt if you can come up with more than a few dozen. If you stretch them out (for example, breaking down "taking other people's stuff" into the various categories of robbery, petty larceny, grand larceny, burglary, and so on) and if you have a good imagination, you can perhaps come up with fifty. There just aren't that many different human actions that are self-evidently wrong in themselves and warrant criminal penalties. It is possible to imagine how this comparative handful of acts might have different definitions in different federal statutes. There might be several laws prohibiting different forms of bribery, for example. But as generously as you try to estimate, it is inevitable that an extremely large proportion of those 4,450 crimes in the federal code are *malum prohibitum*—not things that are bad in themselves but things that warrant criminal penalties because the government has said they do.

Various aspects of the effective lawlessness fostered by the growth in federal law are discussed in the sections of this chapter that will deal with complexity, subjectivity, and discretionary power to enforce the law.

Here, I want to emphasize the degree to which the government has chosen to convert mistakes, or sometimes simply choices with which the government disagrees, into crimes.

It's a complicated topic. For those who want to read into it, I recommend Harvey Silverglate's *Three Felonies a Day: How the Feds Target the Innocent*, and a compilation of articles edited by Gene Healy, *Go Directly to Jail: The Criminalization of Almost Everything.*[7] I will give just one example to illustrate a problem that has spilled into many aspects of American life, the responsible corporate officer (RCO) doctrine.[8]

The RCO doctrine made its appearance in 1943, when the Supreme Court held that a corporate executive could be found guilty under the criminal provisions of the Federal Food, Drug, and Cosmetic Act because the "legislation dispenses with the conventional requirement for criminal conduct—an awareness of some wrongdoing. In the interest of the larger good it puts the burden of acting at hazard upon a person otherwise innocent but standing in responsible relation to a public danger."[9]

So there was the rationale: a public danger involving health and safety. But it was a dodgy argument from the beginning. To find someone guilty of a criminal offense, just how close did the "responsible relation to a public danger" have to be? We're talking not about sleazy corporate executives who are guilty of things that everyone considers *malum in se*—cheating, lying, defrauding—but executives who are going about their jobs at their personal levels of competence, which differ, but acting in good faith. Recognizing how dodgy it was, the RCO doctrine was for many years applied only to misdemeanors or offenses involving light penalties. Also, as one Supreme Court Justice approvingly observed, the RCO doctrine had been enforced in a way that "does not do grave damage to an offender's reputation."[10]

But as time went on the net broadened. In 1975, the Supreme Court ruled that not only could the RCO doctrine dispense with *awareness* that an action was wrong (*mens rea* was unnecessary), it could dispense with the element of wrongful *action*. An executive could be found guilty for a crime of omission.[11] Prosecutors became more aggressive, seeking not only large fines but also jail time for RCO convictions. Here's just one case to illustrate what's happened on this slippery slope.

The defendant was Edward Hanousek, a manager for a railroad company in Alaska.[12] A backhoe operator working under him accidentally ruptured an oil pipeline while removing rocks from a section of track. Hanousek was off duty at the time. He was nowhere near the site. He was nonetheless convicted of unlawful discharge under the Clean Water Act, on grounds that he was guilty of negligent failure to supervise, and sentenced to six months in prison, six months in a halfway house, and a $5,000 fine. The verdict was affirmed by the Ninth Circuit Court of Appeals. The Supreme Court refused to hear his case.

Did Hanousek make any mistakes in his own supervisory role that deserve criticism? As is usual in such cases, the defendant had made judgment calls that the prosecution said were obviously wrong and the defense said were reasonable choices given the circumstances and standard professional practice. But under the Supreme Court's guidance, gross incompetence or negligence was not necessary to send Hanousek to jail. We have reached a state of affairs in which everything that has a bad outcome in an enterprise governed by state or federal law can have a culprit who is liable under standards of civil negligence or even, as in the Hanousek case, criminally liable.

To readers who have even a moderately complicated job, and especially to readers who supervise employees, this is nightmarish. In any complicated job, people make daily judgments about how things should be done. Some are right, some are wrong. Some have consequences, good or bad. Other factors besides one's own decisions are constantly affecting the events that vindicate or discredit those judgments, so that it becomes unclear whether your good or bad judgment is really related to outcomes deemed good or bad. To have *done nothing wrong* but rather to have failed to take an alternative course of action that might (but not necessarily) have avoided the bad outcome, and then be taken to court—and occasionally even to prison—for it is to enter a Bizarro world that bears no resemblance to what most people have in mind when they think of "the rule of law." And it happens in today's America.

In the Hanousek case, Justice Clarence Thomas dissented from the Supreme Court's refusal to hear the case. "I think we should be hesitant to expose countless numbers of construction workers and contractors to heightened criminal liability," he wrote, "for using ordinary devices to engage in normal industrial operations."[13] For that, at bottom, was the environment in which Hanousek's "crime" was committed.

When the rule of law makes us criminals for making an unintentional mistake——or for failing to act as perfect hindsight says we should have acted, even though it is not at all clear that our behavior was even a mistake——how are we defining *lawfulness*?

Civil law that is sufficiently arbitrary and capricious is indistinguishable from lawlessness.

Civil law's counterpart to *mens rea* is negligence. *Negligence* is when you fail to fix the rickety step leading up to your front porch, it collapses under a visitor's weight, and he breaks his ankle. You meant no harm, but you're nonetheless on the hook for the victim's medical expenses, maybe his lost income, and perhaps his pain and suffering. You were negligent, and you are obligated to make the victim whole, or as whole as possible.

This makes sense, in the same way that being punished for doing things that are *malum in se* makes sense. But what if you were not negligent, and are still liable for damages? What if you are fined or even imprisoned for failing to obey a pointless government regulation?

The government's regulation of workplaces no longer consists primarily of sensible precautions involving the safety of tunnels in coal mines or the safety of areas near whirring buzz saws. They include the proper latching devices for storage bins in bakeries.[14] Suppose you're a dentist. To find out what you need to do to comply with government regulations affecting your workplace, you can buy the 2015 *OSHA Manual for Dentists* for just $199, plus shipping and handling, and then work your way through its 307 pages.[15] But you'll be glad to know that your $199 also buys you a "Do-It-Yourself Documentation Kit" that will enable you to "prepare your facility for OSHA inspection." It is 102 pages long.

If you think bakeries and dentists are atypical, Google whatever business comes to mind along with the words "OSHA" or "EPA" and take a look at some sample regulations for yourself. My point is that bakers and dentists alike rarely come across a regulation and say to themselves, "I guess I can't get away with that anymore," or "I guess that really is unsafe; I'm glad it was brought to my attention." As they pore over the regulations, they are instead spending most of their time discovering all the ways they could be breaking laws that have no relationship whatso-

ever to negligence. But they can be fined large sums of money for failing
to do precisely as the government demands.

These thousands of regulations and their interpretations are sometimes so nonsensical, it is hard to believe that the people who wrote them
could be serious. Suppose, for example, that you want to clean a piece
of machinery with a cleansing solvent. I give you two choices. You may
pour the solvent onto a rag, rub down the machine, and throw the rag
into a trash can; or you may pour the same amount of solvent onto the
surface of the machine, use an identical rag to wipe the machine down,
and throw away the rag into an identical trash can. What's the difference
between these two procedures? Using the right one leaves you a law-
abiding citizen. Using the wrong one makes you guilty of an environmental crime. Can you guess which is which? No? Can you guess what
the offenses are? No? Don't worry, the EPA, using the provisions of the
Resource Conservation and Recovery Act of 1976, knows the difference.
They've written a memorandum about it.[16]

The phrase "arbitrary and capricious" that I use to label this form of
lawlessness is a legal term that will return to play a major role in Part II.
It is potentially the regulatory state's point of greatest vulnerability. In
the meantime, I make this simple assertion: Punishment for failure to
observe an arbitrary and capricious regulation is indistinguishable from
punishment for failing to obey the arbitrary and capricious demands of
an absolute ruler. It is a form of lawlessness.

Law that is sufficiently complex is indistinguishable from lawlessness.

An excellent informal statement of the rule of law was given to us by
James Madison in *Federalist #62*:

> It will be of little avail to the people, that the laws are made by men
> of their own choice, if the laws be so voluminous that they cannot
> be read, or so incoherent that they cannot be understood; if they be
> repealed or revised before they are promulgated, or undergo such
> incessant changes that no man, who knows what the law is to-day,
> can guess what it will be to-morrow. Law is defined to be a rule of

action; but how can that be a rule, which is little known, and less fixed?[17]

A large proportion of federal laws passed in recent years fit Madison's description of bad law.[18] Sheer length often defeats clarity. The Sarbanes-Oxley Act of 2002, which overhauled the rules for financial disclosure by corporations, is 810 pages long.[19] The Patient Protection and Affordable Care Act—Obamacare—is 1,024 pages long.[20] The Dodd-Frank Wall Street Reform and Consumer Protection Act, passed in response to the financial crisis of 2008, is 2,300 pages long. It goes without saying that no individual knows how to "obey" those laws in the same way people know how to obey the laws against robbery. You know that you are obeying the law only because experts you have hired to study the law tell you exactly what to do.

Probably you are not a senior executive in a corporation, the financial industry, or the health-insurance business, nor are you a health-care provider. But here's an easy way for you to empathize with their position: If you get a letter from the IRS saying you're going to be audited, do you get nervous even if you have filled out your tax return in good faith?

If you have income that is not recorded on a W-2 form or deductions except the most ordinary ones, being nervous is rational. The tax code as of 2013 consisted of almost four million words—about five times the length of the King James Bible.[21] It is riddled with ambiguities and special provisions. The IRS can almost always find something wrong if its agents look hard enough, no matter what tax preparation software you used and no matter how faithfully you tried to do the right thing.

Nor is that "something wrong" found by the IRS necessarily wrong even according to the IRS's own rules. Periodically, some enterprising journalist gives the same set of tax documents to different tax accountants and pays them to prepare tax returns. Different accountants using the same data invariably come up with tax bills that differ, sometimes substantially. When journalists call the IRS's phone lines asking the same tax question of different IRS advisors, they get different answers. The fact that the IRS says you owe them money doesn't mean they're right and you're wrong.

You know all this. But when the IRS sends you a notice telling you that you underpaid your taxes by $1,529, what do you do? If you know that you honestly reported your financial information and carefully followed the instructions of the tax preparation software, your natural impulse would be to argue with the IRS before paying it. But usually that's not legal. You must pay now (or be hit with penalties and interest), and *then* start a long and complicated legal process for getting a refund, which, even if successful, will take months or longer, many hours of paperwork, and perhaps the cost of a lawyer. If you are sensible, you pay the full amount the same day you get the notice and try to forget about it. You probably haven't done anything wrong, but to fight it will make matters worse.

Sometimes it is impossible to comply with all the laws even when you know what they are. Owners of restaurants get nervous, or simply sigh, knowing what's coming next, when the inspector from the municipal health department walks through the door to do a surprise inspection. They know that the inspector will find that their kitchens fail to meet at least a few of the dozens of standards they are supposed to meet, because no busy kitchen can operate in perfect compliance with all of them. In New York City, for example, a restaurant owner was fined because the temperature of cheese slices was forty-five degrees instead of the maximum permissible forty-one degrees.[22] Why were the cheese slices four degrees hotter than the prescribed maximum? Because they had been taken out of the refrigerator and placed beside a hot griddle so that they could be put on top of sizzling hamburgers. But restaurant owners pay such fines, even knowing that their kitchens are serving safe food to their customers. It's a price of doing business.

The complexity of the law often sets up a situation that is indistinguishable not only from lawlessness but from a kleptocracy. Owners of small businesses of all kinds routinely pay lawyers they can't easily afford in order to get a decision out of a bureaucracy—not an unusual decision, just a run-of-the-mill permission to go ahead with some innocuous business activity. The rules and regulations are so complicated that lawyers are required. The business owners pay the lawyers for the same reason that people pay bribes in Third World countries. It's the only way to get the government to allow you do something that the government would otherwise arbitrarily refuse to let you do. I will return to this theme in the next chapter.

**Law that is sufficiently subjective is indistinguishable
from lawlessness.**

One of the best-known legal maxims is "Hard cases make bad law."
Human affairs are complicated. Any law enforced according to objective criteria of guilt or negligence is bound to yield occasional decisions
that strike just about everybody as unjust. It is for such cases that judges
should have some discretion, so that the injustice may be mitigated. But
that's where "Hard cases make bad law" comes in. Sensible jurists don't
want to use the exceptional case to change the law, because judges are
neither omniscient nor preternaturally wise. *If the objective rules are discarded, then the rule of law morphs into a modern-day version of a primitive
legal system in which people with a quarrel have to accept whatever the headman of the tribe says is right.* For much of American civil law, that's not a
bad description of where things stand now.

GROUNDS FOR DAMAGES. Until late in the nineteenth century,
damages were awarded for tangible damage, usually physical injury or
damage to property. Then the common law gradually began to include
emotional distress and eventually "lost enjoyment of life" as grounds for
damages. These can be legitimate grievances and, in a perfect world,
with perfectly wise headmen, people who behave negligently should be
held liable for such losses. The problem is how to allow such claims to be
made in an imperfect world and still retain a meaningful rule of law. A
broken ankle is associated with a specific range of medical bills, a specific
range of work days lost, and a limited range of pain and suffering (broken
ankles hurt in well-known ways). A damage such as emotional distress
has no similar anchor in objectivity. It can be real, but it can also be
exaggerated or faked altogether. Even when it's real, different personality types experience different levels of emotional distress from identical
events. The reaction of a jury to testimony about emotional distress can
vary radically depending on whether its members are stoics or softies.[23]
Similar problems are associated with estimating lost enjoyment of life.
Juries are routinely called upon to make such decisions, but that doesn't
mean they are in any sense assigning objectively determined awards. The
parties to the suit have to hope that the headman is wise.

COMMERCIAL LITIGATION. It used to be that important commercial promises—for example, to sell property—had to be in writing or they had no standing. With a few specific exceptions, the terms of a written agreement took precedence over anything said orally. Now the courts sometimes permit suits to be filed based on "bad faith" in negotiations, even when no agreement was reached. Alleged oral promises have been enforced by the courts. Alleged verbal agreements have been given precedence over written agreements.[24] Why? The headman said so.

EMPLOYMENT LAW. You are an employer who has fired a woman for incompetence. She files a lawsuit alleging sex discrimination. You provide the court with objective evidence of the woman's incompetence on the job. But she is able to present evidence that you have in the past made sexist remarks. You can still be required to pay damages. It is known as a "mixed-motive firing." The jury will look into your soul and decide whether the degree of your sexism was great enough to trump the woman's demonstrated incompetence. Now you are not just taking it to the headman; you're taking it to the shaman.[25]

Law that is sufficiently discretionary is indistinguishable from lawlessness.

A former member of the US Attorney's Office in New York has written about a popular training exercise among the staff: Name a famous person and then tell the junior prosecutors to figure out a plausible crime that could be pinned on him. The junior prosecutors win the game by finding the most obscure offense that fits the character of the celebrity and carries the toughest sentences.[26]

It's not just a game. Ask Martha Stewart or Michael Milken. Their high-profile cases, involving defendants who could afford the finest legal representation, resulted in jail time for both. Informed legal opinion approaches a consensus that neither Stewart nor Milken committed an offense that ordinarily would have resulted in prosecution, let alone jail time. Stewart was convicted of making false statements to federal investigators about an insider-trading case that, a federal judge ruled, had so little merit that "no reasonable jury could find guilt beyond a reasonable doubt."[27] In Milken's case, the judge threw out the only real criminal charge, insider trading, leaving charges of violating financial regulations that, as the prosecutor in the case later acknowledged, amounted to "criminalizing technical offenses." The regulations in question hadn't ever been charged as crimes before, nor have they been charged as crimes since.[28] Facing a trial that could have sent him to jail for many years, and told that the prosecutors would go after his brother if he didn't capitulate, Milken accepted a plea bargain.

These are the famous cases. Abuse of prosecutorial discretion also happens without publicity to people who have fallen under the scrutiny of a regulatory agency. Suppose the EPA becomes aware of a violation of one of its regulations. Evidence of that violation may be used to initiate informal negotiation with the offender or to seek administrative penalties, judicially imposed civil penalties, or criminal prosecution. The choice can make a life-changing difference to the defendant.

Which does the EPA choose? It has guidelines that look good on paper—the more severe alternatives are to be reserved for severe environmental harm, for example. But if you read more carefully, you discover that the guidelines unobtrusively expand the concept of *harm* to include not just actual releases of pollutants but their threatened release, and permits the definition of *harm* to be satisfied by the failure to report a release, regardless of its significance, and by illegal conduct that represents "a trend or common attitude within the regulated community."[29] In practice, the EPA can rationalize whatever response it prefers. What is true of the EPA is true of all the regulatory agencies. They all have high-minded guidelines—which are just that, guidelines that can be interpreted virtually as the regulators see fit.

A variation on the use of discretion, both by prosecutors in the regular courts and by bureaucrats in the regulatory agencies, is to coerce the cooperation of underlings to go after the real target. The procedure is to go to a little fish, threaten prosecution if the little fish doesn't cooperate, promise immunity if he does cooperate, and build a case around witnesses against bigger fish on the prosecutor's wish list, all of whom are telling the story that the prosecutor wants told (as Alan Dershowitz has put it, such witnesses "are taught not only to sing but also to compose") under the threat of imprisonment or ruinous fines if they don't toe the line.[30]

It also works the other way around. Under the US Department of Justice's "compliance and cooperation" policy, the likelihood that a corporation will be prosecuted can be reduced if the corporation cooperates with the DOJ's investigation of the behavior of individual employees, leading to numerous cases in which, as legal scholar Jeffrey Parker has written, "corporate officers and (more often) mid-level employees were hung out to dry by their firms, who succumbed to the threat of economically devastating charges against them."[31]

Variations on the same theme apply to prosecutors, from the municipal district attorney to the army of attorneys in the DOJ, plus all the bureaucrats in regulatory agencies, from municipalities to the federal government. All of them, in their different ways, can say to the people they've decided to go after: "You can either take your chances on litigating this case and risk everything, or you can plead guilty to a lesser offense."

With prosecutorial discretion goes the potential for prosecutions based on personal animus or arbitrary punishment for being insufficiently respectful. "Some lawyers comment that one of the more difficult aspects of private law practice is maintaining an appropriate level of groveling to government officials," James DeLong writes. Referring specifically to the EPA, he points out that the listed guidelines used by regulatory agencies when they decide whether to prosecute a case do not include a de facto guideline familiar to experienced defense lawyers: "Anyone who argues too hard is unlikely to be regarded as a good person. Also in jeopardy is anyone who questions the EPA staff's intelligence or good faith, and anyone who contends that economic concerns might be as important as environmental ones."[32] If you think this is paranoid, just ask about it with any of your friends who have to deal with regulatory agencies. Many of them will have reached the same conclusion. Don't threaten to fight the case; it will only make matters worse.[33]

There's no alternative to some degree of prosecutorial discretion, both for practical reasons (the court system couldn't handle the load if defendants all chose to go to trial) and moral ones (sometimes defendants should get a break). But we do not have a system in which prosecutorial discretion is limited to those justifications. We have a system in which prosecutors use their enormous discretionary powers in corrupt ways. When that happens, it is indistinguishable from lawlessness.

Law that permits the state to take private property without compensation, or to force the transfer of private property to other private individuals, is indistinguishable from lawlessness.

The last thirteen words of the Fifth Amendment, "nor shall private property be taken for public use except with just compensation," are known as the Takings Clause or Public Use Clause. The founders were referring to the power of eminent domain—the right of the government to say to a property owner, "You have to sell us your property whether you want to or not." Eminent domain is a necessary thing if, for example, public roads are to be built expeditiously in a direct route. It is nonetheless a scary power for the government to hold. Thomas Jefferson opposed it, wanting landowners to hold absolute control over their property.[34] Madison was not so adamant, but the word he chose to put after *public* was *use*, not a broader term such as *purpose* or *benefit*.[35] The plain meaning of the term is that the property in question is transferred to ownership of the government, which in turn employs that ownership for a public good of some sort. That's what the founders had in mind. It's not what the Takings Clause means anymore.

COMPLETE TAKINGS. The founders never even considered the possibility that the Fifth Amendment could justify the compulsory transfer of property from one private owner to another private owner, but that's how the Fifth Amendment is now interpreted. It began in the early 1950s, when Congress passed an urban-renewal program that would condemn large sections of the impoverished southeast quadrant of the District of Columbia for redevelopment activities that would include the sale of some of the land to private developers (Congress at that time controlled the government of the District of Columbia). When a department-store owner objected, the Supreme Court ruled in *Berman v. Parker* (1954) that the District's program was constitutional because it involved a public purpose. *Public purpose* was deemed to fall under the definition of *public use*. It was a classic case of good intentions making bad law. The part of southeast DC to be condemned really was a terrible slum, and it would have been a good thing if somehow it could have been transformed into a livable neighborhood (it wasn't).

The predictable happened: *Berman v. Parker* was the thin edge of the wedge. Over the decades, courts routinely deferred to legislatures and planning commissions that wanted to improve blighted communities. The definition of *blighted* was applied not just to terrible slums but to any neighborhood that wasn't up to snuff, and then to neighborhoods that were just fine, on grounds that, for example, razing the neighborhood to provide space for a General Motors plant would yield "public benefits."[36] By 1984, Sandra Day O'Connor could write that "where the exercise of the eminent domain power is rationally related to a conceivable public purpose, the Court has never held a compensated taking to be proscribed by the Public Use Clause."[37]

In 2005, the Supreme Court put the final nail in the Public Use Clause in *Kelo v. City of New London.* The case was as clear as could be. The home-owning plaintiffs lived in a well-maintained, long-standing working-class neighborhood. The land was being seized to facilitate Pfizer Corporation's construction of a research facility, providing space for a luxury hotel and conference center, a marina, eighty new residences, and a large office complex. There were other outrageous aspects to the case, but it is enough to say that the Court ruled 5–4 in favor of the city, ratifying by Supreme Court precedent the evolution from "public use" to "public purpose" to "public benefit" that had been occurring in lower courts since *Berman v. Parker* in 1954. What it means is that if your property is worth a lot more to someone else than they want to pay, and that person or entity can offer enough goodies to the city where you live, you can be forced to sell so that someone else can make a lot of money, and you don't have a legal leg to stand on, even if your appeal reaches the highest court in the land. It's all perfectly constitutional.

PARTIAL TAKINGS. A de facto taking has also occurred if a government action restricts your free use of your property by declaring that you may not build on the property, or farm on it, or otherwise must refrain from using the property as you see fit. Many of these actions—ones that directly impinge on the public's safety, health, and welfare—have always been widely accepted as legitimate as an exercise of the government's police power. Such is the justification for building codes that reduce the likelihood of fire or collapse, or for sanitation regulations that help prevent epidemics. Zoning regulations have withstood constitutional scrutiny on similar grounds. These limitations on "using the property as you see fit" have another characteristic: almost everyone within a given community shares the cost. All property owners have to build structures

---

Sorry About That

The redevelopment project that was to serve a wonderful public purpose for the people of New London never happened. The private
developer couldn't get financing and abandoned the project. As of
the end of 2014, what used to be a neighborhood of family homes
was still vacant land.

Is this the courts' fault? After all, the courts that heard the case
could not conduct an independent economic analysis of the project.
But the judges could have asked for evidence that commitments of
financing for the proposed project had been secured from banks or
financing was guaranteed by the municipality. They were deciding
whether to expel citizens from their homes so that other citizens could
have their land. Such a momentous violation of citizens' rights should
require more than politicians' assurances to the court that the project
is a really cool idea.

---

that conform to the sanitation regulations, bearing the additional costs of
those regulations. Even people who rent are indirectly helping pay those
costs, which are passed along in the form of higher rents.

When does the government's authority to limit property rights cross
the line from legitimate to lawless? Historically, "using the property as
you see fit" had a simple, elegant formulation in common law: *sic utere
tuo ut alienum non laedas*, meaning "use what is yours so as not to harm
what belongs to others."[38] It provided an intuitively lawful framework for
deciding how the government might limit the rights of property owners,
and distinguishing between the limitations that did and did not require
compensation. Thus a law that forbids a property owner from polluting
his neighbor's water doesn't require the government to compensate him,
because the government isn't taking away anything that the property
owner had a right to in the first place.

When instead the government limits the rights of some property
owners but not all in pursuit of some less immediate public good—
protecting the habitat of an endangered species, for example—it is in
effect asking the property owner to give up some or all of the value of

his property on behalf of others who do not have to pay. The Takings Clause of the Fifth Amendment would seem to require that he receive just compensation. But in *Penn Central Transportation Co. v. New York* in 1978, the Supreme Court decided against the default assumption that compensation is owed. Instead, Justice Brennan, writing for a 5–4 majority, announced that it was the Court's duty to determine "when 'justice and fairness' require that economic injuries caused by public action be compensated by the government, rather than remain disproportionately concentrated on a few persons."[39] In this particular case, the cost to Penn Central was $150 million in lost property rights caused by the designation of Grand Central Station as a New York City landmark. The Court decided that a $150 million loss didn't qualify Penn Central for compensation.

Once the burden of proof was lifted from government, the predictable again happened. The *Penn Central* decision was subsequently and successfully used to dodge the requirement for compensation in a broadening range of partial takings. At the same time, the federal government was getting into the partial-takings business on a massive scale. The National Environmental Policy Act (1970), the Clean Air Act (1970), the Clean Water Act (1972), and the Endangered Species Act (1973), among others, gave federal regulatory agencies the power to prescribe how property owners might and might not use their property, and none of those exercises of power have been subject to a requirement for compensation.[40]

The lawless characteristic of such takings depends on their timing. If laws restricting the use of a given piece of land are already in place when someone is considering whether to buy it, there could be an issue about whether those restrictions are constitutional, but the Supreme Court can (and has) ruled on their constitutionality. One may disagree with the Supreme Court's understanding of the Constitution without justification for calling them *lawless*. If, however, the restrictions are retroactively applied to land that someone has already bought, a tincture of lawlessness comes into play. The more egregious the retroactive taking, the more lawless the behavior of government. In recent decades, those takings have become egregious.

These manifestations of lawlessness by no means exhaust the list. In the interests of concision, I have omitted discussions of issues that are already being widely discussed: the increasing militarization of the police, manifested in indiscriminate use of SWAT tactics in making arrests for people suspected of minor offenses; the increasing aggressiveness of social service agencies in defining parenting behaviors as crimes; and civil forfeiture laws that allow the state to confiscate private property that has been associated with the commission of a crime, even though the owner of the property neither participated in nor had any knowledge of that crime.[41] These manifestations of lawlessness are important but, fortunately, are already meeting increasing public resistance. They backstop the point I have been making through more technical legal developments: lawlessness in contemporary America does not consist of a few aberrant cases but is systemic.

Readers who want to get a more detailed sense of the current state of affairs may go to the sources cited throughout this chapter. The best single compilation of academically oriented analyses is a 2013 collection of articles by leading legal scholars, *The American Illness: Essays on the Rule of Law*, edited by F. H. Buckley. Books for a general audience, in addition to ones already mentioned, are Philip Howard's *The Death of Common Sense*, *Life Without Lawyers*, *The Rule of Nobody*, and *The Collapse of the Common Good*, and Walter Olson's *The Litigation Explosion* and *The Rule of Lawyers*.[42]

How did we get into this mess? To some extent, the increasing complexity and subjectivity of the law have been encouraged by changes in technology, affluence, and the nature of an industrial economy. But these were enabling conditions, not primary causes. Ideas have consequences, and few ideas have had more consequences than those that were originally advanced by the progressives of the late nineteenth and early twentieth centuries. In the case of the legal system, the progressives succeeded in imposing on the nation (for the changes did not arise from any popular demand) a radically new way of thinking about the legal system: the purpose of the law was not only to administer justice but also to serve progressive social purposes. To make a complicated story easier to follow, I will separately trace strands that in reality were intertwined. In this chapter, I discuss the judiciary's unleashing of the lawsuit and Congress's instigation of lawsuits. They transformed the civil legal system. In the next chapter, I take up the creation of a separate legal system for creating and enforcing federal regulations.

Judges Unleash the Lawsuit

L awyers have been prominent in American political life since before the Revolution. In civic life, however, lawyers used to play a surprisingly unobtrusive role. They spent most of their time performing basic legal services—preparing wills, contracts, and deeds, for example—and resolving disputes through mediation. Most potential lawsuits were settled out of court, early and quickly, with modest compensation. Lawsuits that went to trial were almost always completed in a few days. Judgments were small. Punitive damages were not only rare and small; they were declining in the early part of the twentieth century and were even abolished in several states.[43]

Litigation played such a small role in American life partly because it was expensive even then but also because it was seen as something to be avoided whenever possible and never to be encouraged, *and almost all lawyers shared that opinion.* I italicize that point because it must seem so implausible to a contemporary reader.

It was a view that lawyers had held about their profession for two millennia. William Blackstone, writing the *Commentaries* in the eighteenth century, inveighed against lawyers who instigated litigation, calling them "pests of civil society, that are perpetually endeavoring to disturb the repose of their neighbors, and officiously interfering in other men's quarrels," pointing out that lawyers who did such things in Roman times were punished by forfeiture of a third of their goods "and perpetual infamy."[44] Walter Olson describes the view that prevailed as recently as the 1950s in the United States:

> [Litigation] was grossly invasive of privacy and destructive of reputation. It was acrimonious, furthering resentments between people who might otherwise find occasion to cooperate. It tended to paralyze productive enterprise and the getting on of life in general by keeping rights in a state of suspense. It corrupted its participants by tempting them to harass each other and to twist, stretch, and hide facts. It was a playground for bullies, an uneven battlefield where the trusting, scrupulous, and plainspoken were no match for the brassy, ruthless, and glib. For all that, it was sometimes the least bad of the extremities to which someone might be reduced; but

society could at a minimum discourage it where it was not absolutely necessary.[45]

America's legal profession had erected three deterrents to litigation. First, ethics. The American Bar Association's *Canons of Professional Ethics* explicitly forbade "stirring up litigation, directly or through agents."[46] To do so was not only ethically wrong but also against the law in many states. The second line of defense drew on the rules of legal procedure, which at that time made it difficult to bring suits without a clear basis, limited the right of discovery without good cause, and protected a citizen's right not to be sued except in his own court and under the laws of the place where the contested action took place. The third line of defense was based on explicit, objective, legal rules to govern the usual sources of litigation—activities such as the sale of land, terms of employment, and product liability. Sometimes these rules were part of the common law governing lawsuits that involve harm (tort law), but, given the option, the courts preferred well-written contracts as a way of avoiding litigation altogether. A well-written contract relieved the court of having to make judgments about what the rights and obligations of the parties "should" have been. The parties themselves had agreed to their respective rights and obligations, and the court needed only to interpret whether the contract had been honored. With a well-written contract, this was usually so straightforward that lawsuits were not brought: it was too obvious who would win.

Then the progressives came along. In part, they believed that the legal system could serve social justice by shifting the costs of the hazards of modern life from individuals to businesses through reforms in tort law. In part, they believed that litigation was a force for good—if people were given enough access to the courts, and if judges could get enough information, and if the examination of that information was sufficiently thorough, then problems left unresolved or inequitably resolved in the bad old days could be decided with ontological fairness.

The Adoption of Strict Liability

The progressives' victory manifested itself first in its overthrow of the traditional role of negligence. The centuries-old purpose of tort law had been to compensate—"make whole"—a person who had been harmed by the negligence of another. If no negligence was involved, no compensation was owed, no matter what harm the plaintiff had suffered. It was further assumed that a case warranting the intervention of the law was unusual. In the words of legal scholar George Priest, "'Tort law sought no more than to compel redistribution where one person harmed another through an action that substantially departed from the status quo."[47]

As far back as the early 1900s, prominent progressive jurists such as Benjamin Cardozo, Roscoe Pound, and Louis Brandeis began talking about a new way of looking at tort law. It would not merely compensate individuals for harms done through negligence but also redistribute the societal costs of misfortune. The logic went like this:

Accidents and other unfortunate events happen. People suffer losses or harms. When they instigate litigation and are successful, they get relief. When corporations are the defendants, they almost always have more resources than the people who have been harmed. Why not use tort law as a form of insurance that puts the burden of paying for accidents and damages on those who are best able to pay? Why not use tort law as a tool for improving society by making manufacturers and the providers of services so vulnerable to damages that they are motivated to make safer products and provide safer services? It was called *strict liability*—meaning that a defendant could be forced to pay even if no negligence was involved.

STRICT LIABILITY FOR PRODUCTS. Manufacturers of products were the first to be subjected to this new view of tort law. Justice Roger Traynor of the California Supreme Court began the process in 1944 in his concurring opinion in *Escola v. Coca-Cola Bottling Company*. A Coke bottle had exploded in a waitress's hand, injuring her. The case was decided on the basis of *res ipsa loquitur* (the thing speaks for itself), because there must have been negligence somewhere along the line or the bottle wouldn't have exploded. But Traynor's concurring opinion stated that the court should have said that negligence didn't have to be proved, and instead that strict liability applied. His opinion was widely read and attracted an influential legal following. Nineteen years later, in 1963, Traynor wrote the court's majority opinion in *Greenman v. Yuba Power Products, Inc.*, finding for the plaintiff on grounds of strict liability.[48]

Traynor was promoting an idea whose time had come. A year later, in 1964, the American Law Institute came out for strict liability for

defective products in its Second Restatement of Torts. Within a few
more years, strict product liability had been incorporated into tort law
throughout the country. A manufacturer who was in no way negligent
could nonetheless be found liable for damages.

Strict product liability has many attractive features. In the simplest
case, it is merely a subcategory of negligence. Suppose there are two ways
of making a product, both of which cost the same amount of money, but
one of which makes the product safer. Under the old tort system, the
manufacturer had no external incentive to find the second, safer way
to make the product. Under a doctrine of strict liability, that incentive
exists. In technical terms, the goal is efficiency, meaning that the legal
rules lead manufacturers to internalize the cost of undetected harms but
not go to such lengths that the losses outweigh the gains. The field of law
and economics has produced many shelves of books and articles on such
questions.[49]

If that were the end of the story, then strict product liability would be
a clear plus. It's not the end of the story, however, for many reasons that
are not my topic here.[50] One of the simpler ones is that consumers pay
a lot of money for strict liability. In the case of intrinsically dangerous
products such as ladders and machine tools, a large portion of the sticker
price is owed to the high liability-insurance costs the manufacturer must
pay no matter how well designed the product is. A less quantifiable and
yet more serious problem is this: Under a regime of strict liability, the
law requires people to enter a field at their own risk, bearing any costs
from accidents no matter what. That's fine if you want to manufacture
Coke bottles. What if you want to design a new surgical instrument? A
new small airplane? Even if your design leads to a product that is superior
to its competitors, *even one that is safer*, anything that goes wrong with it
will leave you open to lawsuits in a system where settlements can be so
large that they bankrupt you. So do you try to bring your new and better
product to market, or find something less risky to do?

It's not a theoretical problem. The expected liability costs of a new
product are so high that many improvements, including safety improvements, are not brought to market. An empirical analysis of states that did
and did not implement product-liability reform from 1981 to 2000 indi-
cated that tort reform that *reduced* manufacturers' liability was associated

with 24,000 fewer deaths compared to states that did not introduce tort reform.[51]

DE FACTO STRICT LIABILITY FOR SERVICES. At least a product is a *thing*, with a design that can be inspected and conclusions about its functioning that can be drawn based on the laws of physics. For products, a strict-liability regime can be made to work with modifications that protect innovators.

Technically, a strict-liability regime applies only to products, and negligence remains the standard in other kinds of tort actions. But in practice, the economic concept of internalizing the costs of injuries has infiltrated the rest of tort law. The idea is that providers of services should be compelled through the tort system to take the prospective cost of accidents into account as they make their decisions about how to go about their work.[52] Instead of rules of negligence that hold the homeowner responsible for failing to repair the rickety step, for example, they have evolved toward a vague "there's some conceivable way that the defendant could have avoided causing this injury" kind of logic.

That's why you see so many public swimming pools without diving boards. Given the way that the tort system now interprets negligence, putting up warning signs and having lifeguards on duty does not necessarily protect the city from being sued if a diver is injured. It's the same reason that elementary schools dismantle their jungle gyms, and the reason that in so many airports you are driven mildly nuts by the voice endlessly repeating, "Caution, the moving walkway is ending."[53]

Another effect of the de-emphasis on the traditional understanding of negligence speaks to lawlessness. From the lawyers' viewpoint, strict liability simplifies tort law by removing subjectivity. Reaching a decision under the old negligence standard required answers to several questions. What was the defendant's duty? Did the defendant fail in that duty? Did the plaintiff use normal care in the use of the product? Answering those questions can be highly subjective. Strict liability comes down to a simpler proposition: "If you acted and thereby caused harm, you pay that harm."

But that's how lawyers look at it. From the viewpoint of manufacturers of products and providers of services, being found liable these days can feel like being struck by lightning. Under the traditional negligence doctrine, a defendant who had lost a lawsuit might walk out of the court-room feeling that the justice system had failed because the jury wrongly deemed him to be negligent. The jury made a mistake. But under the strict-liability doctrine, *fault*—moral culpability—is not even an issue. The legal system doesn't need to find that you did anything wrong to make you pay. That feels like lawlessness.

Lowering the Bar for Bringing a Lawsuit

If you were hit by a lawsuit prior to the 1930s, you at least had this comfort: the lawsuit was certain to begin with a "pleading" that spelled out the allegations against you in detail. Furthermore, the plaintiff had better come to the court prepared to prove those allegations—he had "to win upon the facts stated in the complaint or not at all."[54] The plaintiff couldn't go on fishing expeditions and could not use a lawsuit simply to vent his grievances against the defendant. The rationale for detailed pleadings was compelling: it meant fairness for the defendant, who had a right to know why he was being hauled into court, and a means of keeping the courts from being filled with frivolous complaints.

The downside was that gathering information for the pleading could be expensive, which might prevent worthy cases from getting a hearing. Once again, the progressives had a better idea: let the plaintiff who thought he had a legitimate grievance come to court unsure of all the facts, after which would come a period during which both sides were compelled to hand over relevant information to the other side before the case was finally heard in court—what we now know as "discovery." When the first Federal Rules of Civil Procedure (FRCP) were adopted in 1938, they changed the old evidentiary requirements for a pleading to what was called a "notice pleading," which put the defendant on notice that he was being sued, along with a general statement of the subject of the allegation, with no need for details.[55] The state courts gradually followed suit.

The floodgates were opened. Attempts to retain any element of seriousness in the initial "notice pleading" fell apart with a 1946 court decision that allowed a frivolous allegation of plagiarism against Cole Porter to go ahead, on grounds that if by some miracle the allegations turned out to have any factual basis, then the plaintiff would be entitled to damages; hence, it was appropriate to proceed.[56] And so fishing expeditions became legal. The plaintiff was free to throw a barrage of accusations against a defendant with no evidence that any of them were true, and then shift the grounds of the suit depending on what was found during discovery.

This is one area in which the Supreme Court has moved to tamp down the worst excesses. In 2007, the Court's decision in *Bell Atlantic Corp. v. Twombly* revised the previous, extremely loose, standard enunciated in *Conley v. Gibson* (1957).[57] The Court did not return to anything resembling the pre-1930s requirement for pleadings. "Here the Court is not requiring heightened fact pleading of specifics, but only enough facts to state a claim to relief that is plausible on its face," Justice Souter wrote for the seven-justice majority. "Because the plaintiffs here have not nudged their claims across the line from conceivable to plausible, their complaint must be dismissed."[58] While the standard remained loose, it did ask for an indication that there was at least smoke, if not fire.

The Broadening of Discovery

Discovery—the process by which each side can compel the other to hand over materials that might be relevant to its case—had been around since the nineteenth century, but the rules limiting the information that could be sought were strict.[59] The same 1938 Federal Rules of Civil Procedure that allowed the "notice pleading" also revised the rules for discovery. Formerly, discovery could be used only for eliciting evidence that supported one's own case, not the opponent's. Under the new rules, each party could ask for anything that related to the "subject matter" of the litigation—which, of course, lent itself to expansive definitions. Furthermore, discovery could probe into hearsay, opinion, and other forms of evidence that would not be admissible at trial if it could be argued (and it always could) that such information could lead to other evidence that *would* be admissible. Depositions went from interviews that usually lasted no more than a few hours to grueling marathons that can go on for days, sometimes weeks. The most intimate details of people's lives could be laid open, with no more justification than that such information might conceivably help the opponent's case.

In 1970, discovery took another ominous turn. The 1938 FRCP had continued to limit the documents that could be requested. In 1970, the FRCP were amended to allow litigators to demand any documents that they wished, with no requirement that a demand had to be accompanied by an explanation of cause.[60] In the case of individuals, this was still another invasion of privacy and a burdensome task, but individuals usually have just a few file cabinets' worth of documents. When corporations are sued, responding to requests for discovery can mean going through millions of documents. Furthermore, these requests can be made of third parties who are neither plaintiffs nor defendants, sometimes costing them millions of dollars when they don't even have a dog in the fight.

The old requirements for filing a lawsuit were not perfect. The demands for particulars in the traditional pleading were arguably too strict, putting too much of a burden on a wronged individual. But the cure—"Let 'em sue, and then sort out whether there's anything to it"—was worse. Walter Olson puts it nicely: "Fearful of being accused of pettifogging specificity, the American courts instead made themselves into a place where nothing was secure and anything could happen. What began as a page out of Dickens ended as a page out of Kafka."[61]

License to Forum-Shop

The last change in the civil procedure may sound innocuous to the layperson: it became possible to file suit in places other than the location where the alleged harm was done. The term of art is *forum shopping*, whereby the plaintiff finds a place to sue where he is most likely to have success.

For a long time, forum shopping was not permitted. The right to be sued at home went back to the Roman legal maxim *Actor forum rei sequitur*, "The plaintiff must pursue the defendant in his forum." The principle was embedded in the English common law and adopted in American common law as well.

Some limited exceptions to the right to be sued at home crept into the common law to accommodate the interstate presence of corporations and, later, the growth in interstate travel by private citizens. But it was once again left to the Supreme Court of the New Deal era to introduce radical change to long-established practice. In *International Shoe Co. v. Washington* (1945), the Court announced that due process requires only that the defendant "have certain minimum contacts with [a state] such that the maintenance of the suit does not offend 'traditional notions of fair play and substantial justice.' "[62] You can't figure out what that means? Neither could anyone else. By the 1960s, both corporations and individuals could be compelled to travel to distant states to defend themselves. As time went on, it even became possible to bring suit in a state that was not where the event happened, nor where the defendant lived, but where the plaintiff lived—a precedent established in 1967 by the California Supreme Court, when a California resident was permitted to bring suit in California against a defendant from Nebraska for a traffic accident that occurred in Nevada.[63]

The issue here is not whether people in one state can be sued by people in other states who feel they were wronged. That has always been possible. The issue rather is *where* the suit must be brought—my place or yours. Different jurisdictions have different laws governing the many issues that a suit might entail. Different localities have different standards: juries in big cities tend to give larger awards than juries in small towns; juries in the Bronx tend to give bigger awards than juries in Staten Island. The result of the practice opened up by *International Shoe* and other decisions affecting federal courts was forum shopping on a grand scale, as plaintiffs flocked to the places where they could expect the best deal.[64]

The Abandonment of Lawyerly Self-Restraint

The ethical stipulation against "stirring up litigation" in the ABA's *Canons of Professional Ethics* still remains, but it has been made toothless by advent of widespread legal advertising. In 1976, the Phoenix law firm of Bates and O'Steen started advertising their rates. The State Bar of Arizona initiated disciplinary proceedings. Bates and O'Steen took their case to the Arizona Supreme Court, which upheld the disciplinary judgment. They then appealed to the Supreme Court, which, on June 26, 1977, rejected the state bar's ban. All those billboards and TV ads you now see urging people who have mesothelioma or who suffered any kind of accident to get a lawyer are owed to *Bates v. State Bar of Arizona*.

Like so many issues involving the law, we have contending values: maximizing the availability of legal recourse to people with unredressed injuries, and minimizing the degree to which lawyers act as "pests of civil society, that are perpetually endeavoring to disturb the repose of their neighbors." It goes without saying that a law banning advertising by lawyers would be a violation of the First Amendment. The first lawyers who decided to test their right to advertise were bound to win, and once that happened, it was inevitable that advertising would become widespread, and it would not be limited to advertising fees. Lawyers would advertise the possibility of getting financial awards at no risk (see contingency fees below). For good or ill, advertising has indeed been a powerful force for stirring up litigation.

The spread of legal advertising interacted with an element of the American legal system that was already in place: contingency fees. Contingency fees pose difficult questions of ethics. Elsewhere in American society, professional conflicts of interest are routinely recognized and guarded against by the professions themselves. Journalists are supposed to disclose relationships they have with people, businesses, or products they write about. Professional sports leagues do not allow their athletes to bet on sports, even if they're betting that their own team will win. Tax accountants do not charge clients based on how many ways to avoid taxes they can find. Physicians do not charge based on whether they cure the patient's health problem. People working in each of those professions understand the incentives for bad behavior that would be created by such practices. The same incentives for bad behavior are promoted by contingency fees for attorneys, which are legal in every state and have been since 1960.

The proponents of contingency fees make two powerful arguments in response. First, contingency fees provide a way for people who can't afford a lawyer to pursue their legitimate legal claims. Second, contingency fees have a built-in safeguard: The attorney makes money only if the suit succeeds; hence, contingency fees weed out weak cases.

Until the revolution in liability, the advantages of contingency fees probably outweighed the conflicts of interest they engendered. In the old days, winning a case involved a single client and a modest reward. A lawyer who accepted a contingency fee knew that he would probably have to take all but the strongest cases to court—it was hard to get corporations to settle out of court when mounting a strong defense didn't take that much time or money.

By the mid-1960s, all that had changed. With strict liability in place, the ability of the plaintiff to impose large discovery costs on the defendant, and the increasing propensity of juries to award punitive damages, made even the richest corporations eager to avoid a trial. Attorneys could profitably accept weak cases that couldn't win in a courtroom.[65] Add in the rise of class-action suits, and the potential rewards of taking a case on contingency rose from "usually modest" to "perhaps wealth beyond the wildest dreams of avarice." Advertising in this milieu gave attorneys a way to chase ambulances on a wholesale basis.

Congress Instigates the Lawsuit

Blackstone's condemnation of lawyers who instigate litigation as "pests of civil society, that are perpetually endeavoring to disturb the repose of their neighbors, and officiously interfering in other men's quarrels" takes on a special irony in the context of today's civil society. One of the chief instigators of that litigation is government at both the state and federal level.

The term of art for this kind of legislation is *private enforcement regime.* Reduced to its basics, legislation that demands compliance with a set of new noncriminal regulations needs to have an enforcement mechanism. Congress can assign enforcement responsibility to a government agency such as the EPA, or it can pass legislation that creates incentives for citizens to enforce the regulation by filing lawsuits against people or businesses in violation of it. The latter alternative is a private enforcement regime.

Creating these incentives is simple. For a plaintiff, the expected value of filing a lawsuit is the expected size of the settlement times the probability of winning, minus the expected legal costs. Legislation can affect all three of those variables. Congress can increase the expected size of the settlement by stipulating that successful plaintiffs can be awarded a multiple of the actual damages (called "damage multiples"). Congress can reduce the expected legal costs by stipulating "plaintiff fee-shifting," whereby defendants are required to cover most or all of a plaintiff's legal costs if the plaintiff wins but not vice versa. Congress can increase the plaintiff's likelihood of winning by wording the regulation so that it gives plaintiffs a low bar for proving their cases.

The first two mechanisms, damage multiples and plaintiff fee-shifting, are the most common components of a private enforcement regime. The use of damage multiples, though unusual, goes far back in common law. The first use of plaintiff fee-shifting occurred in the Civil Rights Act of 1870, in an attempt to help African Americans who were trying to protect their voting rights.[66] Plaintiff fee-shifting was also inserted in the federal government's first significant regulatory legislation, the Interstate Commerce Act of 1887. The Sherman Antitrust Act of 1890 was the first legislation to use both plaintiff fee-shifting and damage multiples (triple). The purpose of these mechanisms was explicitly stated in the floor debate over the bill: it was necessary to depart from long-standing common law on attorney fees and damages so that private litigants could be mobilized in the effort to bring the great monopolists under control.[67]

As in the case of so many reforms that began during the Progressive Era, the short-term results were minor and the long-term results were momentous. In this instance, Congress passed only forty-two private enforcement regimes from 1887 through 1963. The surge of regulatory legislation from the Johnson administration onward was accompanied by an equally steep surge in private enforcement regimes. The figure on page 61 shows what happened from 1887 to 2005.[68]

This is one of the rare instances when social-engineering legislation had its intended outcome. Congress was asking for citizens to litigate, and they did. The rise in the private statutory litigation rate shown in the figure tracks closely with the increase in private regulatory regimes.[69] So effective have these incentives been that lawsuits filed by private citizens to enforce federal statutes have recently been averaging 160,000 annually.[70] By way of comparison, OSHA carries out fewer than 30,000 workplace inspections annually.

Private enforcement regimes are spread broadly among policy areas.[71] Their greatest commonality is the target: 84 percent of private enforcement regimes provide incentives for actions against private entities. Only 9 percent of those regimes also create incentives for citizens to sue state governments; only 17 percent create incentives for citizens to sue the federal government.[72]

Are these incentives a good thing? On the plus side, they make it easier for wronged individuals to obtain redress. On the negative side, they make it easier for plaintiffs to get money from innocent defendants. How those two balance out cannot be determined quantitatively. Even

The surge in private enforcement regimes after the mid-1960s triggered a matching surge in private litigation.

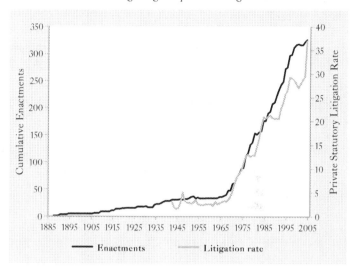

Source: Farhang (2010), 65, Figure 3.1. The litigation rate is per 100,000 population.

if it could, the result would leave open a value judgment. In a completely just world, what would be the appropriate ratio between plaintiffs rightly compensated and defendants wrongly punished? What is known for certain is this: private enforcement regimes enacted by the federal government in combination with the unleashing of the lawsuit by the legal system have transformed the role of the lawsuit. In the words of George Priest, "Tort law in the United States was radically reformed over the past 50 years from a relatively minor mechanism for dealing with a small subset of accidents into, today, an institution that conceptually aspires to regulate all industries and social activities, making it the most significant regulatory body in American society."[73]

Why We Can't Go Home Again

The explanation in four words: the trial lawyers' lobby. Some states have been able to overcome its influence, but it is so influential in national politics that it is unrealistic to expect Congress to accomplish more than cosmetic reforms.[74]

On a more optimistic note, the Supreme Court has moved to clean up some of the excesses of civil litigation. Earlier, I mentioned the somewhat tougher standard for pleadings that the *Twombly* decision promulgated. The Supreme Court has in recent years also handed down decisions that have made it easier for federal judges to issue summary judgments, made it easier to keep junk science out the courtroom, and tamped down some of the worst abuses of the class-action suit.[75]

On a still more optimistic note, I will argue in chapters 10 and 11 that important reforms could be prompted by the systematic civil disobedience I advocate in Part II. But that's for later.

CHAPTER 3

AN EXTRALEGAL STATE
WITHIN THE STATE

*In which I describe the creation of the regulatory state,
operating by rules that wouldn't be permitted in civil
and criminal courts, and enforcing laws that it has
made up on its own.*

T HE CHANGES IN the legal system I discussed in the preceding chapter involved the legal system as we ordinarily think of it. Now we're going to talk about a legal system you may not even know exists: the "administrative law" system, with its own separate courts, prosecutors, judges, and appeals process. It is the governing structure for the regulatory state, which in turn is a largely independent fourth branch of government, only loosely answerable to the executive, legislative, or judicial branches.

Administrative State or Regulatory State?

The extralegal system I describe is usually called *administrative law,* and the entity that it serves is usually called the *administrative state.* I subsequently use *regulatory law* and *regulatory state* instead, believing that they more accurately describe the nature of the beast. When you come across *administrative state* in other reading, the phrase is referring to the same thing I'm calling *regulatory state.*

The Basics of the Regulatory State

To give you a sense of how the regulatory law system works, suppose you're in a bar one night and get into an altercation with another customer. Blows are exchanged, blood is spilled, and the cops are called. You are arrested on a charge of assault. The case goes to trial, with you claiming self-defense.

The lead witness for the prosecution is your adversary's date, Judy Wiseman. The prosecution itself is conducted by the district attorney, Ed Wiseman, Judy's brother. The presiding judge is Rosemary Wiseman, Judy's aunt. You are found guilty. Your attorney takes the case to the Court of Appeals, consisting of a bank of three judges—Ezra, Erasmus, and Geraldine Wiseman, who are, respectively, Judy and Ed's uncle, father, and mother. They affirm the lower court's decision.

You manage, finally, to get your case before the Higher Court of Appeals, which, thankfully, has not a single member of the Wiseman clan in sight. You don't have any new evidence, but aren't you owed a new trial without all these conflicts of interest among the witness, prosecutor, judge, and Court of Appeals? No, the Higher Court of Appeals tells you. Ordinarily, you would have a strong case—"no man may be judge in his own cause," *quis custodiet ipsos custodes*, and all that—but this is the Wiseman family. People named Wiseman are known to be honest, disinterested, and devoted to justice and fair play. So whenever the Wiseman family is involved, the Higher Court of Appeals defers to them.

If you don't like analogies, here is a devastatingly direct statement of how the regulatory law system works by constitutional scholar Gary Lawson, using the Federal Communications Commission (FCC) as the example:

> The Commission promulgates substantive rules of conduct. The Commission then considers whether to authorize investigations into whether the Commission's rules have been violated. If the Commission authorizes an investigation, the investigation is conducted by the Commission, which reports its findings to the Commission. If the Commission thinks that the Commission's findings warrant an enforcement action, the Commission issues a complaint. The Commission's complaint that a Commission rule has been violated

is then prosecuted by the Commission and adjudicated by the Commission. This Commission adjudication can either take place before the full Commission or before a semi-autonomous Commission administrative law judge. If the Commission chooses to adjudicate before an administrative law judge rather than before the Commission and the decision is adverse to the Commission, the Commission can appeal to the Commission. If the Commission ultimately finds a violation, then, and only then, the affected private party can appeal to an Article III court. But the agency decision, even before the bona fide Article III tribunal, possesses a very strong presumption of correctness on matters both of fact and of law.[1]

This is the Orwellian rule of law in the regulatory state.

Making the Rules

The independence of the Wiseman family starts with the rule-making process. The most common procedure is called "notice and comment." The regulatory officials have formulated a rule—occasionally responding to a specific mandate from Congress, but more often to a vague legislative instruction to accomplish some desirable end. The agency publishes this initial version in the *Federal Register* and gives the public a period (usually thirty to sixty days) in which people can submit written comments.[2] In rare cases, the agency will hold some sort of hearing.[3] At the end of the comment period, the agency makes whatever changes it deems appropriate—or none at all. It's entirely up to the agency.

For rules that are deemed to be "significant"—in the Obama administration so far, about 20 percent of the total—the Office of Information and Regulatory Affairs (OIRA), part of the Office of Management and Budget, will get involved in the process.[4] OIRA acts as a coordinator with other agencies, provides additional input, mediates disagreements, and is a conduit for the White House's position on proposed regulations.

If a proposed regulation meets certain criteria (for example, that it will have more than $100 million in financial effect on the economy), the agency is required by presidential executive orders going back to Ronald Reagan to conduct a cost-benefit analysis. To the extent permitted by law, the agency may issue only rules whose benefits exceed their costs, and must select the rule with the greatest net benefits from among the different regulatory approaches being considered.

The problem with this otherwise admirable requirement is that few major regulations have a straightforward set of monetary costs and monetary benefits. Instead, cost-benefit analyses are sensitive to assumptions about how to monetize non-monetary parameters, how inclusively costs are defined, and the magnitudes and probabilities assigned to projected benefits. Miraculously, the cost-benefit analysis conducted by a regulatory agency that wants a certain regulation always concludes that the proposed regulation has more benefits than costs, and has a better cost-benefit ratio than the alternatives.[5] So once again, we are back to a situation in which the regulatory agency has close to total de facto independence. Close, but not complete: The heads of regulatory agencies serve at the president's pleasure, and the president may direct an administrator to interpret and apply statutory law in a given way as a condition of keeping his job. It happens, but only occasionally.

Even as it stands, this is a description of agencies making up rules with limited obligatory obedience to the White House and no obligatory sensitivity to what the public thinks. But it gets worse. Certain categories of regulations can be made up and promulgated without notice and comment. This is known as *exempted* rule making. The categories seem harmless—rules about the agency's management of its own personnel do not require notice and comment, for example.[6] But among those categories is the "guidance" document: an agency's nonbinding interpretations of its regulations. This too sounds innocuous—the agency is just trying to help its "clients" know what's going on. But it often doesn't work that way.

For example, in 2014 the Department of Education's Office for Civil Rights (OCR) offered its interpretation of the "disparate impact" regulations formulated under Title VI of the Civil Rights Act in a "letter to colleagues" that was thirty-seven pages long with sixty-three extended endnotes. It covered everything from courses to teacher qualifications to the physical condition of the school in excruciating detail, in effect telling school districts around the country that "disparate impact" can be found in just about everything about a school. "All this goes a million miles beyond the requirements of the Constitution; of Title VI; and even of OCR's own (legally dubious) disparate impact regulations," writes constitutional scholar Michael Greve. "Yet it can't be challenged in any court, anywhere: unlike a rule or regulation, it's not a 'final' agency action that's subject to judicial review. Obviously, though, the [guidance] is meant to be more than merely helpful: in no uncertain terms, it reminds recipients that OCR can and will investigate suspected evil-doers, including those who have been merely unaware of resource compatibility with respect to paint."[7]

And that gets to the nub of the problem. If a regulatory agency knows you are legally obligated to comply with dozens of existing regulations, to ignore its "guidance" on other matters violates the first commandment of the regulatory state: thou shalt not irritate the regulators. Ignore the "guidance," and they can make life miserable for you on the existing regulations. Michael Greve again: "It's a prescription for a banana republic."[8]

Under Their Thumb

The Orwellian part of the enforcement process in regulatory law begins long before you go to court. Beyond the confines of the regulatory state, the government can seldom unilaterally demand that you tell them what you're doing. Just because you have a child, for example, your local child welfare agency cannot tell you to keep a daily record of your child's nutritional intake. But if your business is under the thumb of a regulatory agency, you can be asked to maintain time-consuming and expensive records without an allegation that you have done anything wrong. The courts will not protect you from such requirements "absent a showing that compliance threatens to disrupt or unduly hinder the normal operations of a business."[9] What constitutes "unduly hinder" is to be decided by the court, which may differ from the way it looks to the people actually trying to conduct the "normal operations of a business." What if the government is requiring you to report information that reveals confidential information or trade secrets? That's no excuse, the court ruled in the same case.[10]

If the regulatory agency decides to investigate whether your business has done something wrong, those requirements for information can escalate virtually without limit. Regulatory agencies have subpoena powers, and they can issue subpoenas for information that are similar to discovery in the civil courts, but with lesser requirements for showing cause. By decision of the Supreme Court, a regulatory agency can issue a subpoena for information merely on the "suspicion that the law is being violated, *or even just because it wants assurance that it is not.*"[11] You are legally required to respond to those subpoenas. There's no basis for a stopping point, no way you can say to a court that the demands are excessive. Clint Bolick, who now directs the Goldwater Institute's Scharf-Norton Center for Constitutional Litigation, recalls that the Equal Employment Opportunity Commission (EEOC), where he worked in the 1980s, "would identify a company it didn't like—but had a flimsy case—and simply issue burdensome nonstop subpoenas." Do that often enough, he observed, and it can "subject companies or individuals to demands for information that can bleed them to death."[12]

Regulatory agencies can also obtain search warrants. Outside the purview of the regulatory state, police requests for search warrants famously require "probable cause"—good reason to think that evidence of a crime will be found in a particular place. Not so with a regulatory agency. Regulators need have only "reasonable legislative or administrative standards for conducting an area inspection"—in effect, a stated policy.[13] They don't need to rely on specific information about the condition of the place to be searched or what might be found there. The Supreme Court still considers your place of business to be your castle if the police suspect you of a heinous crime—they have to come up with probable cause or stay outside—but not if a regulatory agency feels like taking a look around.

Inside an Administrative Court

If you are prosecuted for violating a regulation issued by the EPA, OSHA, HHS, Department of Energy, or any of the myriad other federal regulatory agencies, you appear before an administrative law judge (ALJ) sitting in an administrative law courtroom. An ALJ is selected by the agency whose cases he will hear, and is subsequently an employee of that agency. The agency gets to choose its preferred candidate from among the three top-rated candidates identified by the Office of Personnel Management. An administrative law judge is exempt from performance reviews and other oversight by the regulatory agency, but may be overruled by the head of the agency.[14]

There's no jury. When appearing in an administrative court, you do not get a lawyer unless you pay for it. Most rules of evidence used in normal courts do not apply. The legal burden of proof placed on the lawyer making the case for the regulatory agency is "a preponderance of the evidence," not "clear and convincing evidence," let alone "evidence beyond a reasonable doubt" that you are guilty. If the administrative judge thinks that it's a 51/49 percent call in favor of the regulatory agency that accused you, you're found guilty. If the administrative court judge's decision is adverse, you may, in most cases, appeal that decision to another body within the agency.[15]

It is a system riddled with potential for bias. The degree to which the ALJs themselves are impartial has been the subject of an extensive literature and several Supreme Court cases.[16] But to see the larger problem, imagine that all cases involving disputes between the government and IBM were decided by judges who were employees of IBM, subject to the identical selection procedures and protections of independence associated with ALJs. I cannot imagine anyone seriously arguing that such a legal system offered a fair deal to the government's side of the dispute. By what logic can it be argued that the administrative law system is not similarly biased in favor of the government's position? Because it's run by people whose last name is Wiseman?

Chevron Deference

Once your appeal has been rejected by the agency's review process, you may be able to escape into the normal federal court system (what Lawson called an "Article III court" in his description of the process), and you are once again in the land of ordinary legal procedure.[17] But you still have a large legal obstacle to surmount: courts are bound by Supreme Court jurisprudence to accord deference to the regulatory state.

The Supreme Court jurisprudence has been built up for decades, but received its most authoritative statement in the 1984 Supreme Court decision in *Chevron v. Natural Resources Defense Council*.[18] At issue was the power of the EPA to adopt a new definition of the "source" of air pollution, changing from the one it had previously used (based on the individual devices in a plant) to one based on the total emissions from the entire plant. The Court ruled unanimously that the EPA had the authority to do so. As long as Congress has not directly addressed the precise question at issue, the Supreme Court ruled, the *only* issue that the courts could address "is whether the agency's answer is based on a permissible construction of the statute."[19] In other words, as stated in a major textbook on administrative law, "If the [enabling legislation] is silent or ambiguous, Congress has in effect left a gap in the statute for the agency to fill. If the agency in filling that gap has interpreted the statute in a reasonable manner, the court will give effect to that judgment, deferring to the agency, thus granting *Chevron* deference."[20]

Chevron "caused an uproar throughout the legal community in the United States," said a scholar of administrative law (and a judge on the Oregon Supreme Court), Michael Gillette, speaking to a convention of administrative law judges.

> As well it should have done. Because what it represented was an abdication, in the minds of many, of the traditional responsibility of judges. . . . There are certain conceptual difficulties, are there not, in the idea of allowing agencies to act as "wolves guarding the chickens," *i.e.*, of allowing agencies to define the limits of their own power?[21]

"Certain conceptual difficulties" puts it mildly. The administrative law system is, in fact, an extralegal system. I use *extralegal* not rhetorically but in its technical sense. The most complete exposition of how it is extralegal may be found in Philip Hamburger's *Is Administrative Law Unlawful?*[22] The essentials are simple. Constitutional law evolved first in Britain and then in the United States to bar the use of prerogative power—the ability of a king or dictator to do as he sees fit, independently of the law. The Americans went further than the British, denying absolute power not only to the chief executive but also to the legislature. Regulatory law as it has evolved since the 1930s amounts to an exercise of prerogative power. Thousands of regulations, including ones that carry the penalties of the criminal-justice system, have been written by bureaucrats and are enforced by bureaucrats with legislative guidance barely more specific than "Do what you think appropriate."

Chevron deference augments that characteristic of prerogative power by giving regulatory bureaucrats a pass available to no private citizen and to no other government officials—including the president and cabinet officers—who function outside the regulatory state. For everyone except officials of the regulatory state, judges do not defer to anything except the text of the law in question and the body of case law accompanying it. When it comes to the decisions of the administrative law system, however, judges in ordinary courts defer to the people who made the regulations. Hamburger summarizes the situation as follows:

> The danger of prerogative or administrative power—in contrast to mere executive power—arises not simply from its unconstitutionality, but more generally from its revival of absolute power. Rather than a specialized governmental power exercised through and under law, it is a consolidated government power outside and above the law. It therefore traditionally was recognized as absolute, but whereas it once provoked the development of constitutional law, it now threatens to overwhelm the Constitution.[23]

The regulatory state is extralegal in the most straightforward sense of the term: It exists outside the rest of the constitutional legal order. How did this extraordinary state of affairs come to be?

The Origins of the Extralegal State

Article I, Section 1, of the Constitution begins, "All legislative powers herein granted shall be vested in a Congress of the United States." It is a sentence that seems unambiguous. But ambiguity enters the picture nonetheless because any law has to be administered. None except the simplest legislative acts can spell out every administrative detail. Some degree of interpretation is required of the executive branch. But how much interpretation is acceptable?

The Supreme Court was first asked to supply guidelines in *Wayman v. Southard* in 1825. Chief Justice Marshall observed that "the line has not been exactly drawn which separates those important subjects which must be entirely regulated by the legislature itself from those of less interest in which a general provision may be made, and power given to those who are to act under such general provisions to fill up the details."[24] The wording of that description—subjects of "less interest," "fill up the details"—placed substantial limits on the powers that the Supreme Court would permit the legislature to delegate, and those limits were treated seriously throughout the nineteenth century. In 1892, the Supreme Court stated its position explicitly in *Field v. Clark*: "That Congress cannot delegate legislative power to the President is a principle universally recognized as vital to the integrity and maintenance of the system of government ordained by the Constitution."[25] It subsequently became known as the Nondelegation Doctrine.

Even as *Field v. Clark* was being decided, the progressive movement was getting under way, and the second of the three intellectual themes I mentioned in chapter 1 came into play: the progressives' faith in disinterested expertise and their optimism about the behavior of people given access to power.

The scientific and technological achievements of the nineteenth century had created a hitherto unknown creature: the expert. Scientists and engineers at the end of the nineteenth century, unlike autodidacts like Michael Faraday at the beginning of the century, had been systematically trained at universities and had mastered bodies of objective knowledge. Their knowledge was certified by academic degrees. They were experts in their fields, capable of making objective judgments about matters that fell within their expertise. Furthermore, expertise was not limited to the hard sciences. Psychology, political science, and sociology had all become academic disciplines that claimed for themselves the same kind of expert knowledge. By the end of the nineteenth century there were also supposed experts in business management, accounting, and public administration. Put experts in charge of the administration of government, the progressives urged, with job security to buffer them from meddling politicians, and they would make disinterested, technically correct decisions that advanced the public good.[26]

The first experiments seemed to work pretty well. Political scientist Francis Fukuyama describes the creation of one of the earliest such agencies, the US Forest Service.[27] Its first leader, Gifford Pinchot, was the prototype of the expert devoted to a public-spirited end—in his words, "the art of producing from the forest whatever it can yield for the service of man" through controlled, sustainable logging. He hired agronomists and foresters on the basis of strict criteria of competence and technical expertise. By all available measures, the management of the vast forests owned by the federal government materially improved. Experts left alone to do their jobs could do what politicians could not.

But the Forest Service was initially given a specific mission for which the state of knowledge permitted an unambiguously practicable and positive solution. At the time, no one asked how many tasks of governance fit that description. On the contrary, the progressives had vaulting confidence that the experts could deal with almost any problem. Above all, they believed, it was necessary to give these noble civil servants broad freedom to act. "Give us administrative elasticity and discretion," Woodrow Wilson wrote as early as 1891; "free us from the idea that checks and balances are to be carried down through all stages of organization." Wilson also wanted to give these patriotic, politically neutral, wise administrators the authority to act independently of Congress. "Administration cannot wait upon legislation, but must be given leave, or take it, to proceed without specific warrant in giving effect to the characteristic life of the State."[28] In other words, president-to-be Woodrow Wilson had fully envisioned, and was passionately advocating, the regulatory state we have today.

Standing between progressive theorists and their goal of a regulatory state were the limits imposed on the federal government by the Constitution and, more specifically, by the Nondelegation Doctrine. For the first few decades, the progressives made little headway. In 1928, the Supreme Court clarified the Nondelegation Doctrine by specifying that legislation must give an "intelligible principle" to the executive branch that would guide and limit the regulatory power that the executive branch could wield, but this new requirement did not seriously undermine the Nondelegation Doctrine.[29] In 1935, the requirement for an "intelligible principle" was applied to strike down two elements of the National Industrial Recovery Act.[30]

But the 1930s also saw cases in which the Court ruled that the phrase "public interest" could be sufficiently defined by the context of the legislation to pass constitutional muster.[31] This tendency in the case law was broadened and made explicit in 1943 when *National Broadcasting Co. v. United States* came before the Supreme Court.[32] At issue was the authority of the FCC to write regulations that would govern the conditions under which stations could receive government licenses "as public convenience, interest, or necessity requires." NBC argued that "public convenience, interest, or necessity" was a set of words that let the bureaucrats of the FCC write just about any regulation that struck their fancy. The Supreme Court of 1943 disagreed. What had happened to the necessity of an "intelligible principle"? Nowhere is the phrase mentioned.

National Broadcasting was a declaration of independence for regulatory agencies. A year later, the Court decided that "generally fair and equitable" was a sufficiently precise mandate for the Office of Price Administration to set prices and rents.[33] Subsequently, Congress churned out legislation telling regulatory agencies to make regulations based on concepts such as "just and reasonable," "unfair methods of competition," and "excessive profits."[34] In 1984, the Supreme Court explicitly proclaimed the rules for "*Chevron* deference" that I discussed earlier. Congress can give the bureaucracy a few vague instructions and leave the creation of law up to the bureaucrats. It's perfectly constitutional—if we ignore all constitutional jurisprudence before the 1930s.

At the beginning, I said that the regulatory state constitutes a largely independent state within the federal government, only loosely answerable to the executive, legislative, or judicial branches. Was I exaggerating? Let's run over the bidding.

THE EXECUTIVE BRANCH. The president appoints the heads of the regulatory agencies and a few other top staff. They can affect the atmospherics and exert some drag on an agency's regulatory zeal (as during the Reagan administration) or some intensification (as during the Obama administration). The president can issue executive orders, but he has no power to void regulations created by the regulatory agencies. Those are based on the legislative mandates passed by Congress. OIRA gets a chance to review "significant" proposed regulations, but has no power to quash them or demand specific changes. There's another consideration, true of bureaucracies in all democratic countries: Political appointees come and go quickly. The real control of what a regulatory agency does remains with the career staff.

THE LEGISLATIVE BRANCH. Congress's influence on the budget gives it de facto clout in getting the regulatory bureaucracy to interpret regulations in a desired way (a process described in the next chapter). But most of the regulatory legislation passed by Congress has consisted of broad mandates to give the nation clean water and clean air, make workplaces safe, and prevent bad things from happening, which in turn gives the regulatory state broad discretion in making up regulations as it sees fit, because . . .

THE JUDICIAL BRANCH. If the regulatory agency has followed the rule-making process and there's a rationale for saying that a regulation implements a broad congressional mandate, the courts are to defer to the agency's judgment.

To call the regulatory state an extralegal state within the state is not hyperbole but a reasonable description of the facts on the ground.

Why We Can't Go Home Again

In theory, we could go home again because the rules for governing the regulatory state are so self-contained. The Federal Rules of Civil Procedure are subject to modification by the federal court system, and they have in fact been modified many times since the first version took effect in 1938.[35] If Congress could pass a codification of the rules of administrative law in the Administrative Procedure Act of 1946, it is theoretically possible for Congress to pass a major revision of it. In Part II, I will portray a way that we could conceivably make these things happen. But it won't happen through the normal process of electing the right members of Congress or getting five Madisonians on the Supreme Court.

Congress won't do it, absent the new forces introduced by systematic civil disobedience, because of the corruption of the political process described in the next chapter. The judiciary won't do it, absent those new forces, because it would be so disruptive. Some members of the Supreme Court have signaled their reservations about the free hand that *Chevron* gave to the regulatory state, but jurisprudence since *Chevron* offers an indication of the limits on how far the Supreme Court can be expected to go even with a Madisonian majority.[36]

Recall that in *Chevron* the Court ruled that an agency's regulation will receive deference if it "is based on a permissible construction of the statute."[37] In practice, "permissible construction" means "almost anything is okay." In thinking about the prospects of limiting the power of regulatory agencies, first note that the unanimous vote in *Chevron* included Warren

Burger, Byron White, and Lewis Powell—all constitutional conservatives by today's standards. Next consider that *Chevron* has become one of the most frequently cited cases in administrative law and has been revisited by the Supreme Court several times without significantly limiting its scope.[38]

An attempt to resuscitate the Nondelegation Doctrine underscores how securely the legal regime governing the regulatory state is in place. In 1997, the petitioners in *Whitman v. American Trucking Associations, Inc.* challenged a section of the Clean Air Act that instructed the EPA to set "ambient air quality standards the attainment and maintenance of which in the judgment of the Administrator . . . allowing an adequate margin of safety . . . are requisite to protect the public health." But the Supreme Court held that those phrases fell "well within the outer limits of nondelegation precedents."[39] It was a unanimous decision. The opinion of the Court was written by Antonin Scalia and joined by Clarence Thomas, the two most Madisonian judges of the last half century.

The reality that Scalia and Thomas had to face is that reviving a requirement for "intelligible principles" for regulatory legislation, thereby limiting the ability of regulatory agencies to make up whatever rules they wish, would produce convulsions in the federal government rivaling the chaos that would follow a reversal of *Helvering*. It would open up virtually all of the regulatory legislation of the last sixty years to challenge.

Postscript: Lawlessness and the Obama Presidency

I write in the sixth year since Barack Obama first took the presidential oath. His name occurs rarely in this book, and intentionally so. It is my belief that the arguments in *By the People* would be just as compelling if John McCain had been elected in 2008 or Mitt Romney in 2012.

It is also true, however, that President Obama has significantly augmented a long-term expansion of the discretion exercised by the president in the execution of the law. The most publicized examples are the major changes of the Affordable Care Act (ACA), in which, among other things, President Obama . . .

- unilaterally allowed a one-year grace period during which people could continue to purchase health plans that violated ACA requirements and regulations.
- unilaterally delayed implementation of the employer mandate.
- unilaterally delayed the implementation of the out-of-pocket caps on health-insurance costs.[40]

Apart from his actions regarding the ACA, President Obama . . .

- unilaterally waived the statutory requirement of the Worker Adjustment and Retraining Notification Act that employers must give notice to workers sixty days in advance of plant closings, and unilaterally decided to subsidize companies sued by employees for failure to comply with that requirement.
- unilaterally waived the requirement in the 1996 welfare reform act that participating states require able-bodied adults to work or prepare for work.
- unilaterally provided federal benefits for illegal aliens that had been considered and rejected by Congress.
- unilaterally granted deferred action on deportation to categories of illegal immigrants comprising four to five million people.
- unlawfully (as found by the DC circuit court) halted the processing of the Yucca Mountain Nuclear Waste Application.
- unlawfully (as found by the Supreme Court) treated as recess appointments the selection of the director of the Consumer Financial Protection Bureau and three members of the National Labor Relations Board.
- unlawfully (as found by the General Accounting Office) reached a deal with the Taliban to transfer five detainees at Guantánamo to Qatar in exchange for the release of Bowe Bergdahl.[41]

Presidents have been pushing against the limits on their powers since George Washington, and that tendency has increased as the limits on government have loosened over the last seventy years. Is Barack Obama's administration different from those of his predecessors? Predictably, the current answers are highly partisan. But it is fair to say that the issue of failure to "faithfully execute" the law in domestic affairs has come up more frequently and intensely during the Obama administration than in recent administrations. It is also worth noting that the Obama administration's position on cases argued before the Supreme Court has been rejected on 9–0 votes twenty times, an unusually high rate of unanimous rejections of the Department of Justice's position.[42] As I write, the Supreme Court has yet to rule on the most serious cases: the legality of President Obama's unilateral changes to the administration of the Affordable Care Act and his executive order on immigration.[43]

It is not clear which way the Court will go on those cases. The uncertainty itself is revealing. To me, not a constitutional scholar, it seems obvious. The Constitution says, "All legislative powers herein granted shall be vested in a Congress of the United States." The Constitution's description of the executive power requires that the president "take care that the laws be faithfully executed." *Of course* a president cannot unilaterally delay by a year the legislatively stipulated dates for implementation of a law. *Of course* a president cannot unilaterally decide to ignore existing immigration law. But a broad range of constitutional scholars agrees that President Obama's unilateral actions are not the thin edge of a wedge. He is merely pounding an existing wedge deeper into constitutional limits on presidential power. If the Court invalidates his actions, then the trend may be stopped, at least for a while. If the Court validates them, we should assume that subsequent presidents will treat President Obama's actions as precedents for even more expansive prerogative power. Let's face it: if the Supreme Court can rationalize President Obama's executive order on immigration as merely an exercise of prosecutorial discretion, it can rationalize just about anything. To me, the uncertainty about whether the Court will stand in his way is evidence that President Obama is less a cause of lawlessness in the White House than an illustration of how far lawlessness had already progressed when he took office.

CHAPTER 4

A SYSTEMICALLY CORRUPT
POLITICAL SYSTEM

In which I argue that no significant rebuilding of liberty can be expected from Congress, even a Congress controlled by Republicans, because of the systemic corruption of the political process.

IN THEORY, WE don't need a restored Constitution or a reformed legal system to rebuild important aspects of American liberty. It could happen through a Republican Congress working with a Republican president. Congress has the power to abolish any program, agency, or even cabinet department. Congress could pass amended legislation that contains "intelligible principles" that prevent regulatory agencies from implementing their own agendas. Congress could expand the exemptions of small businesses from regulation. Congress could substitute a consumption tax for the income tax, thereby effectively removing the IRS from Americans' lives.

All this is possible—theoretically. In reality, we live in a world in which none of these things will happen. There will be only tweaks at the margins. The political process in Washington is systemically corrupt in ways that make fundamental reforms impossible. Not improbable but impossible.

Corruption, like *lawless*, is a strong word, so I should begin by clarifying what I mean. I do not argue that American politicians and bureaucrats in the second decade of the twenty-first century are more venal or dishonest than politicians of the past. Rather, the American political process now has reached a stage analogous to that of the legal system.

Just as a technically ruleful legal system now has some of the operational characteristics of lawlessness, today's political process has produced politicians who, while keeping within the law, do things that are operationally indistinguishable from the way Third World kleptocrats operate.

Think of your image of governmental corruption as you imagine it to exist (or perhaps have observed it) in a Third World kleptocracy. Officials who make a modest official salary live in big houses and drive Mercedes, because government service is a way of getting rich. If you are a citizen who runs a business, you are regularly shaken down by officials as a price of doing business. If you have a problem with the government, you have to pay a bribe to get a hearing, and getting action on your request will require an additional bribe. If you want to get contracts for government business, you must give the bureaucrats their cut.

In a kleptocracy, bribes can accomplish many other things as well. You don't want to pay an export duty? The inspectors at the ports can be paid off. You have a bothersome competitor? The officials and the cops can make him decide to close up shop. What you want to do is illegal? A law can be designed especially for you.

The only word to describe those kinds of interactions between government and the private sector is "corruption." Now consider: if for "bribe" one substitutes "financial support for political campaigns and political parties," what I have described is the reality of how Congress and the private sector interact in today's Washington—not once in a while, but as the established way of doing business.

As with the gutting of the Constitution, we are looking not at a problem that has persisted throughout American history but at one that was triggered by events over a short period of time. In the case of the Constitution, the critical period was 1937 to 1942. In the case of systemic corruption, the critical period was 1970 to 1975.

Corruption in Washington Before the 1970s

Corruption in the political process varies directly with the number and value of things that politicians have to sell. This is the fundamental theorem for explaining the behavior of both the buyers and the sellers of political favors.

Applying the theorem, it is easy to look at American history and guess when and where corruption has been most common. For the federal government, the prime eras for corruption in the nineteenth century were the Civil War, when a profusion of government contracts was up for grabs, and during the building of the great railroads after the Civil War, when contracts and land grants were both up for grabs. Read Mark Twain's *The Gilded Age* to get a sense of what Washington was like then.[1] Among state and municipal governments, which accumulated much larger inventories of things to sell, corruption was rampant from the Civil War through the end of century.[2] "Bribery and corruption are as universal as to threaten the very structure of society," a Supreme Court justice told Yale law students in 1895. "Probably in no country in the world is the influence of wealth more potent than in this, and in no period of our history has it been more powerful than now."[3] This was old-fashioned corruption based on payment of bribes. Some politicians and some bureaucrats were bribable; others were not.

Only a few industries engaged in this corruption at the federal level in America before the New Deal. A far larger segment of the business world was completely uninvolved in Washington, because so few businesses had an incentive to sway the vote of a senator or representative. Except for the rare industries that were already significantly regulated in 1928, notably railroads, or ones that urgently needed higher tariffs to protect themselves from foreign competition, the federal government was irrelevant to the way they went about their operations. State and municipal governments were already enthusiastic regulators by 1928, but the federal government was not.

The New Deal expanded regulation, but then and through the 1950s that regulation was targeted—the Civil Aeronautics Board regulating the airline industry and the FCC regulating radio and television, for example. Altogether, about two dozen industry-specific agencies were established.[4] These agencies did not arouse widespread corporate unease. In practice, cozy relationships usually developed between the regulators and the regulated. If you weren't in one of those industries that had been assigned its own regulatory agency, not much had changed even after the New Deal. When John Kennedy came to the presidency in 1961, only a handful of corporations maintained even a small office in Washington.[5]

The pre-1970s environment was also relaxed when it came to campaign funding, because campaigns weren't expensive. The typical House campaign in the 1950s and early 1960s probably cost well under $100,000 in today's dollars, and most Senate campaigns probably cost around $500,000. [6] These were not daunting sums to raise, especially since wealthy individuals were free to contribute as much as they wished.

What about contributions from special interests? Corporations had been banned from making contributions to political candidates in 1907. Corporations that did wish to contribute got around the ban through a variety of techniques, some legal and some not.[7] Unions had remained free to use money from union dues as political contributions, but that changed in 1947 with the Taft-Hartley Act. To get around the new ban, the Congress of Industrial Unions formed an organization to collect donations from union members for use in political campaigns. They called their new organization the Political Action Committee—the first PAC.

For the next two decades, other unions formed PACs, but few industries or nonprofit organizations followed their example. There still weren't many ways in which the federal government could help them or hurt them, and the kind of single-issue politics that motivates PACs on social issues didn't exist.

I am referring to a political climate so radically different from today's that readers who grew up after the 1950s will have a hard time believing me. If you want to get a sense of just how different, read a novel called *Advise & Consent* by Allen Drury, a political journalist who covered the Senate for many years. *Advise & Consent* was published in 1959, became the year's top-selling novel, won the Pulitzer Prize, and was widely acknowledged by political pros to be a realistic portrayal of the way the game was played in 1950s Washington. It is not a kind of politics that today's political pros would recognize. Or you can read Theodore White's *The Making of the President, 1960*, also a Pulitzer Prize winner, to get a sense of how different presidential campaigns used to be. Consider this: For the 1960 election, the first candidate to announce that he was running for president, Hubert Humphrey, did so on December 30, 1959, just ten months and two weeks before the election. It was considered an early announcement.

The Transformation of the Political Environment, 1970–1975

By the end of the 1960s, regulations had been pouring out of Washington in unprecedented volume, adding 27,685 pages to the *Code of Federal Regulations* from Kennedy's assassination through 1969. The Civil Rights Act of 1964 had initiated unprecedented federal oversight of hiring, promotion, and firing. Ralph Nader had demonstrated how much effect lobbying Congress could have on the operations of the auto industry. The stage was set for transformative change, and it happened during the first half of the 1970s. Six events were pivotal.

Richard Nixon Ballooned the Regulatory State

From 1970 to 1974, sixteen new major regulatory agencies were established, including the EPA and OSHA, the two with the most sweeping influence. During the same period, the Supreme Court's decision in *Griggs v. Duke Power* expanded the regulatory clout of the Equal Employment Opportunity Commission (EEOC). What set those three agencies apart from previous regulatory agencies were their unrestricted briefs. Not limited to a specific industry, each had economy-wide authority to regulate.

Corporate America Got into the Game

In 1971, Lewis Powell, later a Supreme Court justice, wrote an influential memorandum for the Chamber of Commerce arguing that a "broadly based and consistently pursued" attack on free enterprise was under way and that there were "few elements of American society to have as little influence in government as the American businessman, the corporation, or even the millions of corporate stockholders."[8] It was time, Powell said, for American business to acquire political power:

> Such power must be assiduously cultivated; and, when necessary, it must be used aggressively and with determination—without embarrassment and without the reluctance which has been so characteristic of American business. . . . Business and the enterprise system are in deep trouble, and the hour is late.[9]

Though little known to the general public, the Powell memorandum marked an inflection point in corporate America's involvement in Washington. Within a decade, most major corporations and industry trade organizations had established offices in Washington.

Television and Polling Revolutionized Political Campaigns

Roger Ailes's orchestration of Nixon's 1968 television appearances and ads had opened an era of rapidly increasing sophistication in the use of the media. Polling techniques had improved, and continued to do so throughout the 1970s, becoming a key tool for crafting campaign positions that maximized a candidate's chances of winning. Television and polling both cost lots of money, and politicians who wanted to stay in office found themselves having to accumulate war chests far larger than they had needed just a few years earlier.

Politicians Became Regulatory Intercessors for Business

The fourth event consisted of obscure procedural changes that never make the news and yet have huge effects.

As described in the previous chapter, regulatory agencies live in a judicial world of their own. In 1975, the Administrative Procedure Act of 1946 was amended in two ways. First, it became easier for outside organizations to participate in the rule-making process. Second, it became harder to appeal against the decision of an administrative law judge. Together, the two changes meant profound unintended consequences for the way that Washington operated. The effect of the first change was to raise the importance of a formal lobbying effort while the rules were being made, thereby giving the lobbying industry a huge new market for its wares. The effect of the second change was to make politicians the de facto court of appeals for overturning the decisions of regulatory agencies. As John Wettergreen summarizes it:

> Appeals against the agencies in courts of law were difficult, and appeals against the agencies in the non-Constitutional, administrative legal system were adjudicated by the agencies themselves. So, in practice, political appeals against the agencies were the most ef-

fective means available. Accordingly, they became so much more common that *ex parte* proceedings . . . which were often felonious in the days before the regulatory revolution, became standard procedure. . . . That is how the main job of the contemporary Congressmen became liaison with regulatory agencies, not legislation.[10]

The confluence of the proliferation of regulations in the 1970s and the congressperson's emerging role as the most effective way to deal with those regulations constitutes an example of what I mean by *systemic corruption*. For most of recorded history, gatekeepers have been an irresistible object of influence peddling and bribery. Changes in the law made members of Congress the gatekeepers for access to the bureaucracy.

Democracy Came to the House

The fifth event was reformation of the internal operations of the House beginning in 1970 and culminating in early 1975, when the Democratic congressional class of 1974, elected in the aftermath of Watergate, took office.

As of 1970, the House was still controlled by the Speaker of the House and the chairmen of the most powerful committees.[11] If you represented a special interest and wanted to get favorable action from the House, corralling votes among the representatives at large was futile. In those days, a substantial majority of representatives could agree on a given policy measure that would nonetheless have no chance of reaching the floor for a vote if the leadership didn't approve. Of the 435 members of the House of Representatives, only a few dozen of them had things of much value to sell.

The early 1970s saw a series of internal reforms that ate into the monopoly power of the Speaker and the committee chairmen.[12] Then the 1974 election brought seventy-five new Democratic members to the House. The first few months of the ninety-fourth Congress saw the revolution completed. Some members remained more important than others, but no longer could a few senior members block legislation from coming to the floor. Unlike the past, it now *did* make sense to corral votes of ordinary members on behalf of your special interest and to engage a member as your advocate with the regulatory agencies.

Congress Inadvertently Magnified the Role of Special Interests

The sixth event was the passage of the Federal Campaign Act of 1974. The act was intended to diminish the influence of wealthy individuals by limiting the amounts of money they could contribute directly to candidates during elections. But it had two unintended consequences. First, it increased the time that members had to spend raising money—"dialing for dollars," as it is called on the Hill—because it now took many more individual contributors to get the same amount of money. Second, it gave wealthy citizens an incentive to use alternative ways of getting their political contributions into the system—and there, ideal for serving that purpose, unexploited for a quarter of a century, was the vehicle known as the PAC.

The increased incentive to use PACs led to the creation of many more of them, which in turn created a third unintended consequence. More PACs created new markets for political contributions. Before the PACs proliferated, suppose you were a citizen with some discretionary income who was passionate about preserving the wilderness. You seldom made contributions to political campaigns, however, because a modest contribution to an individual candidate was unlikely to have any effect on the issue you cared about. But once a PAC exclusively devoted to wilderness preservation existed, that same level of passion for wilderness conservation was much more likely to translate into regular contributions to that PAC—it was a much more focused way of getting political bang for your buck.

The 1974 reform was transformative because it magnified the power of special interests many times over. When individuals could contribute as much as they wanted to a campaign, a member of Congress might have a few large contributors whom he wanted to keep happy. But keeping them happy usually amounted to voting the way that the candidate's publicly held political positions had led big contributors to believe he would vote. Yes, a big contributor in business X might expect the right vote on a bill directly affecting business X, but that would probably amount to one or two votes per session of Congress at most. On the rest of the issues, big contributors usually weren't on the phone pushing the member to vote one way or the other, but were satisfied if the people they supported voted the way they campaigned. As politics goes, it was a fairly benign way for special interests to have influence. In contrast, once the PACs had spread from broad interest groups to ones representing specific industries and causes, votes on major issues and many minor ones were made in the context of past support from the interested PACs and with implications for their subsequent support or opposition.

Together, these ingredients created systemic corruption. As of 1975, the federal government had acquired power over the activities of the private sector that could make millions of dollars' difference to the bottom line of individual corporations, and billions of dollars' difference for an entire industry. Corporate America had finally awakened to that reality. Noncorporate special interests were finding that PACs could attract large sums of money from their constituencies. Large sums devoted to lobbying could tweak the provisions of a proposed regulation, thereby making a big difference to the bottom lines of corporations or advancing the agendas of noncorporate special interests. The way that regulations were administered also meant that soliciting help from members of Congress was the best way to get a favorable ruling or to change an adverse ruling. The way to advance these specific policy objectives was through organizations specifically focused on them—the PACs. And all of this was happening as the cost of campaigns was skyrocketing, making elected politicians frantic to raise enough money to stay in office.

The Maturation of Systemic Corruption

This transformation of the political environment in the first half of the 1970s was swiftly followed by transformations in political practice. The average cost of a Senate campaign in 1974 was $1.9 million, already unprecedentedly high by historic standards. That already-high figure doubled by 1982, tripled by 1994, and quadrupled by 2006.[13] The average cost of a campaign for the House in 1974 had been $236,120. That figure doubled by 1982, tripled by 1996, quadrupled by 2006, and quintupled by 2010, standing at $1.2 million.[14] All of these numbers are based on constant 2010 dollars.

In the first published list of PACs in 1974, only 89 were affiliated with corporations. By 1982, that number had grown sixteenfold, to 1,467. The total number of registered PACs quintupled during the same period, to 3,371 in 1982.[15] Direct campaign contributions by PACs had already reached $114 million in 1978. That figure had more than doubled by 1986 and more than tripled by 2006.[16] But direct contributions drastically understate the real increase in spending on political campaigns by the PACs. PACs are free to spend unlimited amounts on political advertising that does not ask people to vote for a specific candidate—in effect, an open invitation to fund negative advertising about the opponent of the person a PAC wishes to support.

The increasing cost of campaigns and the increasing availability of money through the PACs set the stage for the growth of the industry that has come to symbolize all that has gone wrong with the political process: the lobbying industry. It was inevitable. If you want something from a public official, it's good to have an intermediary seek it for you—someone who specializes in this sort of thing and who has a personal relationship with the person to be influenced. A lobbyist.[17]

The extent of lobbying depends once again on the number and value of things that public officials have to sell. The federal government as of 1975 had a newly expanded inventory of shiny, valuable goods. That alone would have stimulated more business for lobbyists. But the effectiveness of lobbying is also influenced by the distance that separates a member of Congress from substantive knowledge of the issue in question, and this, too, is a key element in the systemic nature of the corruption.

In 1930, the average size of the staff of a member of the House was 2.0—meaning that the average House member had a secretary, and one aide for everything else. The average number of staff for senators was 2.9. Perforce, the members did most of the substantive work themselves. By 1957, those numbers had expanded to 5.6 staff members in the House and 11.6 in the Senate; by 1967, to 9.2 in the House and 17.5 in the Senate.[18] But even at this point, according to Gerry Cassidy, a prominent lobbyist who got into the business in those years, "the Senate was a very different place then: small staffs, members did so much of the work themselves, they were on the floor a lot. . . . And members knew what they were talking about. They had a lot of time. . . . [They] were very familiar with issues."[19]

Just ten years later, in 1977, the average House member had an office staff of 16 people and the average Senator had a staff of 36. The number of issues that members had to vote on had increased. The number of regulatory issues the PACs were bringing to members had mushroomed.

Meanwhile, the time representatives and senators could devote to these issues had been slashed—in part because they were now forced to spend so much time fund-raising. In its briefing for newly elected House members after the election of 2012, the Democratic Congressional Campaign Committee presented a "Model Daily Schedule" for members when they were in DC.[20] It included four hours of "call time"—the term for phoning contributors—and one hour of "strategic outreach," which includes such things as breakfasts and meet-and-greets with supporters. When they're not in Washington, the Model Daily Schedule calls for three hours of daily call time plus one hour of strategic outreach.

The first-order effect was that a large proportion of the decisions members make, and the actions of their offices on behalf of special interests, are not the result of the members' deliberate, considered judgment, but the result of a staffer's recommendation. In his 2009 memoir, Ted Kennedy estimated that staff members handled about 95 percent of the legislative responsibility, representing "an enormous shift in responsibility" from the elected members to staff.[21] Members who rely so heavily on their staff's recommendations aren't being lazy. They are required to make more decisions than they have time to make on their own.

The second-order effect was that lobbyists no longer have just 435 representatives and 100 senators whose influence can produce the desired result; the right recommendation made to a harried member by an aide can also produce the right decision, and the number of people in those positions kept growing. Add in all the people staffing the House and Senate committees, plus all the people in the regulatory agencies who can tweak a regulation, and there has been a population explosion among the people who are worth lobbying.

The lobbying industry flourished commensurately. Here's another of those facts from the past that are hard for today's readers to believe: The first firm that explicitly identified itself as a lobbying firm did not appear until 1975.[22] Coming up with exact figures on what happened since then is difficult. A 1991 study by the General Accounting Office found that of 13,500 individuals and organizations listed as key "influence peddlers" in a widely used book, 10,000 were not registered as lobbyists.[23] At the peak of registration in 2007, before the reform act of 2007 led many lobbyists to deregister (while continuing to lobby), there were 14,837 registered lobbyists, whose annual spending totaled $3 billion.

By this time, politicians needed the lobbyists as much as lobbyists needed them, serving, in Robert Kaiser's words, as "advisors, fund-raisers, even finance chairmen of their campaigns."[24] Former senator Chuck Hagel explained to Kaiser how the campaign financing aspect of the lobbyists' services works. The national committees of the Democrats and Republicans alike use huge fund-raising dinners to finance House and Senate campaigns, raising up to $20 or $25 million per dinner. "Who do we go to, to make sure that we get $20 to $25 million?" Hagel said. "I've run these dinners so I know what I'm talking about. You go to a committee of twenty-five lobbyists, a steering committee. And you say, Okay, you guys each have to come up with a million dollars. . . . So we go to them for that fast money."[25]

The Characteristics of a Kleptocracy as Applied to Contemporary Washington

This is not the place to present the detailed evidence for the corruption now systemic in Congress. That evidence has been presented in many recent books. If you want to pursue it, start with *So Damn Much Money* by Robert Kaiser; *Crony Capitalism in America, 2008–2012*, by Hunter Lewis; and two books, *Extortion* and *Throw Them All Out*, by Peter Schweizer. I can summarize the situation by reviewing the symptoms of corruption in a kleptocracy, and applying it to the contemporary political process.

In a Corrupt System, Government Service Is a Way to Get Rich

In one respect, the current situation is nothing new. In the 1940s and 1950s, Lyndon Johnson became a multimillionaire on a government salary because (among other financial shenanigans) his wife was given a television monopoly for Austin, Texas—something enjoyed by no other owner of a television station in a major city.[26] The same kind of financial exploitation of insider contacts, information, and benefits persists today. Consider investment performance. The average American investor underperforms the market. For the last several years, the average hedge fund has underperformed the market.[27] An analysis of 4,000 stock trades by US senators found that the average senator beat the market by 12 percent per year.[28] A study of stock trades of House members found that they did no better than ordinary investors with most of their stocks but did quite well on stocks with which they were "politically connected."[29] Peter Schweizer gives the gory details of the circumstances leading to specific stock trades by specific members in *Throw Them All Out*. He also documents numerous instances in which members of Congress have used legislative legerdemain to target roads, public transit routes, and federal facilities so that they increase the value of property held by the members.

These are the traditional ways of getting rich through government service that go back to the founding, but they are arguably more widespread than ever before because the enrichment process has been institutionalized through the "revolving door." It is accepted that members of Congress, senior staff assistants, and senior officials in the government will use their government service to secure positions in the lobbying industry, or in the industries they have been regulating, after they leave government service. Those jobs pay many multiples of their former government salaries.

This route to enrichment is most definitely not traditional. Robert Kaiser recounts the disapproving gossip among members and journalists in the late 1970s when, for the first time, a former member reappeared on the floor of the House as a lobbyist.[30] But the practice soon spread, then became standard operating procedure. By 2007, 188 former members of Congress were registered lobbyists. Between 1998 and 2004, half of the senators and 42 percent of House members who left Congress became lobbyists. Three thousand six hundred staffers went through the revolving door.[31] And the same thing was happening among political appointees, especially from the regulatory agencies. As of 2008, 310 officials who formerly worked for George W. Bush and 283 who formerly worked for Bill Clinton had gone to work for lobbying firms, PACs, or industries with which they had been involved while in office.[32] Kaiser presents these numbers and summarizes them as follows:

> These numbers aren't just statistics; they describe the entrenched culture of modern Washington. The essential nature of this culture could not be quickly changed by a ban on congressmen flying in

corporate jets or accepting meals or travel from lobbyists, or even by a two-year cooling-off period. In Washington it had become *normal* to use government experience—in Congress and the executive branch—as a stepping-stone to lucrative work in the "private sector" that is devoted to influencing the government.[33]

There's a phrase for it among Hill staffers: "cashing in." When House Speaker Nancy Pelosi wanted to put a two-year cooling-off period (the time between leaving a government job and coming out the other side of the revolving door) in a proposed bill, one of the arguments used to dissuade her was that House members would have a hard time attracting top-flight talent.[34] Why would talented people want to become congressional aides unless they could expect to cash in?

In a Corrupt System, You Pay for Access to the Authorities

If you are an individual constituent with a good story, you might still get some time with your member of Congress even if you haven't given him a penny. But if you are a corporation or an organization with resources, you are expected to pay for access. Once again, it's standard operating procedure. It doesn't necessarily have to be a payment directly to the campaign of the person you're trying to see, but you had better be listed among the "friendlies" by the member's party, and the way you get listed as a "friendly" is by having contributed. Usually this has been an informal (though universally observed) understanding. After he became Republican Whip in 1995, Tom DeLay brought it nakedly into the open. He prepared "the Book"—a compilation of all the contributions by the four hundred largest PACs made to both Democratic and Republican members over the previous two years. These were used to establish ratings of "friendly" or "unfriendly" for every company, industry, or association that was likely to be a client of the major lobbying firms. The Book was laid on a folder in the anteroom to DeLay's office in the Capitol Building, where any visitor was welcome to leaf through it. "Friendlies" could get meetings with DeLay. "Unfriendlies" could not. You could easily switch your classification. No protestations of ideological solidarity were necessary. Just contribute enough money, and you became a "friendly."[35]

In a Corrupt System, Officials Shake Down Businesses

Members of Congress do not just passively accept corporate contributions as the price of an appointment. They also take the initiative, behaving in ways that look like shakedowns. The former CEO of a major corporation put it this way: "What has been called legalized bribery looks like extortion to us. . . . I know from personal experience and from other executives that it's not easy saying no to appeals for cash from powerful members of Congress or their operatives. . . . The threat may be veiled, but the message is clear: failing to donate could hurt your company."[36]

The shakedowns also occur in what Peter Schweizer calls "tollbooth" charges: donations paid to get a politician to do what he is supposed to do anyway. Thus, for example, the Wireless Tax Fairness Act was expected to come to a vote in the fall of 2011. It was supported by the cell-phone industry, had broad bipartisan support, and was certain to pass. But for months House Speaker John Boehner did not bring the bill to the floor for a vote. Finally, he declared a vote for November 1, 2011. The day before the vote, twenty-eight executives of AT&T wrote checks for John Boehner's campaign fund. The day of the vote, twenty-eight executives of Verizon sent checks to members of Congress, both Democrat and Republican.[37] That's how the tollbooth works. It's not big money—a total of about $50,000. John Boehner was not behaving in some novel way; Speakers of the House going back to Jim Wright have routinely collected tolls. But think about it for a minute: Large numbers of executives do not spontaneously write campaign contributions on the same day. A message had to have gone out from someone that went something like this: "I'm happy to report that our bill is going to be brought to the floor for a vote tomorrow, but I'm told that it would be appropriate for us to come up with X amount of dollars. That works out to Y dollars from each of you." It's corruption. There's no other word for it.

Or take the case of tax extenders. The tax code is riddled with special "temporary" corporate tax breaks that have an expiration date. But Congress can vote to retain those tax breaks through "tax extenders." And so it has become an annual game in Washington: Congress leaves it up in the air whether a given tax will be extended and then, just before the tax extender is approved by the relevant committee (which usually ensures approval by the full House or Senate), a flood of checks arrives for senators or House members who run the key committees that can push through tax extenders. One of the most important of these "temporary" tax breaks is the tax credit for research and development (R&D) expenditures enacted in 1981. Its effectiveness in promoting technological innovation is widely thought to have provided major benefits to the nation as a whole. So why, more than thirty years later, is the R&D tax credit still temporary? "They trot out the R&D tax credit every few years," observed Bob Herbold, former COO of Microsoft, "and it's always with their hands open, looking for money. It's like an annuity for them. They won't make it permanent because it doesn't make sense for *them* to make it permanent."[38] In 1998, there were 42 tax extenders. By 2011, they had more than tripled, to 154.[39]

In a Corrupt System, Public Officials Shower Their Friends with Gifts

In the United States, this has taken the form of pork-barrel projects that members of Congress create for their state or district. It has been going on ever since the government began handing out contracts. This is one type of corruption that has always been systemic: elected officials usually want to be reelected, and reelection is facilitated by getting the government to spend money that directly benefits their constituents. Members who consider themselves to be scrupulously honest can direct these goodies to their constituents without guilt because they tell themselves that their constituents really do need the community centers, roads, jobs, or whatever else the pork consists of, and they, the members, aren't profiting by even a penny. But in reality it amounts to allocation of public money not on the merits of the case but because of political pull for personal political gain. It's not the worst form of corruption, but it's corruption. And it's been growing. An advocacy organization, Citizens Against Government Waste, has tabulated the projects that it defines as pork.[40] The first year of their data goes back to 1991, when fewer than 400 projects counted as pork. That number reached a high of 14,000 in 2006, with a value of more than $31 billion.[41]

In a Corrupt System, Bribes Produce Results Independently of Political Principle

In 2007, Charles Rangel of New York, then chairman of the House Ways and Means Committee, proposed to raise the tax on hedge-fund and equity-fund profits from 15 percent to 35 percent. Rangel's Senate colleague Charles Schumer was among the most progressive members of the Senate, and not shy about saying so. Everything in his avowed political philosophy should have led him to support Rangel's proposal. And yet, as Robert Kaiser reports,

> Rangel's plan was blocked. Its most effective opponent was the congressman's fellow Democrat from New York, Charles Schumer. He became the investment industry's leading advocate in the Senate, a role that benefited him in his job as chairman of the Democratic Senatorial Campaign Committee, which collected millions from investment company executives while Schumer staved off legislation the industry opposed.[42]

Lobbying expenditures by the financial community went up from $4 million in 2007 to $20 million in 2008. Their political contributions to candidates during the same period increased from $11 million to $20 million.

If you want more than individual cases, a scholarly study of 463 executives who had been prosecuted for violations of the rules of the Securities and Exchange Commission found that "accused executives at firms who make political contributions, either via a political action committee or via the CEO, are banned for three fewer years, serve probation five fewer years, prison for six fewer years, and are 46 percent less likely to receive both prison time and an officer ban" than firms that did not contribute. Furthermore, the *amount* of money contributed had an independent effect, with high contributions associated with still lesser penalties.[43] Another study looked at the investigation phase of possible fraud violations. Companies who retained lobbyists were 38 percent less likely to have a charge of fraud levied against them.[44]

Now we come to earmarks—those provisions slipped into large bills, especially the massive appropriations bills, that specify that certain funds are to be spent on a particular private entity's projects, or that exempt a particular business from a tax or regulation. Some of what we now call earmarks are traditional pork instigated by the members themselves. But in 1976, one of the fledgling lobbying firms, Schlossberg-Cassidy, discovered a new way for lobbying firms to attract clients: by acting as go-betweens that could enable entities in the private sector to instigate their own pork. The first such earmark was $20 million for a new nutritional center at Tufts University.[45] What had been done didn't go unnoticed—the *Washington Post* editorialized against it—but over the next few years Schlossberg-Cassidy parlayed their success into more university clients, and then broke still more new ground when they got Ocean Spray, the cranberry-growers' cooperative, to start a PAC. Schlossberg-Cassidy then managed the PAC, deciding which members of Congress got contributions so that Ocean Spray's needs for earmarks could be arranged.

Over the next three decades, earmarks increased from a handful to thousands of provisions slipped into bills. These appropriations were not "approved" by Congress in any meaningful sense of the word. They were just stuck into bills at the behest of one or two members, and the entire bill was passed without anyone but the sponsors even knowing they were in there. Or caring. A study by the Congressional Research Service in 2006 found that the federal budget in fiscal 2005 had 16,072 earmarks by its definitions, up from 4,203 in the first year of its survey, 1994.[46]

The nakedness of the quid pro quos implicit in earmarks became a national scandal. As I write, a moratorium on earmarks passed in 2010 is still in effect. It is unclear how much of the earmark effort has been converted to alternative methods.

Washington is still not nearly as corrupt as real kleptocracies such as Equatorial Guinea, Uzbekistan, or Sudan.[47] The people who run Washington are generally more honest, more committed to the public good, and less thuggish than the officials in a real kleptocracy. The proportional size of the take in Washington is far less than the take in a real kleptocracy. But the parallels in the ways that Washington and kleptocracies operate are many and troubling.

Can the System Be Reformed?

The moratorium on earmarks that began in 2010 shows that Congress is not entirely immune to the public's disgust. But we have two test cases of attempts at deeper reform, and neither gives much reason for optimism. One is the reform legislation of 2007, the Honest Leadership and Open Government Act (HLOGA), intended to reduce systemic corruption. It had a long list of provisions. Members of Congress and lobbyists were required to submit many more, and more detailed, reports on their activities. Lobbyists became criminally liable for gifts to members and staff. The rules for earmarks were tightened.[48] It all looked great on paper. But it didn't do anything to change the way that money would flow into campaigns, and it didn't get to the heart of the revolving door by which former members and their staffs take lucrative positions with lobbyists.[49]

As I write, HLOGA has been in effect for seven years. During that time, the number of registered lobbyists has gone down, but the spending on lobbying has gone up. How is that possible? Because lobbyists, faced with the new restrictions, stopped registering as lobbyists. Thus former Senate majority leader Tom Daschle went to work for the law firm of Alston & Bird as a "special policy advisor." The firm's lobbying income doubled during his first year. Newt Gingrich took home $300,000 a year from Freddie Mac for his work as a "historian."[50] Forty-six percent of those who deregistered continued to work for their same employer, taking advantage of a provision in the law that allows them to continue lobbying without registering if they spend less than 20 percent of their time lobbying—a loophole of gaping proportions. As of 2013, the number of registered lobbyists stood at 12,281. The research of political scientist James Thurber, who has studied congressional lobbying for more than thirty years, puts the true number of lobbyists at around 100,000.[51] I am aware of no dispassionate observer of Congress, from either side of the political spectrum, who has tried to make the case that HLOGA achieved anything close to the goals it promised, or even made government more open.

The second test case is the executive order signed by Barack Obama on his first full day in office. It barred anyone who had been a registered lobbyist in the previous two years from a job in his administration, prohibited new hires from working on issues related to their former employers for two years, and required that persons leaving the administration refrain from lobbying for two years. But within weeks, the new president declared that three new senior officials were "uniquely qualified" for the position the administration had in mind, and therefore the anti-lobbying rules were waived.[52] Within the first year and a half, forty more waivers followed. On top of those were officials—the general counsel for Health and Human Services and the chief weapons buyer for the Pentagon, for example—who had been lobbyists by any ordinary understanding of their careers but were not *registered* lobbyists, and thus were exempt from the president's executive order. The executive order issued with such fanfare at the outset of the administration has become, to borrow a word from the Nixon years, inoperative.

The Final Nail: The Frailty of the Republican Party as an Instrument for Limiting Government

As I write, the Republicans have just won control of the Senate and have their largest majority in the House since 1930. What if they can add a Republican president to those majorities in 2016? To think that it would make any difference in limiting government requires a triumph of hope over experience. Given power, the Republicans have proved themselves to be as embedded in a corrupt system as the Democrats. They aren't worse than the Democrats, but neither have they been better. Since my readers are overwhelmingly on the political right, I think it is important to take a few pages to make that point.

For two decades following the events in 1970–75 that transformed the dynamics of congressional politics, the Democrats were riding high. They controlled the House throughout and the Senate for all but six years. During that period, they took advantage of their prerogatives under the new rules of the game, and encouraged an unprecedented polarization of congressional politics.[53] I don't need to convince most of you of that. What you may not be aware of is the degree to which the Republican majority in the House from 1995 to 2006 not only perpetuated the corrupt practices of the Democrats but extended them.

Democrats first used earmarks in the modern sense of that term starting in the 1970s, and the use of earmarks expanded rapidly thereafter. One of the GOP's themes during the 1994 campaign was Democratic corruption, with earmarks being a prime target. The new Speaker, Newt Gingrich, had it within his power to end earmarks altogether. He chose not to, but at least the number of earmarks did not increase markedly on his watch. At the end of 1998, Gingrich resigned, to be replaced by Dennis Hastert as Speaker, with Majority Whip Tom DeLay as the power behind the throne. The use of earmarks took off. Here are some illustrative numbers from the Congressional Research Service study, ranking the cabinet departments by the number of earmarks affecting them in the 1994 budget.

NUMBER OF EARMARKS IN APPROPRIATION ACTS, 1994 AND 2005

Cabinet Department	1994	2005	Ratio
Energy and Water Development	1,574	2,313	1.5
Defense	587	2,506	4.3
Interior	314	568	1.8
Agriculture	313	704	2.3
Commerce, Justice, and State	253	1,722	6.8
Transportation	140	2,094	15.0
Veterans, HUD	30	2,080	69.3
Labor, HHS, Education	5	3,014	602.8

Source: Congressional Research Service (2006).

Republicans not only multiplied the use of earmarks in the cabinet departments that had seen the most in the past—Energy and Defense—they also took earmarks into departments that had been virtually ignored. Democrats joined in the spree (they accounted for 40 percent of the earmarks), but Republicans led the way.[54]

As Republican whip, DeLay took the Democrats' exploitation of the power of the majority to new depths. I have already described "the Book," which stripped away any pretense that access was not contingent on contributions. But DeLay generated many other stories. For example, there was the letter sent to corporate PACs in the state of Washington when a new Republican member scheduled a fund-raiser. Each letter noted the exact amount the PAC had given to the Republican's opponent in the preceding election and expressed DeLay's surprise that the PAC had supported the opponent—but assured the recipient that the PAC now had "the opportunity to work toward a positive future relationship," concluding with the hard-to-misinterpret sentence, "Your immediate support for Randy Tate is personally important to me and the House Republican leadership team."[55] DeLay also implemented the "K Street Strategy," which forced lobbying firms to hire Republicans by telling them that DeLay wouldn't meet with lobbyists who were Democrats.

The Democrats had done similar things when they ran the House, but it was agreed—and the Republican leadership was proud of it—that Gingrich and then DeLay had expanded and systematized the shakedown of PACs, and done it more ruthlessly than ever before.

If Republican complicity in the systemic corruption had coincided with effective action to limit the size and power of government, Madisonians would have to struggle with whether the ends justified the means. But as things turned out, we don't. Some good things happened in the first years of Republican control of Congress. Growth of regulation was slowed in the last half of the 1990s—in two of those years, the number of pages in the *Code of Federal Regulations* actually went down—and this was largely the effect of a variety of measures initiated by the Republican House. The Congressional Accountability Act of 1995 took away many of the exemptions from federal legislation that members of Congress had formerly enjoyed. The welfare reform act of 1996 marked a significant improvement in the welfare system. From 1998 to 2001, the federal government ran a budget surplus, mostly because of the booming economy, but measures initiated in the Republican House helped.

But in the six years from 2001 to 2006, when Republicans held the White House and both houses of Congress, not only did the GOP fail to limit government, but it's hard to find evidence that its leaders wanted to. And the systemic corruption was untouched. In the House, we witnessed one specific episode, the passage of the Medicare prescription drug benefit in 2003, that represents an abuse of power and betrayal of principle that easily matches anything the Democrats ever did.

Begin with the nature of the prescription drug benefit. A Democratic congress could have enthusiastically pushed for it—it was exactly the kind of bill that the Democrats had been passing for decades. But the bill was antithetical to limited government or fiscal responsibility. It introduced a new multitrillion-dollar entitlement liability at a time when federal deficits were already high, but did not propose any new taxes to pay for it. The benefit was extended to millions of Medicare participants who were financially able to pay for their own medications. There was no public demand for the benefit.

George W. Bush had proposed the Medicare prescription drug benefit in his speech accepting the Republican nomination. It had not attracted much attention at the time, but by 2003, presidential advisor Karl Rove had concluded that passing such a bill would shore up support among the elderly in the coming presidential campaign, and the idea got new life. The House leadership threw its power behind it, against the opposition of a minority of Madisonians in the Republican caucus. The legislation for implementing the Medicare prescription drug benefit came to a vote in the House of Representatives in the early-morning hours of November 23, 2003.

Since the installation of an electronic voting system thirty years earlier, the House had established the custom of allowing fifteen minutes for all votes to be cast. Voting occasionally was left open for an additional minute or two to accommodate members who were delayed getting to the floor, but the only egregious violation of custom had occurred in 1987 when speaker Jim Wright kept the vote open for an additional fifteen minutes. Wright's action was considered to have been unethical even by many Democrats, and was denounced by then-representative Richard Cheney as "the most arrogant, heavy-handed abuse of power I've ever seen in the ten years I've been here."[56]

The roll call on the Medicare drug prescription benefit opened at 3:00 a.m. By 3:15, when the customary fifteen minutes had elapsed, the nays were ahead and the bill should have failed. Voting remained open. By 3:48, more than half an hour after voting should have been closed, an absolute majority of the House had been recorded as voting against the bill. Voting remained open for another two hours. At 5:53, enough representatives had been persuaded to change their votes to pass the bill.

Thomas Mann and Norman Ornstein have provided a detailed account of the arm-twisting, orchestrated by Hastert and DeLay, that went on during the two hours and five minutes between the time when an absolute majority had voted against the bill and when a majority in favor of the bill had miraculously emerged.[57] There is a certain perfection to the House leadership's perfidy: The Republican Party, billing itself as the party seeking to hold back big government, creates a gigantic new giveaway for purposes of winning an election, doesn't even try to pay for it, and then runs roughshod over the House's voting procedures and engages in undisguised coercion and bribery to get enough votes. It is hard to think of anything the Republican House could have done that would have made its betrayal of principle more complete.

For Madisonians, Republican control of Congress is still preferable to Democratic control. The Republican-controlled Congress after 2010 was an indispensable roadblock to legislation advocated by the Obama administration that badly needed to be blocked. But this reality remains: The Republicans controlled both houses of Congress from 1995 through 2006, and the White House as well for the last six of those years. During this period, government expanded on every dimension. The Medicare drug entitlement was just one of the legislative expansions. Even after excluding entitlements (Medicare and Social Security), unemployment insurance (directly affected by the economy), and law-enforcement and border-security expenditures (directly affected by 9/11), domestic spending during the six years from 2000 to 2006 when Republicans had nobody to blame but themselves grew by $38.9 billion per year, more in constant dollars than under any other administration except those of Barack Obama and another Republican, George H. W. Bush.[58] The number of pages in the *Code of Federal Regulations* during 2000–2006 grew more per year than at any time since Jimmy Carter's administration, except for the administration of Bush Sr.[59]

Most depressing of all, throughout the twelve years from 1995 through 2006, when they controlled both houses of Congress, the Republicans demonstrated themselves to be as systemically corrupt as the Democrats. The nature of that corruption ensures that the size and reach of government will increase no matter which party is in power.

CHAPTER 5

INSTITUTIONAL SCLEROSIS AND ADVANCED DEMOCRACY

In which I seek to rid you of any residual optimism that federal power can be rolled back through the normal political process.

A T THIS POINT I need to respond to a position you might reasonably hold. It goes something like this:

Murray is giving up on the political process too soon. He's admitted that some court-ordered reforms have improved the legal system in recent years. Constitutional jurisprudence can get better as well—the Supreme Court has handed down some good decisions over the last twenty years, and would have handed down many more if the Court had included just one more Madisonian justice. The bad effects of over-regulation are more widely recognized than ever before, among moderate Democrats as well as Republicans. And Murray is too hard on the Republicans. The new GOP majority after the 1994 election did many good things in the first few years, and there's no telling what the GOP House and Senate majorities in the early 2000s could have accomplished if George W. Bush had shared Ronald Reagan's mind-set.[1] In any case, the things Murray complains about in the early 2000s were anomalous. The Republican majorities elected in the fall of 2014 will behave better. If we continue to do our best to convey our strong case to the American people and win some elections, we can still make a lot of progress through the political system.

In one respect, I don't disagree. To reiterate what I wrote in the prologue, Madisonians have successfully used the political process to win important policy victories. We should continue those efforts to improve federal policy in welfare, health, education, criminal justice, and the many other domains in which improvements are feasible and badly needed. But this book is not about policy improvements. Rather, I am asking how we can roll back the reach of federal power, something that cannot be done through the normal political process. Let me offer a final pair of reasons for that pessimistic conclusion: the nature of institutional sclerosis in advanced democracies, and the nature of electorates in advanced democracies.

The Dynamics of Collective Action
in Advanced Democracies

The narratives in the preceding four chapters were specific to America's particular history. No other country has ever had the chance to abandon a constitution mandating limited government, as we did. Other advanced countries have avoided many of the lawless features of the American legal system. Our separation of the executive and legislative branches makes our brand of systemic corruption quite different from the types of corruption that have evolved in parliamentary democracies. But in one respect, America is experiencing something that has happened in all the advanced democracies, whether in western Europe, Scandinavia, or Japan. No matter what their initial political or economic systems may have been, the institutions of successful nations eventually become sclerotic.

In 1965, economist Mancur Olson published a seminal book titled *The Logic of Collective Action.* In it, Olson set out the ways in which collective action in a democracy differs in groups of different sizes. Seventeen years later, Olson followed up with *The Rise and Decline of Nations,* in which he applied the argument of *The Logic of Collective Action* on a grand scale.

Both books are technical and closely reasoned. I restrict myself to just two of Olson's many important conclusions. First, advanced democracies inherently permit small interest groups to obtain government benefits for themselves that are extremely difficult for the rest of the polity to get rid of. Second, these successful special interests inevitably pile up over the years until the political system becomes rigid and unresponsive, unable to adapt—the dictionary definition of *sclerotic*.

I will use two thought experiments to illustrate the binds that Olson identified.

Why It's So Hard to End Government Programs That Benefit Only a Few People

The first thought experiment speaks to a question that many Madisonians frequently mutter to themselves: Why is it so incredibly hard to get rid of *any* government program, no matter how small, no matter how unneeded, no matter how outdated? It's understandable that Congress doesn't have the intestinal fortitude to buck huge special interests like the teachers' unions or the oil industry, but why can't it at least lop off the profusion of small, useless programs that litter the federal landscape? The answer lies in the asymmetry of motivation between the few who benefit and the many who pay for that benefit.

Imagine a nation of 100 million coffee drinkers in which 1,000 farmers grow coffee. The country is ruled by a dictator. The coffee farmers pay him an annual $10 million bribe to restrict coffee imports so that the 1,000 coffee farmers can charge twice the world market price for coffee. The bribe is financed by a $10,000 annual contribution to the bribe fund from each coffee farmer. But the import restrictions mean that the average coffee farmer makes an extra $200,000 per year, and anyone who tries to be a free rider comes under intense pressure from the other 999 coffee farmers. So the coffee farmers have no problem maintaining 100 percent participation in their organization.

A public-spirited citizen figures out that people who aren't coffee farmers could collectively save billions of dollars a year if they were paying the world market price for coffee, so he sets out to organize an even bigger bribe to get rid of the import restrictions. In principle, it's an easy win. Suppose, for example, that everyone who didn't grow coffee contributed just $1 to the bribe fund. That would amount to a bribe of $99,999,000. The coffee farmers couldn't possibly match that.

But hard as the public-spirited citizen tries, he can't get his crusade off the ground. The vast majority of coffee-drinkers just don't care enough about the price of coffee to get involved. The small minority who would be willing to contribute stop when they see that almost all of their fellow countrymen want to be free riders. And so for decade after decade, 99.999 percent of the citizens pay twice the world market price for coffee to benefit 0.001 percent of the citizens.

It's not really a thought experiment, of course, if you substitute "sugar" for "coffee." For decades, the federal government has artificially boosted the price of sugar at the behest of a small number of sugar farmers and caused Americans to pay about twice the world market price. The sugar subsidy has survived repeated attempts to end it, most recently in 2013.[2] The reason it cannot be ended is precisely the one that Olson describes: when government favors are up for sale, the comparatively small number of people who benefit are willing to pay a price to acquire and maintain those favors that is far greater than the price the rest of the nation is willing to pay to get rid of them.

Why It's Impossible to Contain the Demand for Government Favors in Advanced Democracies

The second thought experiment speaks to a question that must cross the minds of most politically aware Americans across the political spectrum: What accounts for the feeding frenzy at the government trough? Why are so many Americans so selfish and cynical about profiting at the expense of their fellow citizens?

Mancur Olson has good news in this regard: selfishness and cynicism don't necessarily have anything to do with it. The bad news is that bad motives aren't required to keep the feeding frenzy going. Journalist Jonathan Rauch devised this second thought experiment in *Government's End*, a full-length book treatment of Olson's work as it applies to contemporary Washington.[3]

Four friends sit down to dinner in a restaurant, agreeing to split the bill equally. Three of the four diners order appetizers costing $8, $10, and $12. The fourth realizes that if he orders the $50 snail darter soup, his share of the cost for appetizers will be just $20. That's a 60 percent discount. But as he tells the server what he wants, his friends first razz him and then tell him if that's how he's going to play the game, the deal is off. They'll get separate checks. He orders a $10 appetizer instead—he didn't want the snail darter soup enough to pay the full price.

Now imagine the same menu, but the dinner is in Madison Square Garden with 10,000 diners who are all strangers. Once again, the total bill will be split equally. Everybody knows that's the rule—and so everybody disregards the prices on the menu. Everybody ends up spending $200 for dinner instead of the $50 that almost all of them would have preferred.

The 10,000 people are being rational. If one of them—Mary, let's say—unilaterally orders a $50 meal while the other 9,999 average $200, she will lower her bill by less than two cents. If she has any preference whatsoever, however small, for the more expensive options, Mary is a fool not to get them. Furthermore, no matter how much Mary might want to reach an agreement with the other 9,999 people to behave with restraint, Mary has no way to influence more than a handful of other people around her to restrain their spending.

Mary is in the same position as any organization confronting the reality of Washington today, whether that organization is a business, a union, an advocacy group, or any other organization. We call them "special interests," which makes them sound selfish, but seen from another perspective they are simply doing what we all see ourselves as doing, worrying about legitimate concerns. All organizations have interests that they want to protect, whether it's the Sierra Club's interest in preserving the wilderness or the Weyerhaeuser Corporation's interest in being able to harvest timber. Even if we assume honesty and good faith on both sides, their interests are going to clash. If the Sierra Club is lobbying for what it sees as reasonable restrictions on logging, Weyerhaeuser cannot afford to assume that the Sierra Club's definition of *reasonable* will be reasonable from Weyerhaeuser's point of view. Weyerhaeuser needs to have its own position represented in the fight. Now imagine what happens when thousands—tens of thousands, hundreds of thousands—of parties with competing interests are involved.

The people seeking the favors "are acting not out of greed or depravity," Rauch writes, "but out of the impulse to survive in the world as they find it. Good intentions, or at least honest intentions, breed collective ruin." He continues:

If you see others rushing to lobby for favorable laws and regulations, you rush to do the same so as not to be left at a disadvantage. But the government can do only so much. Its resource base and management ability are limited, and its adaptability erodes with each additional benefit that interest groups lock in. In fact, the more different things it tries to do at once, the less effective it tends to become. Thus if everybody descends on Washington hunting some favorable public policy, government becomes rigid, overburdened, and incoherent. Soon its problem-solving capacity is despoiled. Everybody loses.[4]

The economic consequences of sclerotic institutions are huge because of another dynamic that Olson identified: It's typically much more efficient for a special interest to try to get a larger piece of the existing pie than to seek changes that increase the size of the pie for everyone. Suppose, for example, that a corporation makes widgets. Does it spend its lobbying money to increase the size of the pie for the widget industry, or to acquire a competitive advantage for itself? The payoff of a specific advantage for a corporation is larger and more certain than changes that increase the size of the pie for everybody. Accordingly, the corporation spends its money to get a larger slice.

This aspect of Olson's theory explains why many large corporations are quietly happy about the regulatory state. They have the political clout to shape legislation and regulations to their advantage, and also have the financial and personnel resources to cope with government requirements that overwhelm smaller competitors. The notorious Dodd-Frank bill to regulate the financial industry, excoriated by many businesspeople and economists as the worst kind of incomprehensible regulation, is a case in point. As the chairman of JPMorgan Chase observed with remarkable candor, Dodd-Frank works as a "bigger moat" to protect the large investment banks like JPMorgan Chase, deterring smaller institutions from entering their markets.[5]

Olson argued that each time this pie re-slicing goes on, the society as a whole systematically becomes poorer—re-slicing not only fails to increase the size of the pie; it exacts costs that shrink it. In addition, increasing institutional sclerosis cripples technological innovation. But these are ancillary to my main point: that the United States is in the grip of a process that afflicts all advanced democracies.

Why the United States Avoided Sclerosis for So Long and Why We Ultimately Succumbed

Serendipitously (the founders didn't know about institutional sclerosis), the founders set up a system that by its nature prevents institutional sclerosis from getting out of hand. In America's free-market economy, sclerosis was kept under control in the private sector because sclerotic corporations went out of business or were bought up by companies that were still vibrant. Meanwhile, the enumerated powers restricted the number of favors within the power of the federal government to sell. The cause of institutional sclerosis—the incremental effects of thousands of special interests protecting their benefits—was forestalled because Congress did not have the authority to grant many of the desires of special interests.

The system worked. Recall chapter 4's discussion of corruption in Washington before the 1970s. It was garden-variety corruption, with only the beginnings of sclerosis, attested to by the extremely limited lobbying that went on before the 1970s. But the system that forestalled sclerosis had been destroyed when the Supreme Court trashed the enumerated powers. It took three decades for sclerosis to set in, but once the enumerated powers no longer restrained the goods that Congress could sell, the prognosis—steadily increasing sclerosis, eventually becoming terminal—was inevitable.

The problem with the sclerotic state is not that the wrong people get benefits conferred by government. That happens a lot, and it's too bad. But the truly crippling and ultimately paralyzing effect of sclerosis is what it means for government's ability to act in ways that reduce the net number of problems. Once again, Rauch states the problem well:

The question is not the quantity of activity but how effectively a given amount of activity solves problems "on net." That phrase "on net"—meaning "on balance," after the wins and losses are tallied up—is important. In life, every solution creates at least some new problems. The trick is always to find solutions that create fewer problems than they solve. In the classic example, if you kill a fly with a flyswatter, you come out ahead on net. If you kill a fly with a cannon, you create more problems than you solve. . . . Problem-solving capacity is precisely what seems to have been shrinking for the federal government.[6]

We are living under a political system that has tied itself in knots. "Cleaning house" in Washington will do nothing to untie those knots. The current public-policy debate concentrates on culprits such as the political polarization that is alleged to have immobilized Congress and failures of presidential leadership assigned to George W. Bush by the left or to Barack Obama by the right. Such culprits have some degree of culpability, and have made a difference at the margin. But when it comes to an explanation of why government under both Democrats and Republicans has become so pathetically ineffectual across the board, even at simple tasks, a powerful underlying explanation is that American government suffers from an advanced case of institutional sclerosis.

The Nature of the Electorate in Advanced Welfare States

It is impossible for a government in the grip of the disease to cure itself. The symptoms of the disease prevent the government from acting to cure it. There's only one surefire solution: lose a total war. That's the insight that inspired Mancur Olson in the first place. Why, he asked himself, were the fortunes of Germany, Japan, England, and France following World War II so strikingly different? As of 1945, Germany and Japan had surrendered unconditionally. Many millions of their populations had been killed. Their factories, roads, bridges, dams, railroads, airports, water systems, power systems, and communications systems were in ruins. Almost all of their political and economic institutions had been dismantled. Meanwhile, Great Britain and France had finished the war with far lighter casualties and less damage to their physical infrastructure. Their political and economic institutions were intact.

What happened next was that Japan and Germany experienced explosive economic growth and within three decades after the war's end were among the most prosperous countries in the world. During the same period Great Britain and France languished, with some of the slowest rates of economic growth among advanced countries.

How could countries starting from scratch so quickly catch up to and then race past advanced industrial countries that had been so far ahead in 1945? The short answer is precisely that Japan and Germany *did* have to start from scratch. Losing their physical infrastructure was a problem, but losing their political and administrative infrastructure was a godsend. Their enemies had unintentionally administered the one known cure for institutional sclerosis.

Couldn't Britain and France, both democracies, have mustered the votes to modify their systems when they saw the blazing success of Germany and Japan? Can't the United States now? No, because of the nature of the electorate in advanced democracies. All advanced democracies are welfare states, and welfare states inherently create constituencies in support of the status quo.

In chapter 3, I offered the fundamental theorem for explaining government corruption. Now let me offer the fundamental theorem of democratic politics: *People who receive government benefits tend to vote for people who support those benefits.* The theorem applies as much to middle-class Social Security recipients as to impoverished welfare mothers; as much to farm owners getting agricultural subsidies as to farm laborers getting Food Stamps; as much to defense contractors getting billion-dollar contracts as to nonprofits staying afloat with small government grants.

I use *tend* in a statistical sense. Receiving government benefits may, in the jargon of social science, explain only a small amount of the variance in voting behavior. But elections are binary events in which one vote can make the difference between victory and defeat. Small statistical tendencies drive large electoral outcomes.

For American elections from 1789 through 1932, the fundamental theorem of democratic politics was nearly irrelevant. Military veterans wanted to see their pensions maintained, federal employees wanted to see their jobs maintained, and people who held government contracts wanted to see those contracts continue. But those three groups amounted to a few percent of the population. Apart from them, the number of Americans who received cash or in-kind income transfers from the federal government was zero.

As of the election of 2012, approximately half of all Americans received such benefits.[7] Let's ignore those who received small benefits and limit the argument to those for whom the role of government support is often central to their lives: people getting welfare and Medicaid benefits, and people getting Social Security and Medicare benefits. In both cases, the benefits are large, and the loss of them would often be a personal catastrophe. The continued security of those programs is likely to be near the top of the recipients' political calculations.

The figure below shows the percentage of the population receiving those benefits from the New Deal through Barack Obama's first term.

From 1935 to 2012, the proportion of Americans receiving major benefits from the federal government went from 0 to 35 percent.

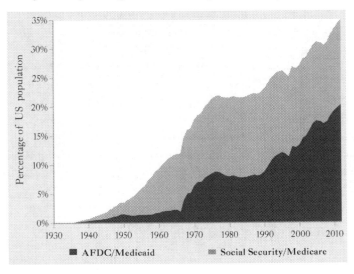

Source: Social Security Administration, Medicaid and CHIP Payment and Access Commission.

When Dwight Eisenhower was elected in 1952, Medicare and Medicaid didn't exist, and the combined number of welfare and Social Security beneficiaries amounted to only 4 percent of the population. Eight years later, when John Kennedy was elected, the percentage had more than doubled, to 9 percent of the population. By the time Jimmy Carter defeated Gerald Ford in 1976, 22 percent of the population fell into those two groups. When Barack Obama was reelected in 2012, more than 1 out of 3 Americans was the recipient of one of those two extremely important packages of government assistance.[8]

Those aren't the only people whose votes are determined in part by the role that government money plays in their lives. First, add the 22 million employees of federal, state, and local governments.[9] Then add all the people who are not carried on federal payrolls but instead are working for contractors in the private sector and nonprofits receiving government grants. Nobody knows how many there are, but the federal government alone spends more than $500 billion on contracts with for-profit firms.[10] Then add all the people who work for nonprofit organizations that depend on government grants for most or all of their income. Again, nobody knows how many people that amounts to, but such organizations got about $700 billion from government in 2012.[11]

Precise estimates of how many votes are swung because people depend on checks written by the government are impossible but also unnecessary to make my point. To illustrate: The voting group that is most intensely interested in Social Security and Medicare consists of those age fifty-five or older. In the typical presidential election, more than 40 percent of the voters come from that age group. In the typical congressional election, they approach half of the voters.[12] In the General Social Survey Polls from 2000 to 2012, only 28 percent of them identified as Republicans, 18 percent identified as "conservative," and 4 percent as "extremely conservative"—and even the votes of Republicans and conservatives can't be counted upon when Social Security and Medicare benefits are on the table.[13] Put bluntly: When more than 40 percent of people who actually cast votes have an active interest in the preservation and expansion of Social Security or Medicare, no Congress will have the votes to pass major structural reform that entails significant cuts in those benefits until fiscal catastrophe is imminent. And perhaps not even then.

The large number of beneficiaries of transfer payments further explains why principled fiscal conservatives are always a minority among Republican representatives and senators. A principled fiscal conservative may win the Republican primary, but winning the general election is nearly impossible in all except the nation's most conservative districts. Instead, the Republicans who actually get elected are mostly fair-weather fiscal conservatives who talk a good game during the campaign, sticking

What About the Growing Size of Ethnic Minority Groups?

The media and Internet are full of analyses predicting that the GOP's future is bleak, but usually focus on the role of ethnic minorities as the cause. Blacks, Latinos, and Asians all vote Democratic by large margins, and they constitute a growing share of the electorate. They will probably constitute a majority of the population by midcentury.

These analyses are correct about the long term, but the consequences in the next few presidential election cycles will be minor, because of the much lower voter turnout among minorities than among whites. See the note for details.[14] The 35 percent of the population who are major beneficiaries of government transfers is already a potent political force regardless of the recipients' ethnicity and will continue to gain strength independently of the growing numbers of ethnic minorities. Ethnicity does not drive the politics of a welfare state. Benefits do.

to generalities, but don't support cuts in the government benefits that are most popular with their constituents once they are in office.

The proportion of Americans who depend on the federal government to put food on the table, whether through welfare, Social Security, a government paycheck, or a paycheck financed by a federal contract, will continue to increase, and it will push the Republican Party to the center in all presidential elections. The number of Madisonians in the Senate will always be in single digits, because only a handful of states have electorates that would conceivably elect someone committed to genuine limited government. Only the House of Representatives will continue to have an active minority of Madisonians elected by extremely conservative congressional districts, but even in the House they will be a minority of the Republican caucus.

Combine the effects of institutional sclerosis with the effects of a growing percentage of Americans who depend on the benefits provided by the welfare state, and the political landscape for Madisonians is already bleak and getting worse. A successful agenda for rolling back government through the normal political process would require Madisonian majorities in both houses and a Madisonian president. It's not going to happen. Nothing will change that situation. It is built into the way that advanced democracies function.

PART II

OPENING A NEW FRONT

But when a long train of abuses and usurpations, pursuing invariably the same object, evinces a design to reduce them under absolute despotism, it is their right, it is their duty, to throw off such government, and to provide new guards for their future security.

—DECLARATION OF INDEPENDENCE

The chapters of Part II propose a program of systematic civil disobedience underwritten by privately funded legal resistance to the regulatory state. This program's first objective is to defend ordinary individuals against government overreach, even if it accomplishes nothing else. Its secondary objective is to make large portions of the *Code of Federal Regulations* de facto unenforceable. Its tertiary objective is to provoke specific, plausible Supreme Court interpretations of existing law that could transform the way that regulations are created and enforced.

CHAPTER 6

ON THE CHOICE OF CIVIL
DISOBEDIENCE

*In which I present two cases for concluding that the
federal government has lost its authority to command
voluntary compliance with its vast edifice of laws.*

THE RULE OF law is the foundation of civilization. Deliberately
choosing to ignore portions of the law is a momentous political
choice. Before I describe how civil disobedience can be employed
to transform the regulatory state for the better, I must state my reasons
for thinking that civil disobedience is ever justified.

The short answer is that the American government does not command our blind allegiance to the law. It is part of our national catechism
that government is instituted to protect our unalienable rights, and that
when it becomes destructive of those rights, the reason for our allegiance
is gone. At that point, revolution is not treason, but the people's right.

I am not proposing revolution, but I am proposing a declaration of
limited resistance to the existing government. I do so because the federal
government has in many respects become destructive of our unalienable
rights. It has lost elements of its legitimacy.

The case that the federal government's legitimacy is waning may be
made on two different grounds, both of which were adumbrated by the
chapters of Part I. One case is sufficient for Madisonians but will not be
sufficient for others. The second should resonate with a wider range of
conservatives, centrists, and moderate liberals.

The Madisonian Case for Lost Legitimacy

L egitimacy in a government is an elusive thing. The Chinese used to
call it the mandate of heaven. Once it was withdrawn, the dynasty
was doomed. In the West, the concept of political legitimacy originally
involved a heavenly mandate as well: medieval kings were thought to
rule through God's will. In the centuries since belief in the divine right
of kings was rejected, political legitimacy in Europe has rested on ties
of ethnicity and culture, faith in the rulers, loyalty to the rule of law, or
combinations of the above.[1]

The United States was founded on a conception of political legitimacy that had no counterpart anywhere in Europe. "It has been our
fate as a nation not to have ideologies, but to be one," historian Richard
Hofstadter observed, and that is especially true of Americans' conception of political legitimacy.[2] It was grounded in John Locke's argument
that, in a state of nature, all political authority resides in individuals. The
social contract that produces a state does not *create* political authority
but *transfers* the political authority that pre-existed in individuals. That
transfer must be voluntary; otherwise, the political authority is not legitimate.[3] The iconic sentence of the Declaration of Independence, beginning with "We hold these truths to be self-evident," is a restatement of
that Lockean position.

For Madisonians today, accustomed as we are to being identified
with an extreme on the political spectrum, it is important to understand
that an overwhelming majority of Americans shared our views about the
foundations of political legitimacy during the first century of the nation's
existence. The breadth of Americans' devotion to the principles of the
founding was one of the features of the new nation that struck European
visitors most forcibly.

Francis Grund, who moved from Germany to America as an adult
and published a two-volume commentary on America in 1837, about the
same time as Alexis de Tocqueville, observed that American patriotism
was quite unlike patriotism in other countries. "It is not an instinctive
attachment to scenes with which they are acquainted from childhood, or
to men to whose familiar converse they are accustomed," he wrote. "It
consists in the love of principles, for which they are ready to make every

sacrifice, and which in the outset they preferred to their homes."[4] By *principles,* Grund meant the principles of liberty that were at the core of Americans' identity: "American liberty is further advanced in the minds of the people than even in the laws themselves," he continued. "It has become an active principle which lives with, and animates the nation, and of which their political constitution is but a facsimile."[5]

Tocqueville made a similar point about Americans' passionate belief that their liberty to pursue their own interests without hindrance was the key to making America work—the principle that he labeled "self-interest rightly understood." It found "universal acceptance," Tocqueville wrote. "You may trace it at the bottom of all their actions, you will remark it in all they say. It is as often asserted by the poor man as by the rich."[6]

Throughout the nineteenth century, these were not issues on which Americans differed. They had other differences that they contested bitterly—so bitterly that the Civil War was needed to resolve some of them—but no American political party disputed the sovereign freedom of the individual and strict limits on the legitimate authority of the national government.[7]

The extent of this bipartisan allegiance is illustrated by the presidency of Grover Cleveland, whose two terms in office came near the end of the century. In 1887 he vetoed a $10,000 congressional appropriation—about $250,000 in today's dollars—that would have allowed the commissioner of agriculture to purchase seed grain for distribution in the Texas counties hardest hit by a prolonged drought. Cleveland's explanation for his veto was a classic statement of the narrow limits circumscribing the legitimate authority of the state:

> I can find no warrant for such an appropriation in the Constitution, and I do not believe that the power and duty of the general government ought to be extended to the relief of individual suffering. . . . The lesson should be constantly enforced that, though the people support the government, the government should not support the people. The friendliness and charity of our countrymen can always be relied upon to relieve their fellow citizens in misfortune. This has been repeatedly and quite lately demonstrated. Federal aid in

such cases encourages the expectation of paternal care on the part of the government and weakens the sturdiness of our national character, while it prevents the indulgence among our people of that kindly sentiment and conduct which strengthens the bonds of a common brotherhood.[8]

It is hard to see any daylight between Cleveland's thinking about the role of government and the one that Jefferson had expressed in his first inaugural address about "the sum of good government" eighty-six years earlier.

Nor had there been much change in the thinking of the population at large. Toward the end of his two-volume study written at about the same time as Cleveland's veto, James Bryce, a leading British scholar of American society at the end of the nineteenth century, reflected on "certain dogmas or maxims which are in so far fundamental that . . . one usually strikes upon them when sinking a shaft, so to speak, in an American mind." These were among the dogmas he cited that today put Madisonians on the political extreme, and that in the late nineteenth century were believed by Democrats and Republicans alike: "Certain rights of the individual, as, for instance, his right to the enjoyment of what he has earned, and to the free expression of his opinions, are primordial and sacred. . . . Where any function can be equally well discharged by a central or a local body, it ought by preference to be entrusted to the local body. . . . The less government the better."[9]

Just as Cleveland's position as president was effectively identical to Jefferson's, the consensus political ideology that Bryce described in the 1880s was essentially unchanged from the one that prevailed in the 1780s and that Grund and Tocqueville described in the 1830s. It amounted to a national civic religion.

Judged by that standard, the federal government lost its legitimacy in theory during the constitutional revolution of 1937–1942, lost its legitimacy in practice during the 1960s, and it has been downhill ever since. It is by that historical understanding that many of us who are devoted to limited government have thought of ourselves as living in a post-American country, governed by people who mouth the clichés about America as the land of the free without understanding what freedom means.

A More Pragmatic Case for Lost Legitimacy

Judging from the polls, only about 10 to 20 percent of all Americans will be persuaded by the argument I just presented.[10] But it is just as clear that a substantial majority of Americans have a sense that something has changed in the federal government's relationship with the American people. I now turn to a way of thinking about waning federal legitimacy that I hope will find broader agreement.

Since 1958, pollsters have periodically asked exactly the same question of representative samples of Americans: "How much of the time do you think you can trust government in Washington to do what is right: Just about always, most of the time, or only some of the time?"[11]

When it was first asked in 1958, 73 percent answered "just about always" or "most of the time." When it was next asked in 1964, an even higher proportion, 76 percent, gave those answers. Then that percentage abruptly began to decline and kept declining. By the time the 1980 election campaign was being contested by Jimmy Carter and Ronald Reagan, only 25 percent of Americans thought they could trust the government in Washington to do what is right all or most of the time—a 51 percentage-point drop in just sixteen years.

That percentage rose somewhat during the Reagan years, then fell, rose again during the last half of the 1990s, and spiked briefly after 9/11. The secular trend has been down. The percentage trusting the government most or all of the time hit a new low in 2014, standing at 13 percent. In other words, we moved from more than 3 out of 4 Americans who trusted the government in 1964 to fewer than 1 out of 7 in 2014.

Part of the explanation for this astonishing drop consists of the problems of lawlessness described in chapters 2 and 3. Americans with a wide range of political views have been disturbed by laws that are so complicated, they are impossible to obey; by a tax code riddled with favors for people with connections and filled with hazards for ordinary Americans; by laws that can send people to jail for things that other people have done; by occasions when property has been confiscated for reasons that seem patently unfair. They've seen people prosecuted for politically motivated reasons or for failing to comply with unreasonable regulations. They've watched politically connected people go unprosecuted. It comes down to a common recognition across political lines: *American government isn't supposed to work this way.*

Another part of the explanation is generated by the problems described in chapter 4. Washington looks like a sophisticated kleptocracy—in the fortunes acquired by people from exploiting their government service, the necessity of paying (in the form of campaign contributions) senators and representatives to get anything done, in the political parties' shakedown of businesses for such contributions, and in the use of government by private interests to make trouble for their adversaries. These practices have led ordinary citizens with a wide range of political views to recognize that both political parties and the bureaucracies of the government are systemically corrupt. *American government isn't supposed to work this way.*

These specific forms of government misbehavior are part of a broader betrayal of the role that the federal government traditionally played in national life. When Kennedy was assassinated in 1963, at a time when 76 percent of Americans still trusted the federal government to do the right thing, most Americans were still in love with the idea that as American citizens they were free and independent, equal before the law with other Americans, living their lives as they saw fit. Americans saw the federal government not only as legitimate but as the best government in the world—an attitude that had characterized us all the way back to the founding.[12] But this happy state of affairs hadn't happened by accident. It was sustained through good times and bad, war and peace, massive immigration and massive social changes, because of three tacit compacts between the federal government and the American people.[13]

The first tacit compact was that the American people wouldn't expect much from the federal government beyond protection of their freedom at home and from enemies abroad. As I noted in chapter 4, few corporations had an office in Washington as late as the Kennedy administration because, with only isolated exceptions, businesses had to worry only about competing in the marketplace, not coping with the federal government. The federal government during the Kennedy administration still had no significant role in K–12 education, local law enforcement, or health care. The federal government had no policies about the practice of religion. Americans of half a century ago still assumed that the task of running daily life was in their own hands. And so when people had complaints about their schools, jobs, products, physicians, or churches, the federal government didn't get blamed for failing to solve problems that Americans didn't think were its business anyway. It's easy to trust the federal government to do the right thing when the expectations of that government are limited.

The second tacit compact was that the federal government would not unilaterally impose a position on the moral disputes that divided Americans. This was exemplified by the dispute over slavery, the most divisive of all American moral disputes. The history of federal policy from the time the abolitionist movement began in the 1820s until the beginning of the Civil War was one long, tortured attempt *not* to impose a federal solution to slavery on the nation. Even the Civil War itself was undertaken as a fight to preserve the Union, not to abolish slavery. That same extreme reluctance to impose unilaterally enacted federal solutions on moral disputes remained through the first half of the twentieth century. The moral dispute over alcohol (a very big deal for more than a century) was resolved by a constitutional amendment, not a federal law. So was the moral dispute over women's suffrage. A constitutional amendment not only requires Congress to pass it and the president to sign it but also requires at least three-quarters of the states to ratify it. When it came to moral issues, the whole nation had to participate in their resolution. Those on the losing side had to recognize that their defeat was national and consensual. It's easy to trust a federal government that doesn't unilaterally decide morally divisive topics by narrow margins in Congress or a one-vote margin on the Supreme Court.

The third tacit compact was that the federal government would make it easy for Americans to take pride in themselves. Americans who made an honest living, took care of their families, and didn't bother anyone else were good Americans—as good as the highest in the land. Elected officials constantly said so and, until the 1960s, the federal government didn't ask more than that in practice. It's easy to trust a federal government that validates your good opinion of yourself.

From 1964 onward, the federal government voided all three compacts.

The first compact is so obviously void that little more need be said. There is no social or economic problem of which a contemporary president can say, "That's not the federal government's responsibility." One consequence is that Americans now do blame the government when things go wrong. When the government creates a Federal Emergency

Management Agency—slow and inept, as so many government agencies are—it gets blamed for the catastrophe in New Orleans after Hurricane Katrina. That New Orleans was built below the level of the Mississippi River and that its own city government responded with spectacular incompetence are irrelevant. The feds get blamed because the feds asked for it. And so it is with every domain in which the federal government has taken on responsibility for fixing things.

The second compact, that the federal government would not unilaterally impose a position on one side of specific moral issues, is also void. Whether by executive action, legislation, or judicial decision, it has imposed policies on the entire nation that large numbers of Americans opposed on grounds of deeply held moral principles. By imposing federal policies on abortion, affirmative action, drug use, education, employment, expressions of religious faith, marriage, and welfare, the federal government has alienated large numbers of Americans from all points on the political spectrum. Thomas Jefferson got it right when he wrote that "to compel a man to furnish contributions of money for the propagation of opinions which he disbelieves, is sinful and tyrannical."[14]

The federal government has always had to face the problem of moral opposition when it has undertaken military action. Every American war has had its conscientious objectors and war protesters. But those reactions occurred in the context of a national consensus that the country must have armed forces and that it must be the federal government that directs them. There is no similar consensus on domestic issues that have caused people to lose trust in the government, either on the issues themselves or on the federal government's right to rule on them. Those who are outraged do not trust the federal government to do the right thing. Add up all the people who have felt this kind of outrage on at least one issue, and you've got a majority of the citizenry.

The breaking of the third compact, the one that made it easy to be a good American, follows from the geometric expansion of law. Just about all of us are criminals now, insofar as almost all of us have broken some of those thousands of laws, and, technically speaking, almost anyone could be successfully prosecuted if the federal government so chose. Many of us watch the experiences of those whom the government has decided to go after, and say to ourselves, "That could be me."

It's not just the expansion of laws that has alienated us from the government. The government's rhetoric has changed. The officials of the federal government no longer celebrate us as fine Americans if we make an honest living and mind our own business. On the contrary, they tell many of us who think we are making an honest living and minding our own business that we are selfish, greedy, racist, or homophobic when we haven't the slightest internal sense that we are any of those things. The federal government has changed from being a vehicle through which the American people celebrate themselves and each other to being a vehicle through which a ruling class hectors and pesters us about our shortcomings. This too helps explain why so many of us have shifted from a broad loyalty and affection for the government to alienation and anger.

In summary, I am arguing that the federal government over the last half century has separated itself from the American people in a way it had never done before. Americans have a long history of getting mad at government. See Pap Finn's rant about "govment" in *Huckleberry Finn*. But something's different now. The federal government has become an entity distinct from our conception of America, with agendas that have nothing to do with serving the American people and everything to do with the health and well-being of the federal government itself. Many of us see that entity as hostile, something against which ordinary citizens must defend themselves. Philip Howard, writing from the political center, has put it harshly but accurately: "A group that no longer shares basic values with the society is categorized by sociologists as a 'deviant subculture.' Washington has become a deviant subculture."[15]

When 87 percent of Americans do *not* trust the federal government "to do what is right" even most of the time, it is also obvious that the alienation does not break along party lines. The legitimacy of the federal government is not gone for a majority of the population, but it has waned. When I propose to use systematic civil disobedience, it is not against a government that has made a few unintentional missteps and should be given the benefit of the doubt. The civil disobedience I propose is against a government that has over five decades earned our distrust.

CHAPTER 7

THE GROUND RULES FOR CIVIL DISOBEDIENCE

In which I present criteria for deciding whether a given regulation may be legitimately ignored in principle, discuss some of the practical considerations, and express what I believe to be an attainable goal.

I WANT TO MAKE it possible for us to safely ignore large portions of the laws and regulations with which we are burdened. But before we get to the *how* of that endeavor, we need to worry about which laws and regulations we're talking about. How do we distinguish between those that should be obeyed and those that may be appropriately ignored?

First, I need to define the specific way in which the concept of civil disobedience is used here, to wit: when a *group* of people agrees to ignore a law or regulation. This is distinct from following one's individual conscience and acting individually, as Henry David Thoreau advocated in *Resistance to Civil Government* (1849).

My use of the phrase *civil disobedience* is also distinct from decisions to break the law because of overriding circumstances, such as the penniless husband who steals medicine to save his dying wife.[1] The law itself often has ways of accommodating these overriding circumstances. I am talking about identifying laws and regulations that may be ignored in general.

One other preliminary: rather than constantly write *laws and regulations*, I will for convenience write just *regulations*, leaving it understood that laws may also be involved.

Regulations That Are Exempt from Systematic Civil Disobedience

I begin with the many rules that shouldn't be subject to systematic civil disobedience. They fall into three categories.

Laws prohibiting acts that are bad in themselves—*malum in se*—are exempt from systematic civil disobedience.

The core set of acts that should be exempt from civil disobedience are the offenses that have been prohibited by civilized societies from the dawn of history: murder, manslaughter, rape, assault, robbery, burglary, larceny, fraud, arson, destruction of another's property, and kidnapping.

The further one moves beyond this core list to things such as treason, perjury, obstruction of justice, and conspiracy, the more the prohibitions contained in the actual law may diverge from *malum in se*. Conspiracy is a case in point. Some conspiracies are *malum in se*. But the law as written is sometimes ridiculously broad, allowing the authorities to use "conspiracy" as a catch-all charge against people whom the authorities want to get but who have not done anything culpable. Even acknowledging the gray areas, however, the default assumption when *malum in se* is plausibly involved should be to exempt the law from systematic civil disobedience. All systematic civil disobedience should involve acts that are *malum prohibitum*: illegal because the state says so, not because they are bad in themselves.

The tax code is exempt from systematic civil disobedience.

The US tax code is terrible, and a product of the systemically corrupt political process I described in chapter 4, but there is a difference between the rules surrounding taxes and the rules promulgated by the regulatory state. There are thousands of regulations about which an American may rightly say, "This is none of the government's business." A constitutionally principled defense for refusing to obey such regulations can be mounted. It will almost always lose in today's courts, but it should win.

In contrast, taxation is one of the legitimate functions of even a Madisonian state. In particular, the income tax, however inferior it may be to other ways of collecting revenue, however badly it has been administered, was authorized by explicit amendment of the US Constitution.

There is also a practical problem. Principled civil disobedience to the tax code would be indistinguishable in appearance from cheating on your taxes. As I will stress in the pages that follow, the success of civil disobedience depends on being able to make a case that the people being charged with violations have done nothing wrong, a case so obviously true that it will persuade a large majority of fair-minded people across the political spectrum. That is impossible for violations of the tax code.

Regulations that foster public goods classically defined are exempt from systematic civil disobedience.

Fostering public goods is also one of the legitimate functions of any government, including the most limited ones, and regulations that really do serve that function should be exempt from civil disobedience.

I have just used a phrase, *public goods*, which has been corrupted in daily use. It does not mean "something that enough people think is good for the public." Strictly defined, public goods fall into two broad sets. One set consists of things that can be done *only* by government because of the nature of the task (for example, national defense is a public good, while feeding the hungry is not).[2] The characteristics of these public goods is that they are both *nonexclusive*, meaning that the good cannot be provided selectively, and *nonrivalrous*, meaning that one individual may consume it without diminishing its availability to others. National defense is one classic example; protection of the environment is another.

Other public goods are those that may or may not be nonexclusive and nonrivalrous, but do entail serious *externalities*, meaning that a cost is borne by someone involuntarily or a benefit is provided to someone who cannot be charged for it. K–12 education qualifies as a public good in this sense. A democracy cannot be sustained without an educated electorate. Everyone who lives in a democracy benefits from the good called *education*. Therefore, it is appropriate that education be publicly funded, with people contributing to its cost whether or not they have children attending school.[3]

How are we to distinguish between regulations that foster public goods and those that do not? Usually common sense goes a long way. Civil disobedience of an environmental regulation is wrong when it leads to factory chimneys belching noxious smoke. When it leads to a modest number of charcoal fires in backyards for cooking hamburgers, it's okay. Advancing this process of winnowing wheat from chaff—discriminating between regulations that really do foster a public good and really must be obeyed, and those that are trivial and may be ignored—is going to be one of the major contributions of systematic civil disobedience. As matters stand, the creators of regulations have far too few incentives to ask themselves, "Is this really necessary?" Systematic civil disobedience will give them those incentives.

Principled Ground Rules

In choosing regulations that may be ignored, two sets of decision rules come into play: principled ones and practical ones. I deal with each set separately, beginning with the principled ones. In doing so, I am going to borrow some legal language for my own purposes. In the famous Footnote Four of the *Carolene Products* decision discussed in chapter 1, the Supreme Court announced that violations of certain constitutional rights (but not others) would be subject to heightened scrutiny, a doctrine subsequently labeled "strict scrutiny."[4] Here, I am going to use *strict scrutiny* to describe categories of regulations that automatically should be high on the list of candidates for systematic civil disobedience.

Regulations that prohibit owners of land from doing whatever they wish with it are subject to strict scrutiny.

The protection of private property is the foundation of freedom. This is true of all property, but property rights for most of our possessions are well protected. The government has no regulations permitting, say, a government agency to use your lawn mower one day a week.

Land is different from furniture, tools, and other personal property—so different that the founders felt obliged to acknowledge the government's power of eminent domain in the Bill of Rights. As discussed in chapter 2, the proper limits on the right to use one's own land as one sees fit trace back to an ancient precept of the common law, "Use what is yours so as not to harm what belongs to others." No property owner has the right to pollute his neighbor's water, for example. When such externalities really do exist, then the regulation in question should be exempt from systematic civil disobedience.

Many regulations restricting land use do not involve such externalities.[5] Zoning laws are suspect, for example. At the state and federal levels, regulations putatively justified by the protection of the environment or endangered species have resulted in egregious infringements on property rights. The "wetlands" provisions of the Clean Water Act have been the source of some of the most well-publicized government overreach (you will get an example at the end of chapter 10), as the EPA and the Army Corps of Engineers have applied absurdly wide definitions of "wetland" and thereby stripped private property of its value.[6] Any farmer or rancher can give you other examples of regulations imposed by the Bureau of Land Management, the Fish and Wildlife Service, and state agencies that prevent them from engaging in innocuous maintenance or improvement of their property. These kinds of regulations are prime candidates for systematic civil disobedience.

Regulations that prescribe best practice in a craft or profession are subject to strict scrutiny.

The satisfactions that come from practicing a vocation can be deep and enduring. Absent a compelling public interest to interfere, people should be left alone to practice their vocations to the best of their ability.

Regulatory agencies have promulgated thousands of regulations that constrain the way that people go about their work. For people who don't work in a profession, those rules are often assumed to be a good thing. Most of us are happy that many agencies regulate the health industry, that the Federal Aviation Administration regulates the airline industry, and that the Securities and Exchange Commission regulates the financial industry. But talk to any physician, pilot, or financial executive about those regulations, and you will get a sense of how different things look from their side of the street. They will agree that certain rules need to be in place—but the necessary rules are a small subset of all the ways in which regulators have made it more difficult for them to do their jobs as they should be done.

The same is true for occupations that have less immediate salience for the health and prosperity of the rest of us but are burdened with numerous regulations. The regulatory arms of the Departments of Interior, Agriculture, Energy, Commerce, Treasury, Justice, Labor, Education, and Transportation reach into the professional lives of just about everyone. Even that most sheltered of professions—college professor—is touched by the regulatory state whenever the administration of a university or the acquisition of a grant is at issue. And I haven't even mentioned the three most visible intruders, because of their economy-wide mandates: OSHA, the EPA, and the EEOC.

The task will be to identify the subset of regulations that are unequivocally exempt from civil disobedience, and then to separate the rest into those that specify acceptable options that apply to some situations and not to others, those that offer okay options that are no better than alternative ways of doing the same thing, and those that actually interfere with best practice. All of the latter three types of occupational regulations are candidates for systematic civil disobedience. Those in the last category are to be aggressively challenged.

Regulations that restrict access to a job are subject to strict scrutiny.

Freedom to try to make an honest living is central to the American project. Absent compelling justification, using the state as a gatekeeper to the labor market is a violation of that freedom. Here, states and localities have been the prime offenders through licensing laws. One may argue that the government has a compelling reason to pass licensing laws when the profession is one that involves life and death. But licensing now affects about 1 out of 3 workers.[7] Should people really be required to get a license to work as an interior designer? Shampooer? Florist? Coffin maker? In addition to licensing laws, states and localities often pile up the permissions required to open a business until they constitute a significant barrier for a person with limited means who wants to open a simple shop or provide a simple service. All of these regulations are subject to strict scrutiny.

Regulations that prevent people from taking voluntary risks are subject to strict scrutiny.

The Lockean conception of freedom has at its core one's unalienable ownership of one's own body. A strict libertarian interpretation of this freedom forbids the state to violate that ownership in any way. Many conservatives disagree with this extreme position (which, for example, forbids any regulation of adult drug use). But a middle ground should find broad agreement among Madisonians: leaving hot-button topics like drugs aside, people should be free to make informed and voluntary decisions to engage in a broad range of activities that put only themselves at risk. They should be free to ski down dangerous slopes, scuba-dive in hazardous waters, climb sheer cliffs, and engage in all the other recreations that can easily break bones or even end lives. Regulations that interfere with the provision of goods and services supporting these activities should be subject to strict scrutiny.

People should also be free to make informed and voluntary decisions about their health care, even if those decisions put them at risk. Regulations that prohibit access to a nontraditional treatment or to a drug that shows promise but hasn't completed the FDA's tortuous approval process are subject to strict scrutiny.

Employment law is subject to strict scrutiny.

To people who are not in positions where they have to hire or fire employees, "employment law" may sound like a matter of avoiding discrimination by ethnicity, gender, age, or disability, plus observing some basic rules about job conditions. People who do have to hire, supervise, or discharge employees know better. A leading resource for employers, *The Essential Guide to Federal Employment Laws*, has separate chapters for twenty major pieces of legislation that impose requirements on employers.[8] The legal defense funds I envision could be kept fully occupied doing nothing but helping people who have run afoul of employment regulations.

**Regulations that are arbitrary, capricious, or an abuse of
discretion are automatically eligible for civil disobedience.**

The Administrative Procedure Act of 1946 specifies that an agency action may be set aside if the court concludes that the action was "arbitrary,
capricious, an abuse of discretion, or otherwise not in accordance with
the law."[9] In the intervening decades, courts have set that standard unreasonably high, but it's a good description of the regulations that are most
eligible for civil disobedience. Chapter 10 takes up this issue at length.

Practical Ground Rules

By definition, civil disobedience means that the person who engages
in it breaks the law. Civil disobedience must therefore be undertaken in such a way that it is obvious to all who watch with an open
mind that they are witnessing free people behaving appropriately—that
the problem is not the person who violated the regulation but the regulation or its interpretation by the bureaucrats. Think in terms of a case
of civil disobedience that comes to trial with attendant publicity: it is
essential that people reading or watching news reports about the trial
are overwhelmingly on the side of the defendant, even though everyone
knows that the defendant is technically guilty. The practical considerations I list below are ways to increase the likelihood of that overwhelming sympathy with the defendant.

Avoid choosing regulations with halo effects.

Certain topics in contemporary life carry with them halo effects. If a
regulation has the putative purpose of promoting a good that has a halo,
a large segment of the population will give that regulation the benefit of
the doubt no matter what.

Protection of the environment is the leading example. Even people
who are not active environmentalists reflexively think that violating a
regulation intended to protect the environment is wrong. Sometimes environmental regulations are so egregiously stupid that the halo effect can

be overcome and systematic civil disobedience is appropriate. But if the regulation's purpose is to save whooping cranes from extinction, trying to make the case that violating the regulation doesn't really harm whooping cranes starts out with two strikes against it.

Many safety regulations also carry a halo effect, so we should avoid arguing that "ignoring this regulation increases the risk of injury only for people who are complete idiots." Sometimes that argument will get support (the woman who sued McDonald's because her coffee was too hot was widely derided), but we live in a world in which a substantial part of the population has become amazingly risk-averse on behalf of others as well as themselves.

Employment regulations involving discrimination carry a halo effect. Affirmative action is a divisive issue in American life. In that context, disobeying regulations that are supposed to prevent discrimination will seldom get the overwhelming popular support that is needed for successful civil disobedience. Disobeying them might get majority support, but a simple majority isn't good enough.

Choose regulations in which the people who might be harmed by violating the regulation are willing parties.

It is possible to take on regulations that involve a halo effect if the person violating the regulation is the person at risk of being harmed, or if it is clear that others involved are willing parties. OSHA already exempts self-employed contractors and farms with fewer than ten employees from OSHA oversight for that reason.[10] That principle could be extended to other small businesses and to behaviors that involve personal risk.

Choose regulations in which the spirit of the regulation is being obeyed even though the letter is being violated.

A second way to take on regulations involving a halo effect is to focus on ones for which the spirit of the regulation can be achieved in more than one way. For example, the spirit behind the use of traffic lights is to facilitate the efficient flow of traffic and to protect pedestrians from being run over. But if there are no vehicles that can possibly reach the intersection before you cross the street, you can walk across the street against a red light without violating that spirit, as thousands of people do on the streets of Manhattan every minute of every working day. A great many of the regulations from OSHA and the EPA fall into the same category. If a defendant can show that his alternative way of doing things achieves the spirit of the regulation even though it violates the letter, the halo effect can be neutralized.

Above all else . . .

The principled and practical ground rules are all subordinate to this overriding consideration: Systematic civil disobedience cannot succeed if it is used on behalf of people who are trying to game the system. It is essential above all else that my proposed measures for supporting civil disobedience be used for defendants who have acted in good faith. Defendants who are technically guilty must be ethically innocent.

An Attainable Goal: A "No Harm, No Foul" Regulatory Regime

The chapters of Part I laid out an indictment of the current legal, regulatory, and political systems for which the natural solution would be a return to Madisonian limited government. In the next two chapters, I lay out a program for attacking the regulatory state that retains—indeed, feeds upon—many of those defects of the present system. I should state explicitly that I propose to exploit those defects without approving of them. If I had a magic wand, this is the regulatory state I would put in place:

Regulations would be limited to ones that implement intelligible principles in congressional legislation.

Regulations would be few, succinct, and written in plain English.

Regulations would overwhelmingly prohibit acts that are *malum in se* or acts that manifestly degrade a public good classically defined.

Regulations would be worded objectively, with clearly defined schedules of penalties.

Regulatory agencies would have limited discretion in the cases they prosecute and the charges they bring. Administrative law judges would have limited discretion in the penalties they impose. The default position would be that all prosecutable cases should be prosecuted (because the acts themselves are manifestly serious), and all findings of a violation should be penalized.

The regulatory legal system would operate efficiently and with dispatch, which among other things would entail reasonable limits on discovery and appeal.

Civil disobedience would be unacceptable, because the system itself is sound and operates on behalf of the interests of the citizenry.

That's my unattainable ideal. I propose instead an attainable alternative that makes the best of a bad situation, using the openings that are offered by the broad discretion that regulatory officials possess, the mass of the regulatory law to be enforced, the sclerosis of the legal process, and the systemic corruption of the political process. It's not my first choice for a solution. It's the one we can realistically seek.

A good way to think about my strategy is that it will force regulators to confront the same reality that faces state troopers on America's interstate highways. Typically, the flow of traffic on an interstate is above the stated speed limit. A majority of drivers on America's interstates are engaged in civil disobedience just about all the time. The state troopers could stop any one of them and fine them. But normal practice is to stop only those people who are driving significantly faster than the flow of traffic or driving erratically. The state troopers are forced by circumstances into limiting enforcement of the law to people who are creating a driving environment that increases the danger for everybody else on the road.

In sports, this enforcement philosophy is called "no harm, no foul." If a violation of a rule has occurred but it has no effect on the action of the game, the officials ignore it and the game goes on, to the greater enjoyment of both players and spectators. As the sports announcers say, "The officials are letting them play tonight." The measures I propose won't get the regulations off the books, nor will they improve the content of those regulations, but they will push the regulatory agencies, kicking and screaming, toward a "no harm, no foul" position. They will be forced to let the American people play.

CHAPTER 8

HELP FOR ORDINARY AMERICANS

In which I describe the Madison Fund, a privately funded foundation to map terrain and probe defenses while helping ordinary Americans who are trying to cope with the regulatory state.

THE OBJECTIVE IS to rebuild the de facto freedom of Americans to live their lives as they see fit, as long as they observe a few simple laws and accord the same freedom to everyone else. The implication of that statement is that they will be free to ignore a great many complicated laws that will still be on the books. How could we possibly get from here to there?

The Government's Enforcement Capability

The beginning of the answer is that the federal government cannot enforce its mountain of laws and regulations without voluntary public compliance. When it is dealing with individual Americans, the government is a fearsome Goliath that can force submission through the threat of a lengthy and ruinously expensive legal process. But Goliath cannot afford to make good on that threat against thousands of Davids. The government can throw huge resources into a case against a Microsoft or Morgan Stanley, where the stakes are also huge. But it can't do that for every little enforcement action. The staff of even the largest government agency cannot afford to carry a large number of small cases that are strung out for as long as the legal system permits.

The table on page 142 shows the number of attorneys, investigative personnel, and administrative law judges in eight of the regulatory agencies that are most likely to affect the lives of ordinary citizens. I omit agencies such as the SEC and FCC that apply to specific industries.

THE IN-HOUSE ENFORCEMENT STAFF OF SEVEN MAJOR REGULATORY AGENCIES

Agency	Attorneys	Investigative Personnel	Administrative Law Judges*
Environmental Protection Agency	1,096	337	3
Occupational Safety and Health Administration	0	205	40
Federal Drug Administration	115	287	74
Equal Employment Opportunity Commission	469	983	0
Consumer Product Safety Commission	37	166	0
Bureau of Land Management	0	385	12
Fish and Wildlife Service	0	559	12

*Refers to the number of administrative law judges for the entire cabinet department in the case of OSHA (Labor), the FDA (Health and Human Services), and the BLM and FWS (Interior).

Source: Author's analysis, Office of Personnel Management's database of federal employees for June 2013. (See www.opm.gov/about-us/open-government/data/.)

Note the qualification "in-house." These resources may be augmented by people who work for other federal entities, state agencies, or for contractors to the regulatory agencies. Getting numbers on these additional resources is difficult even for state agencies and impossible for contractors—the federal government doesn't publish data on the role that private contractors play in the operations of a given agency or cabinet department. But even with these limitations, it is apparent that the enforcement capabilities of the regulatory agencies are wildly out of whack with the breadth of their enforcement mandate.

Consider OSHA. By its own estimate, OSHA is responsible for overseeing 8 million worksites around the nation, and it has issued regulations that all of them are supposed to observe. But OSHA's staff for enforcing all those regulations amounts to about 200 inspectors who actually work for OSHA and another 2,000 who work for state agencies.[1] From 1990 to 2010, OSHA averaged 27,250 site visits per year.[2] The Office of Personnel Management's database of government employees shows no attorneys assigned to OSHA. The Department of Labor as a whole employed 674 attorneys, but how many of these are available to work on OSHA-related tasks is unknown.

Now consider the priorities that drive OSHA's decision to conduct an inspection. In order, they are situations in which (1) there is an imminent threat of serious accidents, (2) fatalities and serious injuries have occurred, and (3) an employee has filed a formal complaint. In addition, OSHA conducts programmed inspections aimed at workplaces such as construction sites that are inherently hazardous.[3] What are the odds that an OSHA inspector is going to show up at a given workplace that is not inherently hazardous? Close to zero.

Or consider the EPA. In fiscal year 2013, the EPA's civil enforcement included 18,000 inspections, 1,440 Final Administrative Penalty Orders, and 873 Administrative Compliance Orders.[4] In a sense, the number of actual penalty and compliance orders is just the tip of the iceberg. In uncounted other instances, the EPA threatened action for regulatory violations and got compliance just by making the threat. In another sense, these numbers indicate how limited the enforcement effort is. The EPA is not responsible just for worksites. Its regulations cover the actions of property owners as well. Eighteen thousand inspections in the context of that mandate is a tiny number.

So we all live under a system with thousands of regulations that we're supposed to obey. But what looks like Goliath to any one of us is actually the Wizard of Oz. Let's have a private-sector counterweight that pulls back the curtain and exposes the Wizard's weakness.

The Madison Fund

How do we establish a private counterweight to government? We can begin with a private legal-aid foundation to provide similar legal assistance to ordinary Americans who are being victimized by the regulatory state. I will call it the Madison Fund.

The best way to give you a sense of the Madison Fund's role is through a specific true example that led to this book. I have to omit details lest the protagonist be identified. "I'd like to write a book about it," he has said of his experiences with regulatory bureaucrats, "but if I did it before I retire, they would destroy me."

The person in question operates one of the many kinds of businesses that use Latino immigrants, legal or illegal. Call him Bob. What makes Bob different from most such employers in his part of the country is that all of his workers are documented. He goes to considerable trouble and expense—$20,000 to $30,000 a year—for the excruciatingly complicated visa process, which never gets simpler even though he brings back the same workers year after year. He pays good wages (his workers make $14–$15 an hour plus overtime and free housing), pays for his workers' airfares, and is in other ways a model employer and member of his community.

Bob has come under relentless harassment by the government. Why pick on him, when his part of the country is full of employers who have 100 percent undocumented Latino workers? Because, by doing the right thing and documenting his workers, he opened himself up to easy inspection by government enforcers who do not have the authority to track down (or do not want to go to the trouble of tracking down) employers of illegal aliens. He made himself a soft target.

The harassment has been continual, and so has been the string of fines and needless expenses that have followed in their wake. But the incident that focused my thinking on the regulatory state ended with Bob becoming so frustrated that he told the official who was enforcing a particularly idiotic regulation that he would fight it in court—at which point the bureaucrat said to him, "You do that, and we'll put you out of business." And Bob knew that is exactly what would happen.

My friend's story made me want to see a mystery man with a briefcase appear from nowhere, tap the bureaucrat on the shoulder, and say,

"We are taking over this man's case. We will litigate it as long as it takes. We will publicize that litigation in ways that will embarrass you and your superiors. None of this will cost our client a penny, and we will reimburse him for any fine you are able to impose. And if you come back and bother him again, we will go through the whole process again."

That's the immediate point of the Madison Fund: to be the champion of individual citizens against Goliath. Its longer-range point is to make clear to other Americans that they don't have to take it anymore. There are ways to force an intrusive government to back off. Specifically, the Madison Fund would have three goals:

1. To defend people who are innocent of the regulatory charges against them.
2. To defend people who are technically guilty of violating regulations that should not exist, drawing out that litigation as long as possible, making enforcement of the regulations more expensive to the regulatory agency than they're worth, and reimbursing fines that are levied.
3. To generate as much publicity as possible, both to raise the public's awareness of the government's harassment of people like them, and to bring the pressure of public opinion to bear on elected politicians and staffs of regulatory agencies.

Those are the goals, and they are achievable. We do not need anyone's permission to achieve them—not the permission of a sympathetic president, Congress, or Supreme Court.

Funding

The emergence of many billion-dollar-plus private fortunes over the last three decades has enabled the private sector to take on ambitious national or even international tasks that formerly could be done only by nation-states. Bill Gates's quest to end malaria through the Gates Foundation is one example. The next American manned space flights are more likely to be achieved by private efforts than by NASA. The private sector similarly has it within its power to provide ordinary citizens with a counterweight against government overreach, even as Congress demonstrates its own powerlessness to do anything. Many billionaires and centimillionaires are principled advocates of limited government. So are tens of thousands of mere multimillionaires.

The Madison Fund could get started if just one wealthy American cared enough to contribute, say, a few hundred million dollars. It could get started if a dozen wealthy Americans cared enough to share the initial cost among themselves. It could get started the way that other Madisonian foundations have begun and flourished, with seed money from a few affluent people who also worked to develop a large network of donors. It could get started the way the Tea Party got started, as a popular movement. Money isn't going to be a problem if the strategy can be shown to be workable.

Institutional Expertise

The Madison Fund will not have to carve out its niche from scratch. Its organizational model can borrow from the Legal Services Corporation, which provides legal assistance to thousands of low-income clients around the nation. It can draw upon the expertise of other institutes that have conducted litigation on behalf of Madisonian causes for decades. The oldest, the Pacific Legal Foundation, was established in 1973 by former members of Governor Ronald Reagan's senior staff. In 2012 it scored a famous victory with the 9–0 Supreme Court decision in *Sackett v. Environmental Protection Agency*, discussed at the end of this chapter. The Landmark Legal Foundation was established in 1976 and has litigated cases on a wide range of limited-government issues. The Goldwater Institute in Phoenix, established in 1988, has a litigation division that has won major victories in promoting federalism. The Institute for Justice, headquartered across the river from Washington in Arlington, Virginia, was founded in 1991 and focuses on cases involving private property, economic liberty, free speech, and school choice. Its most influential case was probably one that it technically lost: the famous eminent-domain case *Kelo v. City of New London*, discussed in chapter 2, in which private homes were condemned so that the land could be turned over to private developers. The national backlash against the *Kelo* decision led to changes in forty-four state laws that strengthened protections of property rights against illegitimate use of eminent domain.

The Madison Fund would also have a rich resource for finding staff and enlisting pro bono resources in the form of the Federalist Society. Dedicated to federalism and the principles of limited government, the Federalist Society's membership numbers more than thirty thousand legal professionals and their allies, distributed across chapters in sixty cities, plus more than ten thousand current American law students who are committed to the same principles.[5]

Getting off the Ground

In the context of America's legal system, the Pacific Legal Foundation, Landmark Legal Foundation, Goldwater Institute, and Institute for Justice are tiny, with combined operating budgets of just $25 million in 2013—rounding error for any of the major regulatory agencies.[6] To serve as a nationwide resource for ordinary citizens in need of defense against the government, the Madison Fund would ultimately need to be much larger, able to spend a few hundred million dollars in litigation annually. But it does not have to be that large right away. On the contrary, it should start small in any case, because much trial and error will be involved. The Madison Fund will have to establish guidelines for the categories of cases it will consider and its screening process for clients. It will have to gain experience with the intricacies of the administrative courts as they function in practice, finding the points of vulnerability. The very task of the Madison Fund—to make enforcement of certain regulations more trouble than it's worth—is novel, and it will take time and experimentation to figure out how best to drain the government's resources while conserving its own. The Madison Fund must develop an active in-house publicity resource: helping the public to understand just how intrusive government has become for ordinary Americans will be a major tool in bringing pressure to bear on the regulatory bureaucracies.

Chapter 10 will discuss some of these practical considerations in more detail. But before getting to them, it's time to introduce a second mechanism for rolling back the power of the regulatory state: the occupational defense funds.

CHAPTER 9

TREATING GOVERNMENT AS AN INSURABLE HAZARD

In which I propose that professional associations shift some of their money from lobbying to insuring their members against mischief from the regulatory state, and then reflect upon the possible consequences when government is seen as just another insurable hazard, like fires or floods.

THE MADISON FUND is to be an altruistic endeavor, funded by people who do not receive its services and operated on behalf of ordinary Americans who are being harrassed by the regulatory state. Now I turn to the way in which the beachhead established by the Madison Fund can be expanded into a full-scale invasion.

The members of professions and crafts have formed guilds since early medieval times. These associations are not altruistic. Historically, they have organized partly as a brotherhood of people practicing the same vocation, but also to increase their leverage in the marketplace—monopolistic leverage, when possible. Today, professional associations lobby in Washington along with corporations, unions, and nonprofit advocacy groups, all trying to use the power of the state to improve their private interests.

But guilds have had another historic function: to establish standards of best practice and qualifications for attaining membership. It is one of the most natural impulses of people who have learned how to do some specific thing extremely well. They take pride in their work, have strong views about right and wrong ways of doing it, and feel a bond with others who are good at the same craft.

Many such associations certify that their members are skilled. In the crafts, the three traditional levels of proficiency have been apprentice, journeyman, and master. To pass from apprentice to journeyman and from journeyman to master has required submission of work samples to a board composed of masters. In medicine, physicians in specialized fields become "board certified," meaning they have met the requirements, which include not only completing specified training but passing extensive tests. Accountants can call themselves CPAs because they have passed the rigorous Certified Public Accountant examination.

For our purposes—creating a private counterweight to the regulatory state—professional associations have enormous potential because they exist both to assist their members and to hold them to standards of professional conduct. That's exactly the combination we need as a method of substituting real expertise for the regulatory proclamations of bureaucracies.

If Dentists Fought Back

Since I have already used OSHA's regulation of dental offices as an example (recall the 307-page *OSHA Manual for Dentists* that I discussed in chapter 2), let's use the American Dental Association (ADA) for a sample scenario. The ADA conducts national board dental examinations and runs centers for disseminating the latest research on best dentistry practice and developing better performance measures.[1] Its Standards Administration Department establishes baseline standards and technical recommendations for the tools of modern dentistry, from toothbrushes to radiographic systems. It issues the ADA Seal of Acceptance to dental products. It has established a code of dental-practice parameters for treatment options. In short, the ADA has all the resources needed to assess whether a dental practice is safe and competent.

Dentists are also tightly regulated. In addition to OSHA's safety regulations, dentists are subject to the labyrinthine body of federal employment law, EPA regulations, and all the other regulations that impinge on any professional running an office and managing personnel.

The ordinary dentist can almost certainly get away with ignoring a lot of those regulations. As of 2011, the United States contained 131,179 dental offices.[2] As noted earlier, OSHA is responsible for 8 million workplaces, and none of the safety priorities used to select workplaces for inspection are likely to involve dental offices. Unless an employee files a formal complaint with OSHA, dental offices are not on OSHA's radar screen, and the chances that OSHA will conduct an inspection are nearly zero.

But they are not quite zero, and the downside risk of ignoring OSHA's regulations if you *are* inspected is substantial. Even though your dental office is safe, you will surely be in violation of a few of OSHA's rules, and you can be hit with fines of up to $7,000 per violation. So risk-averse dentists are not being irrational when they spend an aggravating amount of time and effort to protect themselves against this low-probability risk.

Step back from the situation for a moment. Stop thinking of government as a fearsome entity that must be obeyed, and think of it instead as an insurable hazard. Why not buy insurance against the low-probability event of an inspection by a regulatory agency?

Suppose that the ADA, acting on this way of looking at things, decides to offer its members low-cost insurance against the government, calling it Dental Shield. It charges a nominal $100 per year. About 90 percent of dental offices take up the offer, producing an annual fund of almost $12 million, which is used to reimburse fines and to pay for costs of litigating cases that meet the ADA's established criteria. Suppose that the average inspection results in fines of $10,000. That would permit the ADA to reimburse fines for 200 inspections per year and still leave almost $10 million for litigation costs. Given the rarity of inspections, that should be enough.

What has been accomplished?

An Insurance Business Opportunity?

I have presented a scenario in which professional associations establish the insurance. If it's a sufficiently profitable business opportunity, there's no reason that for-profit insurance companies couldn't do it, in the same way that they provide malpractice insurance for physicians.

First, for a negligible price, dentists can go about their lives as if most federal regulations didn't exist. They will become an insurable hazard on a par with the hazard that a storm will topple a large tree onto the roof of your house. Faced with the risk of a violent storm, you don't fill out extensive annual paperwork. You don't pay an arborist to come in once a year and inspect the root system of the tree. You don't hire a consultant to do a risk assessment of your property. You buy home insurance.

Second, the responsibility for the regulation of crafts and professions will return to the people who care most about it and are most competent to judge. One of the pernicious aspects of the regulatory state is that it makes the operational assumption that large numbers of people engaged in the crafts or professions are either incompetent or charlatans, and only the government's oversight can protect citizens from them. I accept that all occupations have bad apples, but to treat everyone as a suspect is insulting and wrong. In effect, the ADA's Dental Shield program will be saying to its members, "You conduct your practice in a manner consistent with ADA's standards, and we'll defend you against government nitpicking," not "ADA members, right or wrong." If you show yourself to be a reckless driver, your insurance company will cut you off. If Dental Shield, in defending its members, finds itself called upon to defend a dentist who really does run an unsafe office, that dentist faces exclusion from subsequent insurance and other professional sanctions.

The third benefit of a society with many occupational defense funds is more diffuse, but one that I ask you to keep in mind as I work through the ramifications of systematic civil disobedience. A by-product of systematic civil disobedience can be a reinvigoration of civil society. A society in which a central government tries to surveil everyone is on its way to tyranny, no matter what forms of democracy it retains. A society in which people are held to standards of behavior by the approbation and disapprobation of their peers is operating in the way that the great theorists of freedom and the founders both anticipated.[3]

I am not envisioning an end state in which the federal government has withdrawn from regulation. One of the goals of the Madison Fund and the occupational defense funds alike—I'm going to refer to them jointly as "the defense funds" from now on—is to push the government toward the "no harm, no foul" regime I described in the preceding chapter, forcing the government to identify the regulatory roles that it is best equipped to fill and limiting itself to violations of good practice that the government can enforce better than private entities. What we have forgotten over the last half century is how much can be done by private entities. A feature of American life that attracted the amazed attention of European observers throughout the nineteenth century was the genius of Americans in getting things done by coming together voluntarily to solve problems. Of all the ways in which the regulatory state has damaged the American project, I believe the most damning is its suppression of that genius.

Is All This Actually Legal?

What I am advocating through the defense funds is unquestionably subversive. They will be helping people who have ignored regulations evade the consequences of their actions. They will openly be trying to pour sugar into the regulatory state's gas tank. Can such things be legal?

We can be certain the government won't think so, and will try to have their operations declared illegal. Since the Madison Fund will probably be operational before any of the occupational defense funds, one of the Madison Fund's first tasks is likely to be a defense of its right to operate and establishing the limits within which it can do certain things.

Even though its aims are ultimately subversive, most of the Madison Fund's operations, and those of the occupational defense funds, are clearly legal. Providing free legal assistance to people who are charged with crimes or misdemeanors is legal. It's done all the time, by private attorneys working pro bono; by Legal Services; and, for criminal cases, by public defenders.

Does the Madison Fund's openly stated goal of overloading the enforcement resources of the regulatory agencies amount to a criminal conspiracy? It's hard to make that case, since no one involved in the fund would be planning on committing a crime. Lawyers for the Madison Fund are not going to be making up evidence, suborning witnesses, or otherwise meeting the legal definition of obstructing justice. On the contrary, they will be meticulously using the rules of legal procedure to make the litigation as expensive and irksome to the government as possible. But by doing so on behalf of guilty clients, aren't Madison Fund lawyers trying to exploit the system to circumvent justice? Yes—as are attorneys all over the country who use their best efforts to help guilty clients delay convictions on criminal charges or evade them altogether. The only difference is motivation. In the cases we see in the criminal courts, the attorney is helping the defendant avoid the consequences of having done things that are typically *malum in se.* The Madison Fund wants to prevent people from being subjected to punishment for doing things that are *malum prohibitum* for no good reason.

However stridently the government and the *New York Times* might inveigh against the purposes of the defense funds, it is hard to see how their legal advocacy could be shut down. The one area where they are likely to run into snags is in reimbursing clients for fines. This issue will have to be litigated.

In anticipating how that litigation will play out, it is useful to think in terms of the insurance contracts that courts will and won't enforce. The Second Restatement of Contracts (the most authoritative statement of common law principles) says that the general test for enforceability is "a balancing test between the individual interests in enforcement and the public policy weighing against it."[4] The most relevant factors for striking that balance as specified in the Second Restatement are "the strength of that policy as manifested by legislation or judicial decisions" and "the seriousness of any misconduct involved and the extent to which it was deliberate."

Few of the cases that the defense funds take on will have had effects "against public policy" in any serious sense. Remember: one of the criteria for selecting cases is that no real harm has occurred. Furthermore, almost all of the cases will involve regulations that have only a tenuous relationship with anything that Congress spelled out in the legislation—the "strength of that policy as manifested by legislation or judicial decisions" will be low. The most plausible scenario is that the government will litigate the reimbursement of fines, but will usually be unsuccessful.

As time goes on, attorneys at the defense funds will be able to fine-tune the body of cases that permit reimbursement of fines. Insofar as the government contests the reimbursement of fines, it will create a body of case law demonstrating that for many regulations, violation does not involve a significant public interest that prevents reimbursement.

The Empire Strikes Back

E ven after the courts have confirmed the legality of the defense funds' operations, probably with some caveats about the fines that can be reimbursed, the federal government will not stand idly by. We should assume instead that regulatory agencies will be looking for ways to strike back. How might they do so?

Let's go back to the example of Dental Shield. Suppose that you are the administrator of OSHA. You know that Dental Shield is insuring dentists against OSHA inspections. You correctly interpret this as an attempt by Dental Shield to subvert OSHA's authority. You want to re-establish that dentists have to take OSHA regulations seriously. How might you go about it?

Your best weapon is the inspection, so you begin conducting wholesale inspections of dental offices, levying the maximum fines. But Dental Shield contests those fines. Not all of them. In the rare case when a dental office really did have an unsafe condition, Dental Shield pays the fine without contesting it and also cancels that dentist's insurance policy. But in other cases, the insurance company litigates OSHA's citation to the max, appealing adverse decisions to the full Occupational Safety & Health Review Commission, and, when possible, appealing adverse decisions by the commission to an Article III federal court. Dental Shield understands how limited OSHA's enforcement resources are. By contesting citations, Dental Shield makes the pursuit of the dental citations more trouble for OSHA than it's worth.

At this point, you as the administrator are between a rock and a hard place. OSHA cannot afford to devote a grossly disproportionate amount of its limited resources to a vendetta against dentists without degrading its ability to enforce genuinely serious safety regulations elsewhere. But neither can it go to Congress and ask for more inspectors. As OSHA's administrator, you envision the hearing as you sit before the members of House Committee on the Budget. Why is it that OSHA needs these extra resources? Because, you will have to answer, so many of the current staff are engaged in inspection of dental offices and litigating fines of dentists. It's not a pleasant prospect, and it is not going to get you any additional enforcement resources from Congress. If a war with Dental Shield is not practical, you are reduced to three options.

The first is to try to win a battle for public opinion. OSHA's position goes something like this:

> We are a duly constituted agency of the federal government, mandated by law to keep America's workplaces safe. That important mission is being cynically compromised by dentists who, in collusion with Dental Shield, are trying to evade their professional responsibilities, thereby endangering Americans seeking dental care.

It won't fly. Americans generally like their dentists, or they wouldn't have continued to be their patients. The reputation of the federal government, and especially of agencies like OSHA, is dismal. The instinctive response of the American people will be to side with the dentists, not the government. That instinctive response will be reinforced by Dental Shield's ability to cite chapter and verse to demonstrate that the dentists on whom OSHA is levying thousands of dollars in fines were actually running safe dental practices as assessed by the ADA, which knows a lot more about how to go about good dentistry than OSHA does. They just weren't going through the rigmarole that OSHA specifies.

OSHA's second option is to get the courts to declare Dental Shield illegal. I already outlined the reasons for thinking that the defense funds' operations are legal and that such a strategy won't work. In addition to that, taking Dental Shield to court carries a risk for OSHA. Today, few among the general public are aware how the administrative justice system works. One of the oldest and most obviously essential legal maxims is that no one may be judge in his own cause. In America's administrative justice system, the regulatory agency is not only the judge in its own cause but the police, prosecuting attorney, and appeals court as well. To destroy Dental Shield, OSHA will have to take its case into the regular court system, in a highly publicized proceeding, revealing to more of the American public just how loaded in favor of government the regulatory system really is. That's not an attractive option either.

OSHA's third option is to quietly limit its citations of dental offices to cases in which a genuine safety issue exists, not just a technical violation of a regulation. You tell your staff to adopt "no harm, no foul" as OSHA's tacit enforcement philosophy.

CHAPTER 10

FROM SYSTEMATIC CIVIL DISOBEDIENCE TO A "NO HARM, NO FOUL" REGULATORY REGIME

In which I describe a scenario whereby a small change in the courts' interpretation of existing administrative law could lead to a "no harm, no foul" approach to regulation, and argue that we have reason to think such a shift is possible.

F THE MADISON Fund and the occupational defense funds do no more than provide assistance to people who are being harassed by the government, they will have accomplished much. If they deter the regulatory agencies from enforcing the worst regulations, they will be a full-fledged success. But those are not the limits of feasible change. It is not a pipe dream, but possible, that "no harm, no foul" can become embedded in law through a few Supreme Court decisions that five justices could realistically support.

There's an important qualifier to that word, *possible*. Legal experts who have read this chapter and the next have expressed their skepticism, pointing out various technical issues of procedure and precedent. I have no doubt they are right about the barriers, and no doubt that at points in the discussion in this chapter and the next, I am blithely ignorant of still other important barriers.

Despite all this, I feel like I am in a position not unlike that of Steve Jobs when he was shown a prototype of the first iPod. He thought it was too big. His engineers told him that it was a miracle that they had been able to make it as small as it already was. There was simply no way to make it smaller. As the story is told, Jobs walked over to an aquarium and dropped the prototype into it. As it sank to the bottom, bubbles rose to the top. "That means there's space in there," Jobs said. "Make it smaller."[1] I am saying that the regulatory state is out of control because of some basic errors in past jurisprudence. Americans are increasingly aware that it is out of control. The federal government's legitimacy is waning in part because of the regulatory state's unpopularity. Hardly anyone is out there defending the excesses of the regulatory state. Put the whole thing together, and we've got the equivalent of air bubbles. That means there's space in there. A fix is possible.

I have a basis for my optimism in the track record of the Supreme Court. The Court never overturns a decision like *Helvering* or *Wickard*, because such a ruling would not be obeyed and the Court's legitimacy would be shattered. But the Supreme Court has a long history of changing course in less extreme ways when it sees that its decision will have enough support. The Court doesn't always wait for a national consensus; sometimes, it anticipates an emerging one.[2] *Brown v. Board of Education*, which overruled *Plessy v. Ferguson*, is an example. The Supreme Court was as liberal during the constitutional revolution of 1937–1942 as it was in 1954, but it is doubtful that it would have outlawed school segregation if a case such as *Brown* had been brought before it.[3] What made 1954 different were intervening events such as the integration of the Armed Forces. They had altered the national zeitgeist about racial segregation. In 1942, the equivalent of the *Brown* decision probably would have aroused widespread opposition throughout the nation. In 1954, the Court correctly anticipated that a consensus of Americans outside the South would accept it.

To create a new and better regulatory regime, we don't need a flat-out reversal of broad and binding Supreme Court precedent. The regulatory state is vulnerable to a simple shift in its interpretation of the Administrative Procedure Act of 1946, which governs all administrative law.

Applying "Arbitrary and Capricious" to the Enforcement of Regulations

The key to embedding the "no harm, no foul" approach in law is to force the regulatory agencies to be legally accountable for their actions in the same way that all other entities in the United States, from individuals to giant corporations, are legally accountable for their actions. The vulnerability lies in the wording of section 706 of the Administrative Procedure Act, which sets out the scope of judicial review of regulatory actions.

If you read section 706 without any knowledge of how the courts have interpreted it (the section's full text is given in the note), you would think that regulatory agencies are fully accountable.[*] There's nothing that would lead you to predict the great deference the courts have shown toward the regulatory state. And that's the reason for the vulnerability. The actual wording of the law is unobjectionable. It is not necessary to pass a revised Administrative Procedure Act. It is merely necessary to interpret section 706 more straightforwardly.

To that end, the defense funds will be mounting a sustained assault that can potentially affect the judicial interpretation of clause 706(2)(A). This clause says, "The reviewing court shall . . . hold unlawful and set aside agency action, findings, and conclusions found to be . . . arbitrary, capricious, an abuse of discretion, or otherwise not in accordance with law." The defense funds will contend that the phrase "arbitrary, capricious, [or] an abuse of discretion" applies to the *enforcement* of regulations as well as to their creation.

It sounds like a minor point. It could be huge. But as I describe why, I want to emphasize how much of the defense funds' long struggle against the regulatory state will evolve in ways we cannot anticipate. I would be amazed if the scenario that follows is accurate in more than a strategic sense. But it will give you a sense of the possibilities.

Assume that the defense funds have been operating for a few years. Out of the hundreds of defenses they have mounted against regulatory overreach, dozens of them have argued a variation on the same theme: yes, their clients were technically in violation of the regulation, but the enforcement of the regulation itself was arbitrary and capricious (the shorthand I will use for "arbitrary, capricious, [or] an abuse of discretion").

The administrative law judges hearing those dozens of cases are able to throw out all of them because the Supreme Court has set such a high bar for finding that an agency has been arbitrary and capricious. Namely, the Court said in 1971 that it would not find an agency action arbitrary and capricious if it was "based on a consideration of the relevant factors" and there had not been "a clear error of judgment."[5] Imagine you are an attorney trying to demonstrate that an action was arbitrary and capricious. How are you to prove that the agency did *not* consider "the relevant factors" in the face of the agency's paper trail saying that it did? How are you to prove that the agency made a *clear* error in judgment—in effect, a judgment that has no rational basis whatsoever? Answer: It's next to impossible. Lest he leave defendants any chance at all, Justice Thurgood Marshall, writing for the 6–2 majority in *Citizens to Preserve Overton Park v. Volpe*, continued: "Although this inquiry into the facts is to be searching and careful, the ultimate standard of review is a narrow one. *The court is not empowered to substitute its judgment for that of the agency.*"[6]

The sentence I italicized gets to the heart of a problem that explains a great deal of what has gone wrong with the regulatory state: the deference that the courts have wrongly accorded to the regulators. I discussed the origins of the deference in chapter 3. To recapitulate: The progressive advocates of the regulatory state saw regulators as special people—disinterested experts on arcane topics about which elected legislators were ignorant, and able to make technically correct decisions to advance the public interest without fear or favor. None of those advocates seemed to consider the possibility that regulators were as likely to make mistakes as anybody else, as likely to have political biases as anybody else, and as likely to abuse power as anybody else. This idealistic view of regulators persisted, and is reflected in the deference that has been given to regulators by Supreme Court jurisprudence. To this day, the opinions of the bureaucrats in the regulatory agencies count for more in the eyes of federal courts than the opinions of experts in the private sector.

But a few years into the operation of the defense funds, all of those failed defenses they've mounted have not gone unnoticed. The defense funds have learned how to publicize the most egregious cases of arbitrary and capricious behavior by regulatory agencies—a reality TV show showing ordinary Americans being victimized by regulators, *American or UnAmerican: You Decide*, has become a big hit—and over time these cases have affected the nation's consciousness.[7] Just because the administrative judges always say that the regulatory agencies did not act arbitrarily and capriciously, it doesn't mean that the public agrees. Nor are the judges who sit on Article III courts unaware of what's been going on.

In this context, the case of *Lancaster Brick Company v. OSHA* comes before an Article III court on appeal. As the judges study the transcripts of the hearings before the administrative judge and the subsequent rejected appeal within the Department of Labor, they read the following story.

The Source of the Story

The facts about the brick factory and violations of OSHA regulations are all true, drawn from an account of actual violations of OSHA regulations brought against a brick factory as described by Philip K. Howard in *The Death of Common Sense*.[8] Because I have inserted these facts into a fictional legal battle, I have also adopted a fictitious name for the company, and do not identify by name the sources of the quotes. But the quotes are indeed the words of personnel in the real brick company. I have not tried to make my account conform to the technical details of how hearings before administrative law judges and judges in Article III courts are conducted. I'm using a narrative device.

An OSHA inspection of the Lancaster Brick Company's brickmaking facility found the following violations of OSHA regulations, for which it assessed fines that Lancaster is appealing:

1. Some railings in the factory were 39 and 40 inches high instead of the required 42 inches.
2. Lancaster failed to install the required automatic shut-off for a conveyer belt.

3. Lancaster failed to post a POISON sign on a storage shed containing poison.
4. Lancaster permitted a worker with a beard to use a dust mask, violating a rule that requires a close fit between face and mask.
5. Lancaster permitted a fire hazard in a work area.

Lancaster was technically in violation of all five. Its defense is that OSHA's actions against Lancaster should be voided because they are arbitrary and capricious.[9] To make its case before the administrative law judge, the defense fund attorney had taken on the allegations one by one:

1. The lower railings have been in place for decades, and Lancaster has never had an accident involving railings. Why, the defense fund attorney asks, is 42 inches safe and 39 or 40 inches unsafe?
2. The conveyer belt runs through an area that is already partitioned off from workers. There's no safety reason to spend the several thousand dollars the automatic shut-off would cost.
3. The "poison" in the bags in the storage shed is sand. Ordinary beach sand. OSHA wants a POISON sign posted because it classified sand as a poison. How can sand be poisonous? Because it contains silica, which might (just might) cause cancer in certain grinding and mining operations—which, even if correct, has nothing to do with anything that goes on at the Lancaster Brick Company.
4. The dust in the work area is neither heavy nor hazardous, and the dust mask works even when worn over the beard. Furthermore, the man in question is Amish, and if the rule is enforced, he will quit rather than violate his religious convictions. It is cruel as well as senseless to make a man lose his job over principle when there's no safety hazard created by his beard.
5. The work area with the fire hazard is the machinery repair shop. The hazard consists of a few rags (not piles of them) found beside the machines under repair. Rags are needed to wipe down surfaces and clean bearings. You can't run a machinery repair shop without them.

Then the defense had called Lancaster's manager of regulatory compliance to the stand (it's a full-time position at Lancaster, as at most factories). He had testified that each inspection is a kind of "a negative lottery." "Every inspector knows different rules," he said, so the ones that the inspectors cite are their own go-to specialties, unrelated to the actual safety importance of the rule. But with so many regulations on the books (so many that none of the inspectors can remember all of them), they can always find *something* wrong, even though "we have done basically everything they asked for the last twenty years."[10] Even the choice of which regulations to enforce is arbitrary and capricious.

It's even tougher on the factory because OSHA had issued complicated and ambiguous new regulations without explaining how to comply with them. The administrative law judge heard testimony that when a new regulation required Lancaster to make substantial changes to part of the plant, Lancaster's management tried to find out exactly what they needed to do. After a few weeks of working their way through the layers of OSHA's bureaucracy, they gave up. No one would tell them what compliance required.

Lancaster's manager of regulatory compliance then told the administrative judge about another problem: OSHA *creates* safety problems through its fixation on paperwork and the physical layout of the plant. That's not what causes accidents, he says, invoking statistics showing that five out of six accidents are caused by human error. Trying to make everything "idiot-proof," in his words, distracts from real safety considerations. "Workers don't have to think, and bosses get tied down with nitpicking regulations." The plant manager was called to testify. He emphatically argued that OSHA had created safety problems with its demands that workers change long-standing safe and effective habits. "Doing it a new way after years of doing it the old way is just an invitation for an accident," the manager said.[11]

In rendering his decision, the administrative judge had found that the defense had not met its burden of proof. According to the Supreme Court's guidance in *Overton*, the case for "arbitrary and capricious" failed. For each of the five violations, OSHA had offered a paper trail documenting that it had considered the relevant factors in creating the regulations and there was a rationale for each of them. The inspectors were merely applying the regulations to observed conditions at the Lancaster plant.

At the appeal hearing before the Article III court, one of the judges asks the defense fund attorney to respond: Why was the administrative judge wrong? Yes, the appeals court judge agrees, all of the five findings of violations looked pretty silly on their face, but did they meet the *Overton* requirement that OSHA made *clear* errors in judgment? And OSHA could indeed come up with a rationale for each of the five, however far-fetched those rationales may seem to observers who aren't lawyers.

Lancaster's lawyer from the defense fund responds as follows:

> One of the most common criticisms of bureaucrats, so common that it has been a cliché around the world for centuries, is that they interpret the rules according to the absolute letter of the rule without regard to circumstances. Why has this been such a universal characteristic of bureaucrats? For two reasons. One is that they cannot be criticized by their superiors if they have followed the letter of the rule. The other is a sad commentary on human nature, but it has been confirmed by experience over millennia: people who are given the right to order other people to do things tend to exercise that power mindlessly.
>
> Courts such as this one, following the Supreme Court's guidance in *Overton v. Volpe,* have refrained from substituting their judgment for that of the regulatory agencies when applied to complex regulations based on technical analyses of abstruse scientific issues. Our case does not dispute that position. But none of the regulations putatively violated by Lancaster Brick Company are either complex or abstruse. OSHA has given its scientific rationale for requiring that beach sand be labeled POISON—that under some circumstances beach sand may cause cancer. We argue that you as judges are free to decide that such a rationale as applied to the environment of the Lancaster Brick Factory is so devoid of common sense that it is arbitrary and capricious. OSHA has given its scientific rationale for prohibiting dust masks being used by people with beards—that under some circumstances, the worker will be exposed to a health hazard. But you as judges are free to decide that the OSHA inspector who cited it as a violation was so oblivious of the facts of this particular case that the inspector's decision to cite it as a violation was arbitrary and capricious.
>
> We understand that interpreting "arbitrary and capricious" for any specific case is a judgment call. So is the interpretation

of "guilty beyond a reasonable doubt" in criminal cases, or the interpretation of "duty of care" in civil cases. "Arbitrary and capricious" can be explicated as other legal terms of art have been explicated, but in a way that captures this elemental truth: a regulatory agency's actions, findings, and conclusions can have gone through the motions of taking relevant considerations into account, and can appeal to some rationale, and still be obviously arbitrary and capricious when viewed in the context of the specific real-life situation in which they are applied.

To evaluate "arbitrary and capricious" in the context of specific real-life situations would bring regulatory law into the realm in which ordinary civil law and criminal law have abided for centuries. In common law, circumstances surrounding the actual event in litigation have always been at the center of attention. In criminal law, mitigating circumstances have always been taken into account. Only regulatory law has been sheltered from the requirement that it be enforced in the context of circumstances.

The deference of administrative judges and the Article III courts to the regulators has gone too far. Even assuming that it is appropriate for highly complex regulations—a point we do not reach in this case—it is inappropriate for simple regulations. In those instances, as in any other kind of law, the citizen must have the ability to appeal to a jury's or a judge's common sense. Since administrative courts shelter the regulatory agencies from juries of ordinary citizens, you are the only repository of common sense left.

In this scenario—which leaves open the probability that exactly the same argument will have failed many times previously—the Article III court does not rule on the *content* of the regulations, but holds that the *enforcement* of those rules in the Lancaster case was arbitrary and capricious, and on that basis it finds for Lancaster Brick Company.

The adverse decision leaves OSHA with a painful choice. Should the agency accept the court's finding and hope that it will be a one-off result? Or does the agency appeal the decision to a higher court, all the way to the Supreme Court if necessary, to overturn the decision and preserve the more restrictive interpretation of "arbitrary and capricious"?

If the defense funds did not exist, the first option would be attractive.

The case might get a news story in the local paper, and maybe a few defense attorneys elsewhere in subsequent cases would pick up on it, but not much else would happen. But the defense funds will not allow the ruling to go unnoticed. It will be widely publicized in the news media and then cited as precedent in subsequent cases that the defense funds bring. If the regulatory state does not get a higher court to overturn the ruling, its way of doing business will be forever altered.

So *Lancaster Brick Company v. OSHA* is appealed up the ladder and reaches the Supreme Court. What then? I think we are at a point in the history of the regulatory state analogous to the state of legal segregation in 1954. The Supreme Court will discern an emerging social consensus: Americans across most of the political spectrum are fed up with the excesses of the regulatory state. They don't want to get rid of it, but they want it to be reasonable. They want it to stop being arbitrary and capricious. The Supreme Court upholds the ruling that *enforcement* of a regulation can be arbitrary and capricious regardless of whether the content of the rule rises to that level.

How the Reinterpretation of "Arbitrary and Capricious" Can Lead to a "No Harm, No Foul" Regulatory Regime

What difference does a single court victory make? Until the *Lancaster* decision, the defense funds will have been fighting a war of attrition based on overwhelming the limited enforcement resources of the regulatory agencies. Once that Supreme Court decision is available as a precedent, and the regulatory agencies know that the defense funds will be using it constantly, a large part of the battle will have been permanently won.

Once again, put yourself in the position of an administrator at OSHA. For the enforcement of big, complicated regulations, little has changed. The courts will still accord deference if the rules in formulating the regulations have been followed and the issues are sufficiently abstruse. Regulatory bureaucrats may feel a frisson of apprehension that didn't exist before (What if some deep-pocketed corporation goes all out to demonstrate that even a complicated regulation is prima facie idiotic in its content?), but no more than that.

But when it comes to routine inspections and the small stuff, the shift in the interpretation of "arbitrary and capricious" will have created a new dynamic. Consider the sequence of events at that point.

Before legally supported systematic civil disobedience began: The ordinary citizen or small business was completely vulnerable. The regulatory agency could issue compliance orders with no downside risk whatsoever.

After the formation of the defense funds: The agency then faced a downside risk. It could still ultimately get its way, but when a defense fund took a case, the regulatory agency was forced to expend resources, knowing as it did so that even when it finally prevailed, the defendant's fine was going to be reimbursed. Before the advent of the defense funds, only the defendant had to ask, "Is it worth it?" when the regulatory agency came after him. After the defense funds, regulatory bureaucrats also had to ask themselves, "Is it worth it?"

The day after the Supreme Court has issued the reinterpretation of "arbitrary and capricious": Now the downside risks of a confrontation in an Article III court have qualitatively increased. Every time the defense fund wins a case, the regulation in dispute is at risk of being undermined. Go back to the Lancaster example of the requirement for a POISON sign where bags of sand were stored. After an Article III court has ruled that the requirement for labeling sand was arbitrary and capricious when it was enforced against a brick factory, a precedent has been set that means any other similar violation of that particular definition of poison can be contested successfully—and so can comparable cases involving other substances that don't require a warning in many work settings. Multiply that by hundreds and eventually thousands of regulations. Prior to the reinterpretation of "arbitrary and capricious," the defense funds could succeed in making regulations unenforceable de facto; afterward, they can make those regulations unenforceable through the power of judicial precedent.

And now we come to the point at which systemic change in the regulatory regime begins to unfold. Let's continue with the POISON example. In principle, the regulation has merit. If I'm in an area where I could accidentally knock over a jar, break it, and release poison gas into the air, I'd like to be informed of that fact by a sign that says POISON. So if

OSHA wants to keep a regulation requiring workplaces to let people know that dangerous stuff is being stored, fine. What the reinterpretation of "arbitrary and capricious" does is force OSHA into an internal review process of substances that fit a commonsense definition of "dangerous stuff." Sand comes off the list right away. Cyanide stays on the list no matter what. But in between those two extremes, as OSHA makes choices about what substances are dangerous in what contexts, this consideration has to come into their mind: "Could we defend this decision in front of a judge?"[12]

The final list of things and places that require a POISON sign will still probably be too inclusive, but it will be much shorter than the current list. The storage conditions that are deemed dangerous will be more realistically defined than they currently are. That's a major improvement in itself. The formation of regulations will be constrained by the prospect of having the regulation undermined in court—something that the regulatory state has not, for practical purposes, had to worry about.

The reinterpretation of "arbitrary and capricious" will also force a degree of common sense onto the assessment of local conditions. Here, the example of the conveyer belt at Lancaster is applicable. Having an automatic shut-off on conveyer belts is a good idea in workplaces where workers behaving with normal caution are at risk of being accidentally pushed into the conveyor belt. But the need for an automatic shut-off varies according to the size of the conveyor belt, its speed, the things that the conveyor belt is carrying, and how exposed workers are to the conveyor belt in the course of their movements around the workplace.

OSHA's real goal is to see that conveyor belts are not a safety hazard in the workplace. After the reinterpretation of "arbitrary and capricious," it knows that it can't just have a broad requirement for automatic shut-off devices, because it will be vulnerable to a defense like *Lancaster*. One would hope that this would push OSHA to rewrite the regulation so that it allowed for alternative ways of making conveyor belts safe, and limited the conditions under which conveyor belts pose a significant safety hazard at all. But even if OSHA doesn't formally rewrite the regulation, it will have incentives to pursue a violation only in those circumstances when it is not vulnerable to a *Lancaster*-like defense.

The same will be true throughout the regulatory system. Sometimes the wording of regulations will change; more often, the change will consist of the enforcement of the wording. Enforcement will more often be framed in terms of principles rather than blind enforcement of the letter of the law—just as (most of the time) speed limits on interstate highways are enforced according to principles of safety, not the precise miles per hour posted on traffic signs. In short, regulatory bureaucrats will be pushed toward a "no harm, no foul" approach to regulations. It won't be perfect. It will be a huge improvement.

Evidence That the Strategy Might Work

Thus my reasons for thinking that it is realistic to hope that systematic civil disobedience, backstopped by legal support, can result in a major change in the jurisprudence of "arbitrary and capricious." We have a recent and directly applicable case in point that says it's realistic: *Sackett v. Environmental Protection Agency* (2012).

In 2005, Mike and Chantell Sackett purchased two-thirds of an acre of land on which to build their new home. As the owners of a small construction company, they were familiar with all the rules that surround house construction, and followed all of them. They began excavation for the foundation. Then they received a compliance order from the EPA saying that their two-thirds of an acre was wetland subject to the Clean Water Act. If they failed to restore the land to its original condition within five months, they would begin incurring fines of more than $37,000 a day. If the EPA then initiated an enforcement action, all of those days would count in the Sacketts' liability if the administrative court ruled against them.

The Sacketts knew that the allegation was absurd by any meaningful definition of *wetland*. But the EPA refused to give the Sacketts a hearing where they could make that case because a compliance order is, technically speaking, only a warning.

The EPA gave the Sacketts a choice: They could refuse to comply and wait until the EPA issued an "enforcement action." *Then* they could argue their case in an administrative law court. But while they waited for the EPA to issue an enforcement action—which could take whatever amount of time the EPA chose—their $37,000-per-day meter would start running five months after the compliance order was issued. So at the moment they stepped into the hearing room to make their case, they could already be facing hundreds of thousands or millions of dollars of accumulated fines if their appeal failed. It was a classic example of regulatory strong-arming: give the citizen a choice of knuckling under right away, with all the costs of restoring the land to its original condition plus losing the value of their land (because no one could build on it), or risk being financially ruined if the same administrative system that called their plot "wetland" persisted in that judgment.

Let's pause for a moment before I tell you the ending, and consider the enormity of what was being done to ordinary American citizens *even if the land genuinely qualified as wetland.* A family wants to build a home on two-thirds of an acre of land they have legally purchased. Would the public good associated with preserving wetlands have been compromised if Congress had provided for individual families to build homes on small plots of land that are not part of a larger wetland tract? And even given the ham-handed way that Congress actually wrote the legislation, would the public good associated with preserving wetlands have been compromised even the tiniest bit if the EPA had turned a blind eye to the Sacketts' plot?

But we don't need to fret about that point. As you may go to the Internet and see for yourself, no reasonable person would have said that the Sacketts' lot, sandwiched between a paved road on one side and a row of tightly spaced lakefront houses on the other, was even wetland in any meaningful sense of the word, let alone part of any kind of wetland tract that could be preserved even if it should be.[13] With the help of pro bono lawyers from the Pacific Legal Foundation, the Sacketts fought their case all the way to the Supreme Court. They showed great courage in doing so—even though they were getting free legal help, they were vulnerable to millions of dollars in fines if they lost.

But the Sacketts won, at least on this issue (they were just given the right to be heard in court; the actual compliance order was not voided).[14] On March 21, 2012, the Supreme Court unanimously overruled the lower Article III court that had heard the case, holding that the Sacketts could bring a civil action under the Administrative Procedure Act to challenge the EPA's compliance order.

The Sackett case is applicable to our goals in two ways. First, it is exactly the kind of situation that the defense funds will seek to litigate: one in which reasonable people, looking at what the regulatory state has done, will conclude that the federal government is behaving outrageously and even tyrannically. Everyone was on the Sacketts' side except the EPA and the looniest environmentalists. If the Supreme Court had ruled against the Sacketts—in effect saying that if the EPA comes after you, you don't even have the right to fight—it could have created a public backlash similar to the backlash against *Kelo.* So point number one is that if the cause is not only righteous but obviously seen as righteous by the public at large, and if the regulatory agency is behaving with sufficient arrogance and stupidity, the Supreme Court will sometimes find a constitutional justification for doing the right thing.

My second point is that the EPA fought this case all the way to the Supreme Court. One's first reaction is to ask why. True, the same issue had been litigated several times before and the EPA had always won. But the facts in this case were so ludicrous that senior officials at the EPA surely understood they would take a major public-relations hit. Perhaps they wished they could have rewound history and left the Sacketts alone. But they nonetheless persevered all the way to the Supreme Court.

We have reason to hope that the effort to change the application of "arbitrary and capricious" will follow the same pattern. The defense funds will lose many cases, but sooner or later some spectacularly indefensible enforcement action will get in the pipeline to the Supreme Court and the regulatory agency at fault will not have the good sense to back off. And the Supreme Court itself will be faced with the question: Do we want another *Sackett*, at a time when the public's disgust with an overweening government is even greater than it was when *Sackett* was decided?

It is not just a possibility that the worst aspects of the regulatory state can be rolled back. Given a sufficiently relentless focus on the proposition—the manifestly true proposition—that the regulatory state is routinely "arbitrary or capricious," that rollback can happen.

CHAPTER 11

A NECESSARY CRISIS

*In which I discuss the possibility that the courts can
be brought to realize that they founded the regulatory
state on false premises, that they must meet their obligation to undo some of the damage they have caused,
and that doing so will require a broader reform of civil
litigation.*

HAMMERING ON THE arbitrary and capricious enforcement
of regulations is the easiest point of attack on the jurisprudence
that created the regulatory state. Better law does not require the
courts to nullify regulations but merely to nullify enforcement actions.

But going after enforcement doesn't get to the bottom of things.
Recall that the full phrase that holds regulatory agencies accountable
is "agency action, findings, and conclusions found to be . . . arbitrary,
capricious, an abuse of discretion, or otherwise not in accordance with
law." The core problem isn't that so many regulations are badly enforced
but that so many regulations represent an abuse of discretion. Regulatory
agencies take advantage of vague language in the legislation to create regimes of rules that a majority of Congress would not have countenanced
if those rules had been explicit in the legislation.

Is there any chance that systematic civil disobedience backstopped by
the defense funds can get the courts to accept that truth? Possibly. The
difficulty isn't making the case. Demonstrating that regulatory agencies
abuse their discretion in creating regulations is as easy as demonstrating
that they enforce regulations arbitrarily and capriciously. But the federal
courts will rightly fear an explosion of their caseload if they open that
door even a crack.

Coming to our aid will be some strategic truths about the legal system. At some point, the combination of the system's sclerosis and its workload will lead to a crisis and some sort of resolution. A carefully crafted campaign to distinguish mandated regulations from discretionary ones could be instrumental in demonstrating to the courts that they have no choice but to act.

The Parable of the Dirt-Eating Children

In 1977, Louis Ottati of Kingston, New Hampshire, had been working for a storage drum reconditioning company for seven years and decided he knew enough to go into business for himself.[1] He got his father-in-law, Wellington Goss, to help him finance the enterprise. They incorporated as Ottati & Goss, Inc.; leased a one-acre site in the midst of a thirty-four-acre site where other drum-reconditioning companies were operating; and bought a front loader, a mixing bin, and a platform truck. They did good business for a year, processing up to a hundred drums a day. Like the other drum-reconditioning companies around them, Ottati & Goss deposited the waste products from the reconditioning into dumpsters that were then taken to an approved disposal site. But then the EPA discovered that the drum-reconditioning companies, including Ottati & Goss, had allowed some of these waste products to leak from the dumpsters or had otherwise contaminated the ground. The EPA filed a complaint under the Resource Conservation and Recovery Act.[2]

In 1980, the EPA undertook the cleanup of the entire thirty-four-acre site and collected reimbursement of its costs from the companies at fault. But then the EPA decided that further cleanup was needed, and, among other things, required Ottati & Goss to incinerate the dirt on their acre to remove a small residual amount of diluted PCBs and components of benzene and gasoline. The incineration of the dirt would cost $9.3 million.

Ottati & Goss refused, arguing that the cleanup already completed was adequate. The EPA filed suit to compel them to undertake the cleanup. After five years of litigation, the case reached the United States District Court of New Hampshire, which ruled in favor of Ottati & Goss. But that wasn't the end of it. The EPA appealed to the First Circuit Court of Appeals. After another five years, on April 4, 1990, the First Circuit affirmed the district court's ruling.[3] After ten years and who knows how much in attorneys' fees, Louis Ottati and his father-in-law were vindicated.

What was the benefit of incinerating the dirt that drove the EPA to go to such extraordinary lengths? Here is the answer, in the words of one of the First Circuit's judges, Stephen Breyer, later appointed to the Supreme Court:

> How much extra safety did this $9.3 million buy? The forty-thousand-page record of this ten-year effort indicated (and all the parties seemed to agree) that, without the extra expenditure, the waste dump was clean enough for children playing on the site to eat small amounts of dirt daily for 70 days each year without significant harm. Burning the soil would have made it clean enough for the children to eat small amounts daily for 245 days per year without significant harm. But there were no dirt-eating children playing in the area, for it was a swamp.[4]

To Breyer, the case represented "how well-meaning, intelligent regulators, trying to carry out their regulatory tasks sensibly, can nonetheless bring about counterproductive results."[5] To me, it represents regulators who have lost all sense of proportion, and also lost sight of what they are doing to the lives of the people they go after. Louis Ottati and his father-in-law were not engaged in a criminal enterprise. They were making an honest living and performing a useful service. They had not been deliberately polluting the earth, and they had paid for cleaning up their mistakes. Surely "well-meaning" and "intelligent" officials, conscious that they are public servants, would want to make sure they weren't asking Louis Ottati and his father-in-law to financially ruin themselves and their families for no good reason. Surely they made that $9.3 million demand for incineration only after determining, with all the technical expertise available to the EPA, that the remaining contamination posed a genuine risk. They apparently did neither of those things.

But Breyer is correct in one sense: the "counterproductive results" of *United States v. Ottati & Goss, Inc.* are not the result of idiosyncrasies of individual EPA officials. *Ottati & Goss* is a parable illustrating the intersection of two ingredients of an eventual but necessary crisis: the dysfunction of the legal system, and the bankrupt premises on which the regulatory state is based.

The dysfunction of the legal system was the subject of chapters 2 and 3. *Ottati & Goss* exemplifies that dysfunction. That it took ten years and forty thousand pages of case record to decide the issues *when both sides agreed on how little would be accomplished by the extra cleanup* is ridiculous.

The second ingredient—the bankruptcy of the regulatory state's premises—introduces some new themes that need elaboration. After I finish that task, I will describe how the dysfunction of the legal system and the dysfunction of the regulatory state might collide.

The Bankrupt Premises of the Regulatory State

Eventually, reasonable observers will reach a point at which it is clear that the premises of the regulatory state are wrong. I don't mean "wrong" from a particular political point of view, but empirically, indisputably wrong. An analogy with economics may clarify what I mean. Economists still fight about many things that are grounded in political ideology, from socialists at one end to libertarians at the other. All of the contending parties have empirically grounded arguments they can bring to the debate. But the range of debate has narrowed. Ninety years ago, Marxist economic theory was the ideological foundation of the young Soviet Union and was still considered by intellectuals throughout the world to have revealed laws of history. Today, Marxism is not taken seriously by anyone who has kept up with the state of knowledge about economics. The premises of Marxist economics turned out to be wrong—wrong about human nature, wrong about capitalism, and disastrously wrong in practice. The premises of the regulatory state are just as empirically wrong.

I could parse them more finely, but to simplify the argument I will put the premises this way:

- Problems of public policy can be analyzed so that they yield objectively correct solutions.
- The people who frame those solutions are disinterested experts

who can put aside their own biases and institutional self-interest as they go about their work.

When the Supreme Court decided in 1943 to discard the requirement that regulators be constrained by a legislative "intelligible principle," the justices had to believe both premises to be true because that decision, *National Broadcasting Co. v. United States*, turned over de facto legislative power to unelected bureaucrats. As I noted in chapter 4, that is a dicey thing to do, considering that the first words of the Constitution after the Preamble are "All legislative powers herein granted shall be vested in a Congress of the United States." Delegating power to bureaucrats made sense only if, in the eyes of the Court, vague policy goals would be reliably implemented in a way that reflected what Congress had in mind. That belief is unsustainable without the two premises. Both premises required to make the logic work turned out to be wrong.

"Problems of public policy can be analyzed so that they yield objectively correct solutions."

This premise is true of a subset of policy problems that meet the following three criteria:

1. The problem is extremely simple and can be objectively described.
2. The problem is perceived as a problem by a consensus of the people who will be affected by the solution.
3. The problem has a known technical solution (preferably only one technical solution).

The size of that subset of policy problems is greater than zero, but not much. Sewage and water systems usually meet the three criteria, for example. The size of the pipes, the location and capacity of the pumping systems, and the design of the sewage treatment facility are all engineering concerns. Everybody in town wants clean water and good sanitation, and they are indifferent to the technical choices made by the engineers as long as clean water flows from open taps and toilets flush (and as long as a proposed new sewage treatment facility is not going to be located in their backyard).[6]

Other examples of that subset are the great regulatory success stories. Earlier, I cited the Forest Service as one of the earliest success stories for the progressives' ideal of independent agencies run by experts. That success was a reflection of an objectively describable problem (destruction of forests) that the public saw as a problem, with an obvious cause (indiscriminate logging), and a technical solution (sustainable logging). Also, the forests in question were owned by the government—a crucial caveat for creating consensus agreement that a problem existed.

Another great success story also occurred early, following the passage of the Pure Food and Drug Act of 1906, and it followed the same pattern: a simple, objective problem (adulterated or misleadingly described products) that just about everybody agreed was a problem, and a simple technical solution (require manufacturers of the products to list the ingredients on the package).

The EPA's successes in reducing smog in major cities and restoring rivers to health are also classic examples. The problems and solutions were both simple. If a few million cars and trucks are on a city's roads every day, emitting large quantities of the stuff that constitutes smog, something that everyone in the city hates, then a regulation requiring a device on auto exhaust systems that reduces those emissions is going to have a big positive effect on that city's air pollution. If factories along a river are disgorging millions of gallons of contaminated wastewater into a river every day, requiring those factories to clean up their wastewater before releasing it into the river is going to have a big positive effect on the quality of water in the river.

Once one moves from problems that are simple and objective, consensually seen as problems, with known technical solutions, the ideal of objectively correct public policy recedes beyond our grasp. To see how even the simplest policy problems spill over into subjective preferences, suppose we talk about traffic control.

Aren't traffic problems fairly simple and objective from a technical point of view? Don't citizens, by consensus, want traffic to flow efficiently? Aren't there well-analyzed technical solutions? "More or less" is the answer to all three questions—and in that mild qualification, "more or less," lies a tangle of complications.

Do you support or oppose synchronized stoplights on main arteries? Right turn on red? One-way streets? Limited-access highways running through the city? Bike lanes? Bus lanes? Traffic circles instead of stop-lights? Speed bumps? No matter what your answers might be, I assure you that a substantial number of your fellow citizens disagree. A traffic expert can calculate and describe objective truths about the pros and cons of each of those options. But opinions differ on whether those objective truths describe outcomes to be desired or opposed. The choice of which options to employ is thus intensely political. If a city council were to establish a traffic department and give it authority to create "an efficient and orderly traffic system" independently of any more specific (that is, "intelligible") principles to guide the traffic experts' decisions, the city council would have no way of predicting what mix of solutions the experts might come up with. It would depend on the definitions and priorities that the traffic experts attached to "efficient" and "orderly."

That's why most cities don't turn over discretionary power to their traffic experts. Instead, any major change in the traffic system usually ends up coming before the city council for a vote. It's too politically sensitive to leave to the experts. The experts explain the options, but the politicians vote on the ones to adopt.

The federal regulatory state is established on exactly the opposite approach: the Congress legislates vague mandates, then turns the job over to the experts and lets them do as they think best. It asks the experts to do something that is usually impossible to do. With the rarest exceptions, there is no such thing as objectively correct public policy. Tip O'Neill famously said that "all politics is local." Similarly, all public policy is ultimately political.

"The people who frame those solutions are disinterested experts who can put aside their own biases and institutional self-interest as they go about their work."

There are two problems with this premise. First, expertise in the policy sciences isn't the same as expertise in, say, electrical engineering. Second, bias is inevitable.

THE TECHNICAL IMMATURITY OF THE POLICY SCIENCES. Even when regulations involve the hard sciences or engineering, the state of knowledge keeps changing, and what was thought to be the right solution twenty years ago is no longer thought to be the right solution now.

The Forest Service once again is a case in point. The Great Idaho Fire of 1910 led to a new mission for the Forest Service: preventing forest fires. The Forest Service pursued this new goal energetically and succeeded in lowering the annual number of forest fires. But whereas the science of timber harvesting was already reasonably well understood in the early part of the twentieth century, the science of maintaining healthy forests was not. At the time that the Forest Service started its fire-prevention work, it was not yet known that fires are a necessary part of maintaining healthy forests. The policy that the Forest Service pursued for more than fifty years turned out to be scientifically wrongheaded.[7]

For policies informed by the social sciences, the situation is much worse. Science, good or bad, is often irrelevant. The latest received wisdom about best practice is more often driven by ideology than evidence. Education is the leading case in point, with numerous policies—No Child Left Behind is the poster child—that were already known to be scientifically wrongheaded when they were promulgated.[8]

I hesitate to mention a topic as emotional and divisive as climate change, but it is such an appropriate illustration of the immaturity of policy analysis that I must. Is the state of hard scientific knowledge about climate change good enough to tell us *what* has been happening to the world's climate? Yes, with some caveats. Is the state of hard scientific knowledge good enough to justify the inference that human activity is playing some role in climate change? Yes, with still more caveats. Are the hard-science models of climate change good enough to tell us what will happen in the future? No, the models are constantly being modified because new data persistently fail to conform to predictions. Are the social sciences good enough to tell us how effective proposed policy measures will be in slowing climate change once the practical problems of implementation are taken into account? Not even close.

The essence of the scientific method is the acquisition of explanatory power—to be able not only to observe phenomena systematically but to explain those phenomena so well that we are able to predict what will happen if the same causal conditions are replicated. To do that requires accurate measures of both the phenomena themselves and powerful analytic techniques for measuring how different phenomena are related, both of which must be quantitative. In the hard sciences, that process started four hundred years ago. In the social sciences, it started fifty years ago.[9]

As someone who has been a practicing policy analyst for more than forty of those fifty years, I am unable to come up with a single example of an important social phenomenon we can predict precisely and consistently. We have ascertained that certain phenomena are correlated at predictable levels given adequate sample sizes. But even though we can predict the correlation within a fairly small range, the size of the correlation is usually modest. Even a correlation of 0.5, large for the social sciences, means that 75 percent of the variance in a phenomenon is unexplained. Besides that, the causal reasons for the correlations can seldom be clearly distinguished from the noncausal reasons. Today's social scientists are to social scientists a century from now as alchemists are to chemists. The idea that scientifically objective social policy is feasible today is risible.

THE INEVITABILITY OF BIAS. In the traffic example, I could stipulate that traffic experts might disinterestedly project the changes in traffic flow resulting from, say, synchronizing traffic lights on a main artery. The first premise is still wrong. There is no objectively right policy answer to the question "Do you want traffic flow on Main Street to have a median observed speed of 15 mph or 25 mph?"

In reality, however, experts within the regulatory bureaucracies are not saints, and the range of things they can do disinterestedly is narrow. Only at the lowest levels of authority can specialists go about their work disinterestedly. A fingerprint specialist in the FBI forensics labs can analyze fingerprints disinterestedly. An expert on bear habitat in the Fish and Wildlife Service can count bears disinterestedly. A hydraulic engineer in the Army Corps of Engineers can calculate a dam's energy output disinterestedly.

But as soon as people with these nonpolitical expertises move into managerial jobs, their ability to be disinterested is constrained. The fingerprint specialist who becomes a manager in the FBI will be pulled in all sorts of directions dictated by political considerations. So will the expert on bear habitats who becomes an administrator of the Endangered Species Act. And as for managerial positions held by engineers, the Army Corps of Engineers is notorious for its enthusiasm for building dams indiscriminately.

Apart from the influences of personal opinions and personalities, the decisions of bureaucratic managers are influenced by institutional self-interest. The FBI is constantly fighting over turf with a half dozen other agencies that deal in crime and domestic security. The Fish and Wildlife Service is constantly trying to protect its programs and prerogatives in each new budget cycle. So is the Army Corps of Engineers.

Such observations were formalized into a field of academic study known as *public choice theory.* Mancur Olson, who figured so prominently in chapter 5, is one of its major figures. So are noted scholars from the left (Kenneth Arrow and Anthony Downs, for example). The indispensable book on public choice theory is usually identified as *The Calculus of Consent: Logical Foundations of Constitutional Democracy* (1962), coauthored by two economists of the right, James Buchanan and Gordon Tullock. For our purposes, the main contribution of public choice theory has been to systematize an observation that will not come as news to anyone who has been around a functioning government agency: Officials in bureaucracies are like everyone else. They have opinions, passions, and interests, and their decisions are influenced by them.

Many of these influences are not political. For example, people have different levels of tolerance for risk. Some people enjoy risk; others want life to be as risk-free as possible. If someone is working for a regulatory agency, that personality trait makes a big difference in how regulations are framed. But political ideology does play a role as well. It should not be necessary to belabor that point. To list just some of the major areas of government regulation—employment, environment, safety, energy, health care, and drugs, for example—is to make it obvious how ideologically charged regulatory decisions must be.

Whether the influences are personal or political, what it comes down to is that the EPA's experts are no more disinterested about the correct operation of oil refineries than are the experts at Exxon; the experts at the EEOC are no more disinterested about proper grounds for firing an employee than the experts at Walmart. I am not picking out bureaucrats for special criticism on this score—to repeat, they're like everyone else.

They are not like everyone else, however, when it comes to the effects of their preferences. The EPA's built-in biases are well known. Sometimes, those biases will lead to choices that Exxon's experts think are clear mistakes *even given EPA's priorities.* But there's no way to force the EPA to back off those mistakes. EPA's choices are imposed on refineries nationwide. Once again, demonization is unnecessary. We may assume that the EPA's experts believe in their innermost heart of hearts that their policy judgments are in the public interest. But it cannot be assumed that they have been able to reach those judgments disinterestedly. We're all biased, but only people within government have the power to impose those biases on their fellow citizens with the force of law. For the leaders of the progressive movement to have believed that experts are disinterested, and for the Supreme Court to have accepted that position in *NBC* in 1943, was monumentally naïve.

A Scenario for Collision

As with the Lancaster Brick scenario, I offer a scenario that surely won't work out exactly this way, but gives a sense of the possibilities.

We again assume that the defense funds have been operating for several years. The public's awareness of the regulatory overreach has been raised. The success of the defense funds' strategy has forced regulatory agencies to move tacitly toward a "no harm, no foul" enforcement policy.

But something new has been emerging as well: cases that challenge the content of regulations instead of their enforcement. Like the *Sackett* case, many of these have been high-profile cases brought by ordinary people of modest means helped by the Madison Fund. In other cases, an occupational defense fund has challenged the content of a regulation on behalf of a member of a particular craft or profession. In still others, corporations have challenged the content of regulations on their own.

These various cases have all been batted down by the administrative courts, but occasionally a defense fund has obtained review by a federal appeals court. This is the generic argument that the defense fund's counsel has made:

> This case brings to the court a dilemma of the federal judiciary's own making. In 1943, the Supreme Court made an error in deciding *NBC*. Whether it was an error of constitutional law is not at issue. Rather, the Supreme Court made an error in assessing reality, akin to a formula for antifreeze based on the assumption that ice forms at 28 degrees Fahrenheit. In *NBC*, the Court assumed

that good public policy can be defined objectively. More precisely, it thought that general goals stated in legislation imply an appropriate, objective set of regulations that can be created by disinterested public officials. More than seventy years of experience since *NBC* have proved that the Court was wrong.

General goals can be implemented in radically different ways depending on the necessarily subjective operational definitions applied to words such as "fair," "equitable," "just," "reasonable," "safe," or "healthy" that are used to express the goals.

General goals can be implemented in radically different ways depending on readings of the state of knowledge on which experts disagree, and depending on the results of analyses using methods and data on which experts disagree.

General goals can be implemented in radically different ways depending on the political ideology and on the personal preferences and proclivities that regulators bring to implementation.

In sum, the Supreme Court's practice of ignoring its own previous requirement of "intelligible principle" has been a mistake. Policy formation doesn't work the way that the Supreme Court in 1943 thought it did. Bureaucrats don't work the way that the Supreme Court thought they did. The Court's decision in *NBC* was a mistake that allowed the construction of a vast edifice of law that is based on the decisions of unelected officials, not on the will of elected representatives expressed in legislation. That edifice of law affects the lives of all Americans, directly or indirectly. Some unknown but large portion of those laws would never have been passed by Congress if they had been specified in the legislation. This body of law by bureaucratic proclamation is illegitimate.

We understand that a federal court's de facto freedom to act is circumscribed, and therefore do not ask you to reinstate the requirement for an intelligible principle. To do so would call into question the constitutionality of hundreds of laws passed by Congress since 1943. As a practical matter, that is impossible.

But consider the position of our client as a matter of justice. We believe we have presented clear and convincing evidence that the content of the regulation he is accused of violating is technically unsound and counterproductive. It is a bad law. Let us assume for the moment that the court agrees with that conclusion. If this regulation implemented an intelligible principle in the authorizing legislation, we would not be here. As the court has clearly stated in the past, it is not the judiciary's function to throw out laws just because they are bad. When Congress, a state legislature, or a city council passes a bad law, there's nothing to be done about it except try to get the law changed. But the regulation our client is accused of violating does not have that standing.

We do not ask you to void the regulation because it is "arbitrary, capricious, [or] an abuse of discretion." We ask you to recognize that it was, in fact, discretionary and extralegal—a regulation that government officials chose to create, not one that they were legislatively obliged to create—and accord it no special deference. In other words, we ask you not to reverse *NBC* but to modify *Chevron.* We ask that our client's dispute with the government regulatory agency be treated the same way the courts treat disputes between private parties—to be decided on the merits of the cases made by the opposing parties without favoring either side a priori. If, having done so, you agree with our position that this regulation is not only extralegal but bad, we ask that you rule that our client was justified in not complying with it.

We began by saying that this case poses a dilemma to this court. We used the word *dilemma* in its true meaning: a problem in which all of the alternative solutions have defects. It is wrong that citizens of the United States are subject to thousands of laws that are the creation of unelected government officials, but it is impossible to get rid of them without creating chaos. At the same time, it is wrong for the courts to continue to allow citizens to be punished for breaking bad laws created by unelected officials. It violates a foundational principle of American democracy. Some corrective measure, however imperfect, is required. The withdrawal of deference from regulations deemed to be discretionary and therefore extralegal is both appropriate and practicable.

As that argument is repeated time and again, in cases where reasonable observers agree that the regulation in question is obviously bad, we can hope that it will begin to get traction in public opinion. As in the case of "arbitrary and capricious," the objective is to develop an emerging social consensus: a recognition that the real problem with the regulatory state is not just that the execution of its rules may be bungled but that it is a dysfunctional system founded on wrong assumptions.

This much is within the power of the defense funds to accomplish. But is it realistic to hope that the Supreme Court will ever withdraw *Chevron* deference from regulations judged to be discretionary and therefore extralegal?

On the optimistic side, this argument allows the Supreme Court to modify *Chevron* without provoking a constitutional crisis. It's not as if modifying *Chevron* would require dismantling the regulatory state. All of the agencies, all of their staffs, and all of the 200,000-odd pages of the *Code of Federal Regulations* would be left in place after a *Chevron* modification.[10] Agencies would still be permitted to create regulations that are not mandated by an intelligible principle in the legislation. The only difference is that the courts would distinguish between two kinds of regulations. Those that follow directly from the expressed will of Congress—to resurrect the old language, follow from an intelligible principle—would continue to be upheld as long as they are also constitutional. Regulations that are deemed to be discretionary—were not mandated by an intelligible principle—would not be accorded deference. In defending discretionary regulations, a government agency would be subject to the same treatment that all other entities in American society are supposed to get: When you walk into the courtroom, you have exactly the same standing as your opponent. What matters is not who you are but how strong your case is. Being a member of the Wiseman family doesn't help anymore.

But at this point comes the collision. Even if they wanted to, five justices would still be understandably reluctant to modify *Chevron* because of the dirty little secret illustrated by the parable of the dirt-eating children: The legal system is so sclerotic that it could not possibly cope with the flood of litigation that would be unleashed against the regulatory agencies if they were not shielded by *Chevron* deference. As matters stand, even corporations with the deepest pockets are reluctant to challenge bad regulations, sometimes paying billion-dollar fines instead, because *Chevron* deference sets the bar so high for making their cases. Given a level playing field, fighting all sorts of bad regulations would make economic sense. Added to that are all the cases that would be brought by the occupational defense funds, and the rich new vein of cases that the Madison Fund could take up. The Supreme Court must expect that even modifying *Chevron* deference would swamp the legal system.

But envision the situation if the Supreme Court refuses to budge on *Chevron* deference for that reason, in the face of an emerging social consensus that the regulatory state is out of control, and with growing acceptance by the public (which is happening already) that overregulation is having terrible effects on the economy, technological innovation, and the provision of services. What does it say about the state of the American legal system if the only reason not to allow Americans to challenge extralegal laws is that the court system can't handle the workload?

Therein lies the possibility that systematic civil disobedience and the defense funds will trigger a badly needed crisis: the courts will realize they have to give people a chance at their day in court, but things have got to change so that those days in court don't become ten-year cases with forty-thousand-page case files. The courts will get the push they have needed to reform civil litigation.

What needs to be done to fix the legal system is not mysterious. The civil legal system once worked pretty well. Civil legal systems in other advanced societies of the West work pretty well. As described in chapter 2, the changes that produced the current mess are known, and so are the fixes that could incrementally create new case law that moves us toward a more sensible system. The Supreme Court can do much to push that process along. But the only way to get the justices to do that is by giving them no alternative. That's what the pressure brought on the courts by the defense funds might accomplish: force the courts to reform or be overwhelmed.

What are the odds of this scenario, or something like it, actually happening? Probably small. But reality has a way of ultimately forcing confrontations. Herb Stein's law is true: "If something cannot go on forever, it will stop."[11] Two compelling realities are that the legal system really is broken and must eventually be fixed, and that Americans really are forced to comply with thousands of rules that legislators would not have passed on their own. The Supreme Court might prefer to turn a blind eye to both realities. But systematic civil disobedience and the defense funds can make that hard to do.

PART III

A PROPITIOUS MOMENT

We the people of the United States, in order to form a more perfect union . . .

—CONSTITUTION OF THE UNITED STATES

The program of systematic civil disobedience described in Part II doesn't require a favorable alignment of the stars. We don't have to hope for a charismatic Madisonian president or rely upon a friendly Congress. Changing the constitutional jurisprudence on "arbitrary and capricious" or *Chevron* deference requires five sympathetic Supreme Court justices, which would require some luck, but we don't need the Supreme Court's permission to implement the defense funds, which can have great impact even without changes in constitutional jurisprudence.

The possibilities described in Part III are different. I am no longer talking about changes that can be implemented given concrete and practicable private-sector initiatives. Rather, I argue that in the middle of the second decade of the twenty-first century the stars are in fact aligning for a much broader rebuilding of liberty than we could have imagined even a decade ago.

The forces leading to that potential outcome are fairly easy to describe. I've already alluded to some of them in Part I—some of the things that I treated as problems then become assets now. But it's one thing to discern potentials; it's quite another to forecast how the policy changes will play out. I must speculate, and my crystal ball is cloudy. But the moment is propitious, and the opportunities are open-ended.

CHAPTER 12

THE RETURN OF
DIVERSIFIED AMERICA

*In which I argue that America's cultural diversity in
the second decade of the twenty-first century resembles
the America of the eighteenth and nineteenth centuries,
and that the mood is favorable for returning to a system accommodating that diversity.*

IN EARLY DECEMBER 1964, Lyndon Johnson held a celebratory
reception in the East Room of the White House for the new Democratic members of Congress. The election had given the Democrats two-thirds of the seats in each house of Congress, supermajorities
that would enable LBJ to pass just about everything he wanted during
the next two years. The president was in an understandably expansive
mood. He concluded his remarks by quoting the words of his mentor,
Sam Rayburn, from Rayburn's maiden speech as a member of the House
in 1913. Rayburn had said he dreamed of a country "that knows no East,
no West, no North, no South, but inhabited by a people liberty-loving,
patriotic, happy and prosperous; with its lawmakers having no other purpose than to write such just laws as shall in the years to come be of service to humankind yet unborn."[1] It was a philosophy, Johnson concluded,
that "had served this country greatly."

It's poetically perfect: The words had originally been spoken in the
year Woodrow Wilson, the first progressive Democratic president, was
inaugurated. They were quoted by Sam Rayburn's protégé in the year
that saw the high-water mark of New Deal liberalism. Together, 1913
and 1964 are excellent bookends for an era in America's history when it

was indeed thought that we should, and could, be all one people, not just indivisible but unitary.

In the eighteenth and nineteenth centuries, that notion would have struck most Americans as nonsensical. It is just as nonsensical for Americans in the twenty-first century.

A Heritage of Cultural Diversity

The received wisdom about multicultural America goes something like this:

> At the time of the founding, America's free population was not only white but almost entirely British, and the nation's culture was based on their common heritage. That monocultural domination continued through the nineteenth and twentieth centuries as other white European immigrant groups were assimilated into the Anglo mainstream. In the twenty-first century, with people of color soon to become a majority of the population, the United States faces unprecedented cultural diversity.

Here is the alternative view that the rest of this chapter propounds:

> America was founded on British political and legal traditions that remain the bedrock of the American system to this day. But even at the time of the founding, Americans were as culturally diverse as they are today. That diversity was augmented during the nineteenth and early twentieth centuries. Then came an anomalous period from roughly the 1940s through the 1970s during which cultural diversity was dampened in some respects and masked in others. Since the late twentieth century, America has returned to its historic norm: obvious, far-reaching cultural diversity that requires room for free expression.

At the Founding

You may reasonably question whether America at the founding was truly as culturally diverse as it is today—after all, the free population consisted almost entirely of Protestants whose ancestors were English or Scottish. I therefore describe that period in some detail.

Historian David Hackett Fischer's magisterial *Albion's Seed* describes how the British came to America in four streams.[2] From East Anglia came the Puritans seeking freedom to practice their religion. They settled first in Massachusetts. By the time of the Revolution, they had spread throughout New England and into the eastern part of New York and had become known as Yankees.

From the south of England came the Cavaliers, who had lost out during the English Civil War, accompanied by large numbers of impoverished English who signed contracts to work as their indentured servants.[3] The first wave settled in Virginia's tidewater, and the second around the Chesapeake Bay. They spread southward through the tidewater regions of the Carolinas and Georgia.

From the North Midlands came the Quakers, who, like the Puritans, were seeking a place to practice their religion unmolested. They settled first in the Delaware Valley and then spread throughout eastern and central Pennsylvania, with some of them drifting southward to Maryland and northern Virginia.

The fourth group came from Scotland and the northern border counties of England. Some of them arrived directly from their ancestral homelands, but the great majority arrived in the New World after an extended stopover in the north of Ireland—hence the label by which we know them, the Scots-Irish. They landed in Philadelphia but quickly made their way west on the Great Wagon Road to settle the Appalachian frontier running from west-central Pennsylvania to northeast Georgia.

The four groups did indeed share a common culture insofar as they had all come from a single nation with a single set of political, legal, and economic institutions. But my topic is cultural diversity as it affects the different ways in which Americans think of what it means to "live life as one sees fit." That consists of what I will call *quotidian culture*: the culture of everyday life. In terms of quotidian culture, the four streams shared the English language, barely. They differed on just about everything else, often radically.

Religion was culturally divisive. Anglican Christianity among the Cavaliers retained much of the pomp and ritual of Catholicism, and it permitted a lavish, sensuous lifestyle that the Yankees' religious heritage,

Puritanism, and Quakerism forbade. But Puritanism and Quakerism were also very different from each other. The Puritans saw themselves as God's chosen people—"the saints"—and the religion they practiced was as harsh and demanding as reputation has it, epitomized by the title of the most famous sermon of the eighteenth century, Jonathan Edwards's "Sinners in the Hands of an Angry God." The Sunday service, which might last five or six hours, even in unheated churches in the dead of a New England winter, consisted mostly of long lecture-like sermons and long teachings of the Word. It also included a ritual of purification, as members who were known to have committed specific sins were compelled to rise and "take shame upon themselves," which sometimes included crawling before the congregation.

The Quaker First Day meeting was completely different. Whereas the congregation in a Puritan church was seated according to age, sex, and rank, Quakers were supposed to take the seat nearest the front according to the order of arrival. There was no multihour lecture or even a preacher. Anyone who was moved by the spirit could speak, including children, but the strictly observed convention was that such interventions lasted only a few minutes. Sometimes nothing would be said for the entire meeting, and those were often thought to be the best—"gathered" meetings during which the spirit of God was felt wordlessly by all. Instead of trying to live blamelessly to avoid the wrath of an angry God, Quakers worshipped a God of love and forgiveness. Sinners in need of forgiveness were "held in the light."

Meanwhile, the Scots-Irish in the Appalachian backcountry combined passionate enthusiasm for Protestant teachings with equally passionate hostility toward the religious establishment. Thus an Anglican missionary to the region was told by one family that "they wanted no damned black gown sons of bitches among them," and was warned that they might use him as a backlog in their fireplace.[4] Others to whom he intended to minister stole his horse, drank his rum, and made off with his prayer books.

The nature of the family varied across the four streams. Yankee and Quaker families were nuclear. To them, marriage was a covenant that must be observed by both husband and wife, and could be terminated when one party failed to live up to the bargain. But Yankees and Quakers differed in the roles assigned to each party. Among the Yankees, marriage was a strict hierarchy with the man in charge; among the Quakers, marriage was seen as a "loving agreement," and was a partnership between man and wife. Among the Cavaliers, the father was the absolute head of an extended family that embraced blood relatives, other dependents, and sometimes slaves. Marriage was not a covenant but a union before God, and indissoluble. A Scots-Irish family was a series of concentric rings, beginning with the nuclear family and successively widening to include extended family and American versions of Scottish clans, lacking the formal structure of clans in their ancestral home but consisting of related families with a few surnames who lived near one another and were ready to come to one another's aid.

Marital and premarital morality varied among the four streams. The criminal laws of Puritan Massachusetts decreed that a man who slept with an unmarried woman could be jailed, whipped, fined, disfranchised, and forced to marry the object of his lust. In cases of adultery, both Yankees and Quakers punished the man as severely as—sometimes more severely than—the woman. Among the Cavaliers, it was just the opposite: Men who slept with women not their wives were seen as doing what comes naturally and were treated leniently. Women were harshly punished for accommodating them.

Once people were married, Puritanism wasn't all that puritanical. Surviving letters between Yankee spouses commonly expressed their love in ways that leave no doubt about their mutual pleasure in sex. It was the Quakers, more gentle and consensual in many aspects of marriage, who were more likely to see sex as sinful in itself. Many Quaker marriages included long periods of deliberate sexual abstinence.

Yankees, Quakers, and Cavaliers alike looked down on the morals of the Scots-Irish, who practiced an open sexuality that had no counterpart among the other three groups. That persecuted Anglican missionary to the Scots-Irish I mentioned was scandalized that, among other things, the young women of the backcountry "draw their shift as tight as possible round their breasts, and slender waists" in a deliberate display of their charms.[5] He calculated that 94 percent of the brides in the marriages he performed in 1767 were already pregnant.

There's much, much more. People in the four cultures had radically different parenting styles. They ate different foods and had different attitudes toward diet and alcohol. They dressed differently. Their approaches to formal education were different, and so were their opinions and practices regarding recreation, social rank, death, authority, freedom, and good order. Their work ethics and attitudes toward wealth and inequality were different.

The table on the next two pages adapts Fischer's summary of some of the differences (his table in *Albion's Seed* has many more) separating the four peoples who made up America's free population at the founding. If Fischer had included a description of the folkways of the African Americans, it would have constituted a fifth culture as distinct as the other four.

Thus my reasons for arguing that the differences separating Yankees, Quakers, Cavaliers, and Scots-Irish at the founding were at least as many and as divisive as those that separate different ethnic groups in America today. Go through each of the categories in the table and ask yourself about the differences in quotidian culture that now separate whites, blacks, Latinos, and Asians. In some respects, the differences are substantial—but seldom greater than the ones that separated the four original streams of Americans.

The Anti-Federalists believed that the cultural diversity of the thirteen new states was so great that a strong central government was unworkable, as expressed in the following passage from Brutus (the Anti-Federalists' counterpart to the Federalists' Publius), writing in the *Anti-Federalist Papers #18*:

> The United States includes a variety of climates. The productions of the different parts of the union are very variant, and their interests, of consequence, diverse. Their manners and habits differ as much as their climates and productions; and their sentiments are by no means coincident. The laws and customs of the several states are, in many respects, very diverse, and in some opposite; each would be in favor of its own interests and customs, and, of consequence, a legislature, formed of representatives from the respective parts, would not only be too numerous to act with any care or decision, but would be composed of such heterogenous and discordant principles, as would constantly be contending with each other.

The Federalists prevailed not because they refuted these arguments but because the powers of the federal government were so constrained.

FOUR REGIONAL CULTURES IN ANGLO-AMERICA, CA. 1700–1750

Label	Yankees	Quakers	Cavaliers	Scots-Irish
Region of Origin	East Anglia	North Midlands	S. & W. England	Scotland and bordering
Original destination	Massachusetts	Delaware Valley	Virginia	Backcountry
Region	Greater New England	NJ, DE, PA, No. MD	Tidewater MD to SC	Highlands VA to GA
Religion	Puritan/ Congregational	Quaker	Anglican	Presbyterian, Calvinist
Worship style	Lecture-centered	Spirit-centered	Liturgy-centered	Field meeting and fellowship
Family identity	Strong nuclear	Moderate nuclear	Extended	Clan and derbfine
Family cohesion	High	Moderate	Low	Moderate
Marriage ceremony	Civil contract	Meeting and agreement	Sacred ceremony	Abduction rituals
Males never wed	Low (2%)	Moderate (12%)	High (25%)	n.a.
Male dominance	Moderate	Moderate	High	Very high
Premarital pregnancy (P)	Low (10–20%)	Very low (5–15%)	High (20–40%)	Very high (40%)
Child nurture	Will-breaking	Will-bracing	Will-bending	Will-building
Old-age ideals	Saint	Teacher	Patriarch	Thane
Burial customs	High austerity	Extreme austerity	High ceremony	Folk ritual
Eating patterns	Age-dominant	Communal	Rank-dominant	Gender-dominant
Color display	Sad colors	Neutral colors	Bright colors	Folk colors

(continued on next page)

Four Regional Cultures in Anglo-America, ca. 1700–1750

(continued)

Label	Yankees	Quakers	Cavaliers	Scots-Irish
Sexual display	Moderate to low	Very low	Moderate to high	Very high
Amuse-ments	Town and team games	Useful recreations	Blood sports	Field contests
Work ethic	Puritan	Pietist	Leisure	Warrior
Time ethic	Improving the time	Redeeming the time	Killing the time	Passing the time
Rank system	Truncated	Egalitarian	Hierarchical	Segmented
Deference	Moderate	Low	High	Mixed
Wealth inequality (G)	Low (.4–.6)	Very low (.3–.5)	High (.6–.75)	Very high (.7–.9)
Settlements	Hamlets	Farm clusters	Plantations	Isolated
Local polity	Town meeting	Commission	Parish and court	Court
Internal migration	Low	High	Moderate	Very high
Honor	Grace-centered	Holiness-centered	Rank-centered	Primal honor
Crime profile (C)	Mostly property (.4)	Balanced (1.2)	Balanced (.9)	Almost all violent (5.2)
Level of violence	Very low	Low	Moderate	High
Freedom ways	Ordered liberty	Reciprocal liberty	Hegemonic liberty	Natural liberty

Definitions of quantitative indicators

P   Proportion of first births within 8 months of marriage.

G   Gini coefficient, ranging from .00 (perfect equality) to .99 (the uppermost percentile has all the wealth).

C   Ratio of violent crimes to property crime.

Source: Adapted from "Four Regional Cultures in Anglo-America: A Summary of Cultural Characteristics, ca. 1700–50," in Fischer (1989), 813–15.

Americans at the founding, Federalist and Anti-Federalist alike, demanded a Constitution that severely restricted federal power not just because of an abstract attachment to federalism or because of the single issue of slavery but because of the many concrete ways in which peoples with different ways of life didn't want a government that would interfere with those ways of life.

The Post-Founding Immigrants

The cultural variegation of America had just begun. The nineteenth century saw a series of surges in immigration that brought alien cultures to our shores. In the single decade from 1846 through 1855, 1,288,000 Irish and 976,000 Germans landed on the East Coast.[6] They brought not only the Irish and German cultures with them—both different from all four of the British streams—but also Catholicism, which until then had been rare in the United States.[7]

The Irish who arrived during that surge were not like earlier generations of immigrants who had been self-selected for risk-taking and optimism. They were fleeing starvation from the potato famine. More than half of them spoke no English when they arrived. Most were illiterate. They did not disperse into the hinterlands but stayed in the big cities of the east. Since those cities weren't actually that big in the mid-nineteenth century, the Irish soon constituted more than a quarter of the populations of New York, Boston, Philadelphia, Providence, New Haven, Hartford, Jersey City, and Newark. Large urban neighborhoods became exclusively Irish and Catholic—a kind of neighborhood that America had never before experienced.

The Germans were the antithesis of the Irish, typically farmers who practiced advanced agriculture or highly skilled craftsmen. Michael Barone's description of the culture they brought with them is worth quoting at length:

> As soon as they could they built solid stone houses and commercial buildings. They built German Catholic, Lutheran, and Reformed churches, and they maintained German-language instruction in private and public schools for decades. They formed fire and militia companies, coffee circles, and especially singing societies, staging

seasonal Sangerfeste (singing festivals). They staged pre-Lenten carnivals, outdoor Volkfeste, and annual German Day celebrations. They formed mutual-benefit fire insurance firms and building societies and set up German-speaking lodges of American associations. Turnvereine (athletic clubs) were established in almost all German communities and national gymnastic competitions became common. German-language newspapers sprung up—newspaper baron Joseph Pulitzer, a German-speaking Hungarian Jew, got his start in one in St. Louis—and German theaters opened in New York, Philadelphia, Cincinnati, Chicago, and Milwaukee. Some German customs came to seem quintessentially American—the Christmas tree, kindergarten, pinochle.[8]

In the 1870s, large numbers of Scandinavian immigrants began to augment the continuing German immigration, and most of them headed straight toward what Barone has called the "Germano-Scandinavian province," consisting of Wisconsin, Iowa, Minnesota, and the Dakotas, overlapping into parts of Missouri, Kansas, Nebraska, and Montana. The mixed cultures of Scandinavia and Middle Europe in the small towns of those regions persisted long into the twentieth century, famously chronicled by Willa Cather in the early twentieth century and over the last forty years by Garrison Keillor.

The Civil War created or intensified several kinds of cultural diversity. First, its conclusion marked the emergence of African American culture from the shadows. Communities of American blacks in the South were no longer limited to the size of a slaveholder's labor force but could consist of large neighborhoods in Southern cities or the majorities of populations in rural towns. All the categories of folkways that distinguished the various white cultures from one another also distinguished black American culture from the white ones.

The Civil War also led Southern whites, whether descendants of Cavaliers, indentured servants, or the Scots-Irish of the backcountry who had never owned slaves, to identify themselves as Southerners above all else. In many respects, they walled themselves off from the rest of the country and stayed that way for a century. White Southern culture was not only different from cultures in the rest of the country; it was defiantly different.

In the 1890s, America's cultural diversity got yet another infusion from Eastern Europe and Mediterranean Europe that amounted to 20 million people by the time restrictive immigration laws were enacted in the 1920s. They came primarily from Italy, the Austro-Hungarian empire, and Russia, with this in common: Almost all of them had been second-class citizens in their homelands. The Italian immigrants came from rural, poor, and largely illiterate southern Italy and Sicily, not from the wealthier and more sophisticated north. Austro-Hungary's immigrants were overwhelmingly Czechs, Serbs, Poles, Slovaks, Slovenians, and Jews, not ethnic Hungarians or Austrians. The immigrants from the Russian Empire were almost all Poles, Lithuanians, and Ukrainians, not ethnic Russians, with large proportions being Jewish as well. Occupationally, the Ellis Island immigrants had usually been factory laborers, peddlers, and tenant farmers, near the bottom of the economic ladder.[9]

The size of these immigrant groups led to huge urban enclaves. In New York City alone, the Italian-born population at the beginning of the twentieth century was larger than the combined populations of Florence, Venice, and Genoa, mostly packed into the Lower East Side of New York. A few blocks to their west were 540,000 Jews, far more than lived in any other city in the world. To enter either of those neighborhoods was to be in a world that bore little resemblance to America anywhere else. And that doesn't count New York's older communities of Irish, Germans, and African Americans. When in 1913 Sam Rayburn voiced his hopes for an America that knew no East, West, North, or South, the four points of the compass barely began to describe the patchwork of cultures that was America.

The Anomaly of Mid-Twentieth-Century America

O ver the next sixty years, events combined to both dampen and mask cultural diversity. First, World War I triggered an anti-German reaction that all but destroyed the distinctive German culture. In the 1920s, new immigration laws choked off almost all immigration from everywhere except Britain and northern Europe, and even that was reduced. With each passing year more children of immigrants married native-born Americans and fewer grandchildren of immigrants grew up to carry on the distinctive features of their Old World culture. By the

middle of the century, the percentages of Americans who were immigrants or even the children of immigrants were at all-time lows. Most
of the once-vibrant ethnic communities of the great cities had faded to
shadows. No longer could you find yourself in an American street scene
indistinguishable from one in Palermo or the Warsaw ghetto.

Among native-born Americans, our long-standing tradition of picking up and moving continued, with surges of the population to Florida
and the West Coast. Then came World War II.[10] Almost 18 million out
of a population of 131 million put on uniforms and were thrown together
with Americans from other geographic, socioeconomic, and ethnic
backgrounds.[11] The economic effects of war production also prompted
a wave of African American immigration from the South to the North
and West.

These demographic changes occurred in the context of the culturally
homogenizing effects of mass media. Movies were ubiquitous by the beginning of World War I, and most American homes had a radio by the
end of the 1920s. These new mass media introduced a nationally shared
popular culture, and one to which almost all Americans were exposed.
Given a list of the top movie stars, the top singers, and the top radio
personalities, just about everybody under the age of sixty would not only
have recognized all of their names but have been familiar with them and
their work.

After the war, television spread the national popular culture even
more pervasively. Television viewers had only a few channels to choose
from, so everyone's television viewing overlapped with everyone else's.
Even if you didn't watch, you were part of it—last night's episode of
I Love Lucy was a major source of conversation around the water cooler.

In these and many other ways, the cultural variations that had been so
prominent at the time of World War I were less obvious by the time Lyndon Johnson came to office. A few cities remained culturally distinct, and
the different regions continued to have some different folkways, but only
the South stood out as a part of the country that marched to a different
drummer, and the foundation of that distinctiveness, the South's version
of racial segregation, had been cracked by the Civil Rights Act of 1964.
When, in December 1964, Lyndon Johnson evoked Rayburn's dream
of an America "that knows no East, no West, no North, no South," he
was giving voice to a sentiment that seemed not only an aspiration but

something that the nation could achieve once the civil rights movement's triumph was complete.

But even as he spoke, the US Congress was only a year away from an immigration bill that would reopen America's borders. Johnson's own Great Society programs—plus Supreme Court decisions, changes in the job market, and the sexual revolution—would produce a lower class unlike anything America had known before.[12] Changes in the economy and higher education would produce a new upper class unlike anything America had known before.[13]

The Culturally Segregated America of the Twenty-First Century

Half a century after Johnson's speech in the East Room, America is at least as culturally diverse as it was at the beginning of World War I and in some respects more thoroughly segregated than it has ever been. To put it in terms of the argument of this book: Today's America is once again a patchwork of cultures that are different from one another and often in tension. What they share in common with the cultures of pre–World War I America is that they require freedom. In one way or another, the members of most of the new subcultures want to be left alone in ways that the laws of the nation, strictly observed, will no longer let them. They need to be left alone if they are to live their lives as they see fit.

Towns, Small Cities, Suburbs, Big Cities

The primary driver of quotidian cultural diversity throughout American history and continuing today, independently of ethnicity, religion, wealth, politics, or sexual orientation, is the size of the place where people live. At one extreme, in big cities of a million people or more, those other elements of cultural diversity all have room for expression. Neighborhoods are still segregated by ethnicity (though that has been slowly diminishing), but the megalopolises also have rich neighborhoods and poor ones; neighborhoods where families predominate and ones where singles do; neighborhoods where churches are active and ones where they are empty; tough neighborhoods and genteel ones; neighborhoods where bankers live and ones where artists live; and, in recent decades, gay and lesbian neighborhoods. Some cities have identifiably liberal neighborhoods and conservative ones.

If you live in a big city, enough money will let you choose to live in a neighborhood with just the right combination of characteristics to fit your priorities. Your "community" also probably consists of many pockets. Just as anywhere else, you can acquire close friends, but those friends tend to be scattered. Some of them live in the same geographic neighborhood but others live in virtual communities defined by your vocation or avocations.

So living in a big city does not mean living without community, but most of the city is anonymous, and so are almost all the interactions you have when you leave the confines of your immediate geographic neighborhood. If you've got a problem with a water bill or getting your trash picked up, you must deal with an anonymous city bureaucracy. The policeman who arrives when your apartment is burgled is someone you've never seen before and will never see again. If you get into a dispute with a neglectful landlord or an incompetent contractor, there is likely to be no personal relationship that you can use to resolve the dispute; you will have to take it to the authorities.

By its nature, the big city itself is an unfathomably complicated machine. It has large numbers of people with serious needs of every kind, for which there are a profusion of government agencies that are supposed to provide assistance. The technological and administrative complexity of the infrastructure that provides police protection, firefighting, water, sewers, electricity, gas, and transportation in a congested and densely populated place is staggering.

Now consider the other extreme, a small town or city. It might be 500 people, 3,000, or 15,000; it's surprising how similarly communities function below a certain size. There's no sharp cutoff point. In the quantitative work I've done for this discussion, I chose 25,000 as the upper bound, but that's arbitrary.

First, it's important to note that some things are the same everywhere. If a town or small city has an ethnic minority of more than a few families, its members will probably be clustered in the same blocks. Even small towns tend to have some clustering by socioeconomic class as well;

they have a right side and a wrong side of the tracks. The residents don't all know one another except in the tiniest places. Even people living in a town of just several hundred people cannot have what the anthropologists call "stable social relationships" with more than about 150 people, because that seems to be about the most that *Homo sapiens* can handle at one time.[14]

But daily life in a town or small city has a much different feel to it from life in the big city. For one thing, people of different ethnicities and socioeconomic classes are thrown together a lot more. There are only a few elementary schools at most, sometimes only one, and usually just a single high school. The students' parents belong to the same PTAs and attend the same Little League games. The churches are centers of community activities, and while there are some socioeconomic distinctions among their congregations, the churches mix people up a lot.[15]

Small towns are not idyllic. The most bitter community disputes I have been part of occurred not in Washington, DC, but in a town of fewer than 200 people. My point is simpler: Hardly anyone in a town or small city is anonymous. Policemen, sales clerks, plumbers, and landlords are often people you know personally. Even when you don't, you're likely to know *of* them—if the plumber's last name is Overholtz, your parents may have known his parents, or your friend's daughter married an Overholtz a few years ago, or in a dozen other ways you are able to place that person in the matrix of the town.

The same thing is true of whatever interactions you have with government in a town or small city. In the big city, postal clerks are so often brusque and unhelpful that the stereotype has become notorious. In a small town, the postal clerk is more likely to add the necessary postage when you've understamped and collect later, or may phone to let you know that a package you were expecting has arrived. It's not because the United States Postal Service assigns its friendliest postal clerks to small towns but instead is the result of age-old truths about human interactions: When you know that an encounter is going to be one-time, it's easier to be brusque and unhelpful than when you expect the encounter to be repeated. Repeated encounters tend to generate personal sympathies, understandings, and affiliations.

The mayor and city council members of a small town are people you can phone if you have a problem. In a small city, solving your problem may involve as little as a phone call to the right person in a municipal bureaucracy that numbers a few dozen people. Not all problems will get solved that easily, but as a rule the representatives of government in a town or small city are more reluctant to play the role of an "I'm just following the rules" official than someone working in the bureaucracy of a city of a million. They are more willing and able to cut their fellow citizens some slack. It's a variation on the reason why a village postal clerk is likely to be helpful. Bureaucrats in towns and small cities aren't faceless. They have to get along with the citizens they govern. In fact, they can't even get away with thinking of their role as "governing" their fellow citizens. They have no choice but to be aware that they are, in fact, public servants.

As for social capital—the potpourri of formal and informal activities that bind a community together—the range and frequency of things that still go on in towns and small cities is astonishing. Such places have not been immune from the overall reduction in social capital that sociologist Robert Putnam documented in *Bowling Alone*.[16] Social capital has been hardest hit in the most distressed communities in parts of the country where jobs have disappeared.[17] But in towns and small cities that still have a stable core of middle-class and blue-collar citizens, the traditional image of the American community survives in practice. These are still places where people don't bother to lock the door when they leave the house and the disadvantaged are not nameless "people on welfare," but individuals whose problems, failings, and virtues are known at a personal level.

As cities get larger, the characteristics I have discussed shift toward the big-city end of the scale, but it happens slowly. The earliest change, and an important one, is that socioeconomic segregation becomes more significant. When a city is large enough to support two high schools, you can be sure that the students who attend each will show substantial mean differences in parental income and education. The larger the population, the more that churches will draw their congregations from different social classes.

But many of the activities that go under the rubric of social capital continue. The churches remain important sources of such social capital, and so do the clubs such as Rotary, Kiwanis, American Legion, Veterans of Foreign Wars, and others that are still active in cities of up to a few hundred thousand people (and sometimes beyond). Mid-size cities often have strongly felt identities, with solidarity and pride that carry over into concrete projects to make the community better. Even in cities of 300,000 or 400,000, the local movers and shakers are a small enough group that they can be brought together in a variety of ways, as members of a local civic organization or more informally, and they are often able to deal with local problems without a lot of red tape.

I could discuss these characteristics of life for still another kind of community, the suburbs of the great metropolises, but by now the point should be made: The simple size of the places where people live creates enormous diversity in daily life, in the relationship of citizens to the local government, in the necessity for complex rules, and in the ability of communities to deal with their own problems.

We aren't talking about a small, quaint fraction of American communities that can deal with their own problems. Madisonians are often chastised for confusing today's highly urbanized America with an America of a simpler time. I think the opposite mistake is a bigger problem: assuming that most of America is like New York or Chicago. As of the 2010 census, 28 percent of Americans still lived in rural areas or in cities of fewer than 25,000 people. Another 30 percent lived in stand-alone cities (i.e., not satellites of a nearby bigger city) of 25,000–499,999. Fourteen percent lived in satellites to cities with at least 500,000 people. Twenty-eight percent lived in the sixty-two cities with contiguous urban areas containing more than 500,000 people—the same proportion that lived in places of fewer than 25,000 people.

What Does "Contiguous Urban Areas" Mean?

For each of the largest fifty cities, I defined a "Greater X"—e.g., "Greater Kansas City"—that is based on contiguous high-density census tracts rather than the official city limits. City limits often bear no relationship to the actual extent of a city, especially on the East Coast, where the city limits may have been defined in the eighteenth century. The map and the discussion in the text are based on those modified city definitions.[18]

The 28 percent who live in the large contiguous urban areas don't take up much space, as the map below shows.

Cities of 500,000 population and above

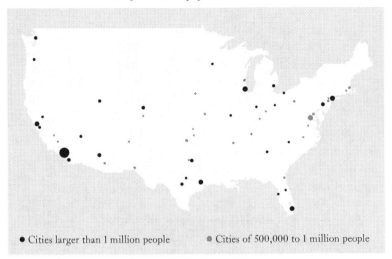

● Cities larger than 1 million people   ● Cities of 500,000 to 1 million people

The black circles represent cities of more than 1 million people. They contain 21 percent of the population. The gray circles identify cities of 500,000 up to 1 million, with 7 percent of the population. The sizes of the circles roughly correspond to the size of the geographic spaces they encompass (that's why the circle for New York is so much smaller than the one for Los Angeles). Now look at all that space outside the circles. Specifically, look at the area including the state in which you live, and consider that a small geographic portion of your state consists of big cities—something that's true of even the most urban states.

My proposition is that the people in that space, comprising fully 72 percent of the population, need a lot less oversight from higher levels of government than they're getting. The municipal governments in that space need a lot less supervision from state and federal government than they're getting.[19] For cities under 500,000, a compelling case can be made that their citizens should be given wide latitude to live their lives as they see fit. Once we're down to cities under 25,000, I think that case becomes overwhelming, with access to a few block grants (carrying only the most basic bureaucratic strings) being nearly the only role that higher levels of government need to play.

The Ethnic Overlay

I now turn to the topic that dominates the national conversation about growing American cultural diversity: growing ethnic diversity. My message is that it's important but not revolutionary.

In 1965, America reopened immigration to people from around the world, and in so doing opened a new era. The figure below shows the story from the earliest census data in 1850 to the 2010 census.

In terms of its foreign-born population, America now is about where it was from 1860 to 1930.

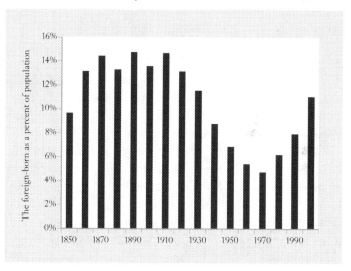

Source: Author's analysis, decennial census data from Social Explorer (www.social explorer.com).

The chart gives a specific example of two themes of this chapter: Mid-century America was anomalous, and America today bears some striking similarities to America of the nineteenth century.

The inflows of different ethnic groups since 1965 has indeed led to a major change in the ethnic composition of the American population. In 2012, non-Latino whites (hereafter just *whites*) constituted only 63 percent of the population, compared to the 80-plus percent that had held true from the founding through 1980—a big drop.[20] The second largest ethnic group in 2012 was Latino, amounting to 17 percent of the population, surpassing the group that had hitherto been the largest minority, blacks, who in 2010 were 13 percent of the population. Asians in 2010 had reached 5 percent of the population. By now, almost everyone is familiar with the Census Bureau's projection that whites will be a minority of the American population before midcentury.[21] These are momentous changes in America's ethnic mix at a national level. But they have caused, and will cause, little change in quotidian culture in the vast majority of American towns and cities, because changes in the ethnic mix of specific places have been so intensely concentrated.

LATINO AMERICANS. Start with the great surge in Americans from Mexico, Central and South America, and Cuba. In 1970, 9.3 million Latinos constituted less than 5 percent of the American population, concentrated in the border counties of Texas and Arizona, all of New Mexico, southern Colorado, and southern California, plus a growing Cuban presence in southern Florida and a large long-standing population of Latinos, mostly Puerto Ricans, in New York City.

From 1970 to 2010, the census shows an increase of 41.2 million Latinos. That's a huge increase—but 71 percent of it was in the places I just mentioned, leaving just 29 percent of the increase in the Latino population to be scattered everywhere else in the country.[22]

The upshot is that county-by-county maps of the Latino presence in 1970 and 2010 look remarkably similar. Typically, the increase in the Latino population means that a local culture already influenced by Latinos is somewhat more influenced. With the exception of a few cities—mainly Chicago; Washington, DC; and Atlanta—places that had a minor Latino presence in 1970 still had a minor presence in 2010. So two different thoughts about cultural diversity fostered by Latinos need to be held in one's mind at the same time:

1. *The last fifty years saw the advent of a Cuban American culture in South Florida and the spread of an existing Mexican American culture in parts of Southwest America and California that have importantly affected quotidian culture in those places.* The increase in the proportion of Latinos in those

areas has also affected the political power balance. As of 2010, Latinos constituted an absolute majority of the population in 28 incorporated cities of more than 100,000 people. In some much larger cities, Latinos were approaching an absolute majority, constituting more than 40 percent of the population as of 2010 in Dallas, Houston, Albuquerque, Phoenix, Tucson, Los Angeles, Long Beach, Fresno, and Bakersfield.[23] In all, 18.2 million Americans in the Southwest and California lived in zip codes that were majority Latino.

2. *America as a whole is not being Latinized.* Outside the areas where the Latino presence is concentrated, Latinos constitute a small portion of the population—6 percent. That's far short of a percentage that has much effect on quotidian culture. Furthermore, the surge in the Latino population is in a prolonged pause and may be over. According to analyses by the Pew Foundation, net Latino immigration stalled after the Great Recession of 2009.[24] Michael Barone points out that the other great ethnic surges of immigration have petered out after about twenty-five years, and the Latino immigration may well be doing the same thing.[25] Based on past experience, most of the Latino immigrants who do arrive will go to areas that already have large Latino populations. The best guess is that towns and cities with small Latino populations now will continue to have small ones for the foreseeable future.

AFRICAN AMERICANS. Similar generalizations apply to the African American minority: in certain specific parts of the United States, the influence of blacks on quotidian culture is large, but most American places have very small black minorities.

African Americans have been concentrated in the same places for many decades: the former states of the Confederacy and large urban areas in the Northeast and Midwest, plus large concentrations in Los Angeles and Houston. Adding up the black population in the onetime states of the Confederacy and the nineteen cities outside those states with at least 100,000 blacks in the 2010 census leaves only 12.8 million blacks living in the rest of the country, less than 7 percent of its population.[26] The diversity in quotidian culture introduced by African Americans is great, but isolated. There is no reason to think this pattern will change.

ASIAN AMERICANS. The most intriguing, least predictable cultural change being fostered by ethnicity is where you might least expect it: with Asian Americans. Amounting to only 5 percent of the population,

Asians would seem to be too small a group to have much influence on the culture. For almost all of the country, that's true. We have become accustomed to seeing Asian physicians in medical centers all over the country, and Asians running restaurants, dry-cleaning establishments, and convenience stores all over the country, but these amount to isolated moments in daily life.

Yet in a few geographic areas Asians are establishing a presence that already affects quotidian culture. The New York City and Los Angeles metropolitan areas each had almost 2 million Asians in 2010, and San Francisco had over 1 million. Four other metropolitan areas had more than 500,000 Asians, and nine others had over 200,000. What makes these numbers especially interesting is that Asians are heavily overrepresented in the elite zip codes of those cities. If the Asian population continues to grow—and, unlike immigration from Latin America, immigration from Asia is not slackening—the population of America's elite zip codes could easily be one-quarter Asian by the 2020s. To my knowledge, no one has given any thought as to how that might play out in the elite culture.

The most dramatic current example of an Asian presence that already affects quotidian culture is in Silicon Valley, which effectively stretches from the southern suburbs of San Francisco to San Jose.[27] Silicon Valley, with a population approaching 2 million, is unique in its concentration of people in the top percentiles of IQ—surely a higher concentration than in any other American geographic area with such a large population. Their talents are being put to work in the information-technology industry, which is the single most important industry in reshaping daily life for people around the globe. And 33 percent of the population of Silicon Valley is Asian. In ten of Silicon Valley's zip codes, Asians constitute a majority of the population. How might this affect the culture of Silicon Valley and, more broadly, the evolution of the IT industry? It is another intriguing but unanswered question.

ETHNIC DIVERSITY IN PERSPECTIVE. The day a few decades from now that a majority of the American population consists of nonwhites will be historic, but in my view it will not have much effect on daily American life. Opinions to the contrary are abundant. They range from ugly nativism of the kind America has known since the 1840s to thoughtful argumentation. For an example of the latter, see *Who Are We?* by the late Samuel P. Huntington, one of the most distinguished social scientists of the past half century.

My discussion of the ethnic overlay is intended not to minimize the degree of cultural diversity that growing proportions of minorities will create, but to place it in perspective. Suppose that American towns and cities had always mirrored the national ethnic distribution. In that case, the typical place where we lived in 1970 would have consisted of 83 percent whites, 11 percent blacks, 5 percent Latinos, and 1 percent Asians. Forty years later it would have consisted of just 63 percent whites, 17 percent Latinos, 13 percent blacks, and 5 percent Asians. That change would have betokened a transformative shift with many effects on quotidian culture.

That's what has happened in America's largest cities, most of which have become genuinely multicultural now in a way they were not in 1970. I don't see that as a bad thing. Large cities are the ideal place for multiple ethnicities to flourish and to make local life more interesting.

But outside the largest cities, it has been exceedingly rare for town and city populations to mirror the national distribution. Instead, America has had a combination of one-ethnicity towns or cities (mostly with a dominant majority of whites, but some with dominant majorities of African Americans, Latinos, or American Indians) and two-ethnicity towns or cities (white-black, white-Latino, and a few that were white-Indian). Most of these local mixes are decades or even centuries old, and the charms of life in different parts of the country are decisively affected by them. The distinctiveness of life in Charleston or Savannah would be impoverished without its black-white mix. The unique culture of New Orleans depends on its black-white-Cajun mix. Miami has its unique mise-en-scène because of its many Cuban Americans. San Antonio, Albuquerque, Phoenix, and Los Angeles are all richer and more textured places to live because of their large Mexican American populations.

It's not just cities. If you want to think of it that way, the enriching element of ethnicity is still in play in nearly all-white communities. The distinctiveness of quotidian culture in some places in Maine is owed to the centuries-long predominance of Yankee stock, while daily life in parts of Tennessee and Kentucky reflects the continuing predominance of the Scots-Irish. All of these and many other ethnically grounded cultural differences are an essential part of what makes America special. They aren't about to disappear anytime soon, for reasons that I have tried to explain, and it's good that they aren't going to disappear.

The Cultural/Political Overlay

Places of the same size and similar ethnic mixes can nonetheless be culturally at opposite poles, because for the last three decades America has been busily segregating by socioeconomic status and politics.

The United States has always been a mobile country, with people pulling up stakes and moving long distances. But until the 1980s, the motivation for Americans to move around within the country was usually economic. People moved to escape a place where jobs had disappeared, moved to where job opportunities were attractive, or both. When it wasn't economic, the motive often had to do with climate, as people left the cold winters of the Northeast and Midwest for the sun of Florida, the Southwest, and California. From the 1980s onward, large numbers of people have been choosing where they wanted to live for other reasons. They moved to places with a lifestyle that appealed to them, which also usually meant moving to places where people shared their politics, their socioeconomic class, or both.

The degree to which Americans have sorted themselves according to their class and politics has been described by Bill Bishop in *The Big Sort: Why the Clustering of Like-Minded America Is Tearing Us Apart*.[28] You are familiar with the basics of the situation just from following the news. For example, you have surely seen many versions of the red-state/blue-state map. They vary depending on the election, but the consistent theme is a mass of red states in the interior of the country and solid blue in the Northeast and along the West Coast. Red/blue maps based on counties reveal a more accurate picture: The blue is concentrated in the largest cities and surrounding areas. It's not that California, Oregon, and Washington are entirely blue, but that the coastal strips of those states are blue. Away from those coastal strips, California, Oregon, and Washington are bright red—those parts of the state just don't have nearly as many people as the coastal strip. Colorado is not blue all over but mainly in a narrow corridor running from Boulder to Colorado Springs plus an island of blue in Aspen. The same phenomenon can be found in most states.

In one sense, there's nothing new here. Since the solid South broke up in the 1960s, urbanized areas have always generally voted Democratic while rural and small-city areas have generally voted Republican. What's different is that those tendencies have changed from mild to extreme. *The Big Sort* opens with two maps of the American presidential vote by counties, one for the 1976 contest between Gerald Ford and Jimmy Carter and the other for the 2004 contest between George W. Bush and John Kerry. In terms of the national vote, the results were nearly evenly divided—50.1 percent to 48.0 percent in 1976, 50.7 to 48.3 percent in 2004—but the electoral maps look completely different. In 1976, 73 percent of America's counties were defined as "competitive," meaning that the difference between the winner and loser was fewer than 20 percentage points.[29] The electoral map everywhere outside the South and Texas was dominated by competitive counties. In 2004, only 52 percent of counties were competitive, and the electoral map was dominated by huge blocks of counties between the coasts, especially in the plains states and mountain states, that went for George W. Bush by more than 20 percentage points, while the landslide counties for John Kerry were concentrated in the counties with the nation's largest cities.[30]

A 2014 Pew Foundation study gives us additional ways to calibrate the change. Historically, both major political parties in the United States have been dominated by centrists. In the last few decades, those on the ideological extremes have grown dramatically. Among politically engaged Democrats, the percentage who hold consistently liberal views grew from 8 percent in 1994 to 38 percent in 2014. Among Republicans, the proportion of the politically engaged who hold consistently conservative views rose from 10 percent in 2004 to 33 percent in 2014.[31] Furthermore, people increasingly associate only with those who share their politics. Forty-nine percent of consistent liberals and 63 percent of consistent conservatives say that most of their close friends share their politics.[32] That's the kind of polarization that produces neighborhoods sorted by politics.

The political sorting is symptomatic of a deeper class sorting. It was led by the emergence of a new class in America during the 1980s. It has gone under many labels. Robert Reich called them "symbolic workers"; Richard Herrnstein and I called them the "cognitive elite"; David Brooks memorably called them "Bobos," short for "Bourgeois Bohemians"; and Richard Florida called them "the creative class." All of us have been referring to the population of very smart, highly educated people for whom the economy of the last thirty years has been tailor-made. For an acute (and often hilarious) description of the new class, I refer you to David Brooks's *Bobos in Paradise*, still as accurate today as it was when it was published in 2000. For a summary account of how this new class came to be and where they live, I refer you to the first four chapters of my own *Coming Apart*.[33]

Briefly, a revolution in higher education beginning around the 1950s subsequently produced a much larger cohort of college graduates than the nation had ever known and, within that population, a subset distinguished by high levels of intellectual talent and common socializing experiences in the nation's elite colleges and universities.[34] They developed a culture with distinctive tastes in everything from food and alcohol to sports and avocations to marriage and child rearing. It's not primarily a matter of money. An associate professor at Oberlin making a modest salary is probably as fully immersed in the new elite culture as a programming genius at Google with millions of dollars of Google stock. In contrast, an affluent business executive in Des Moines who likes living in Des Moines probably has a lifestyle that is largely indistinguishable from that of a middle-class American. He probably has a bigger house (not a mansion) than someone in the middle class and drives a more expensive automobile (not a flashy one), but that's about it.

The members of the new elite culture have flocked to the cities where they will find the most like-minded people. In the tenth-anniversary update of *The Rise of the Creative Class*, Richard Florida presents a "creativity index" that measures the attractiveness of cities to the creative class.[35] Within the twenty-five top-ranked places are a dozen that are home to the nation's most highly regarded research universities, including Harvard, Princeton, MIT, Stanford, Caltech, and Duke. Others of the top-ranked places are synonymous with hip and high-tech: Silicon Valley, San Francisco, Portland, Austin, Seattle, Denver. Others are large cities that don't fit the pattern so obviously but have quietly become places with high-tech industries whose workforces have led to an ambience that attracts still more members of the creative class—Atlanta, the Boston area, Minneapolis, San Diego, Sacramento, the Los Angeles area, and the Washington, DC, area.

The ethos and values of this new elite are seldom directly political. It is not political that the new elite watches hardly any television at all except for a few fashionable series (as I write, *Downton Abbey*), while the average television elsewhere in the United States is on for thirty-five hours a week. It is not political that new elite mothers typically have their children in their thirties while mothers in mainstream America bear their children in their early to mid-twenties. Such lifestyle differences sometimes have political implications, but the more important point is that the differences are substantial. Tell a member of the new elite that he is being relocated from San Francisco to Des Moines, and he is likely to be so unhappy about the prospect that he looks for a new job rather than accept the transfer. He won't feel at home in Des Moines. It works both ways. Go back to my affluent Des Moines businessman. If he is a devout Christian, for example, with traditional views about the definition of family, San Francisco probably won't feel like a good match. If he is politically conservative, it will feel even worse. In San Francisco, he won't be able to live his life as he sees fit as well as he can in Des Moines.

I have only touched on the other kinds of sorting that have been at work. I have not mentioned, for example, the massive influence that an aging population has had on the culture of retirement regions of the Sun Belt. But spelling out all those kinds of sorting here would be overkill. My point is not really a matter of dispute: Cultural sorting has added a complex array of ways in which American communities differ from one another. "Living life as one sees fit" has different definitions in different cultural pockets of the country.

Chapter 13

THE BEST OF TIMES

In which I describe some resources for rebuilding liberty that are coming together in the second decade of the twenty-first century.

MUCH OF WHAT has happened to the United States is not new. Cultures age. Political institutions become sclerotic. To that extent, ours is the story of all regimes that last long enough.

What's new about the United States is that resurrecting the American project in an altered form is not an exercise in nostalgia. We don't want to restore a bygone Golden Age. I don't know of any Madisonians who want the 1950s back, let alone the 1780s. We just want to put government into its proper box, using a definition of "proper box" based on eighteenth-century principles but one that also accords with twenty-first-century realities. That's a call to shape the future, not restore the past.

Charles Dickens's famous opening of *A Tale of Two Cities*, "It was the best of times, it was the worst of times," applies to us. Part I of this book described some of the ways in which this is the worst of times. But the last few decades have also given us new assets that the founders couldn't have imagined. Along with them are new problems confronting our adversaries. Right now is also the best of times.

Liberation Technology

Of the things we have going for us, one stands out: technology that makes liberty practical as never before. Limited government and a high level of individual freedom no longer pose some of the problems that they used to pose.

Replacing Government Oversight with Public Oversight

Suppose we are back in 1900 and I am arguing with a progressive, trying to make the case for Madisonian freedom and limited government. There are reasons why the progressives won. In 1900, they have strong arguments in their favor.

First, my progressive adversary can point to numerous examples of local tyranny that go unchecked in the America of 1900. There's the company town, where the dominant employer forces workers to shop at the company store and borrow from the company bank. Anyone who tries to unionize the workforce will be fired and perhaps physically attacked. In the South, local tyrannies are directed against African Americans. Local police ignore any inconvenient laws that interfere with keeping African Americans "in their place." State governments are often indifferent to these abuses because the legislature and senior officials have been bought off or, in the case of the Southern states, share the mind-set of the localities. In 1900, it's easy to argue that only the federal government can stand up to these local tyrannies.

Next, my 1900 progressive adversary can point to the helplessness of ordinary consumers. Information is hard to acquire and hard to share. Lack of information enables unscrupulous middlemen to buy crops at below-market prices or sell products at inflated prices. Lack of information enables food and drug producers to sell adulterated products to consumers who have no way of knowing what is in them. Lack of information enables people to pass themselves off as teachers or attorneys who actually know nothing about teaching or the law. Lack of information allows manufacturers to get away with selling inferior products, because bad reputations spread slowly. The only way to cope with these problems, my progressive adversary says, is through government oversight, licensing, and regulation.

Over the course of the twentieth century, technology turned out to be an extraordinarily powerful and efficient way of countering these problems. With regard to local tyrannies, the civil rights movement is the obvious case in point. It succeeded because of the development of news media over the twentieth century, especially television. The evening news showed videotape of black elementary-school children being escorted to school by National Guardsmen past whites shouting abuse at them, of Medgar Evers's widow comforting her son at the funeral of that murdered civil-rights activist, and of a burning bus carrying Freedom Riders firebombed by a mob in Georgia. Such images drove a sea change in the consciousness of the white electorate about what was being done to black Americans in the segregated South that was impossible before television and became inevitable thereafter.

In the decades since, the competition among local television news programs has led to a nationwide capacity for searching out local tyrannies and getting them on camera. It is a way to win the ratings war. If the scandal is juicy enough, it will get picked up by one of a dozen network and cable news shows specializing in scandal and exposés. Letting the news outlets know about such behavior is as simple as an e-mail. For that matter, traditional media outlets are no longer necessary. Twitter, Facebook, YouTube, and a profusion of blogs specializing in such topics can be tapped by almost anyone with a grievance. There is no such thing as a local fiefdom immune from exposure to the rest of America.

The changes have been even more revolutionary in the availability of information about products and services. Commercial exchanges in a free market need two characteristics: they must be both voluntary and informed. Now they can be both in a way that was difficult in 1900. It doesn't make any difference what you're in the market for. There's information on everything. Whether you're looking for a new smartphone or a better pepper grinder, just Google *smartphones* or *pepper grinders*, and in a few minutes you will know everything about the merits of alternative choices. You'll also have a choice of vendors from which to purchase the smartphone or pepper grinder of your dreams at the lowest price— usually for delivery tomorrow.

You need a plumber? You can go to Angie's List and read about the experiences of your fellow citizens with different plumbers in your area. Looking for an apartment? You can go to Craigslist. You name it, and the Internet has an abundance of usable, reliable information. It also has a lot of unusable and unreliable information, but only members of the hard left think that the government should step in and run the Internet. We can figure it out for ourselves. With the Internet, freedom really does work. An unregulated Internet has empowered us to make informed choices about an incredibly wide range of goods and services. The government has become nearly irrelevant to this process. Cast your mind over the hundreds of questions you have used the Internet to answer during the past year, and consider how little you used government websites. For those of you who have needed to use government websites, how well did they meet your needs compared to commercial websites?

In the early 1900s, Upton Sinclair's *The Jungle* led to government inspection of meat, for good reason. But suppose that the government stopped inspecting meat in 2015. What would Safeway do? Try to make money by selling contaminated meat? That would mean catastrophe; Safeway's customers would know about it right away. Instead, Safeway would start touting its tough internal inspection system in an advertising campaign. Or the major food-store chains would get together and establish industry meat standards and inspection mechanisms that are more impressive than the government's sketchy inspection process. The vulnerability of bad behavior in the total information environment of the Internet is much more important to the prosperity of corporations than their vulnerability to government inspection.

Overseeing Public Safety

Technology is revolutionizing public safety. Historically, the interrelationships of crime, the police, and the public were among the toughest for a free society to handle. Somebody must have a monopoly over the right to physically coerce malefactors—the maintenance of public safety is one of the most elemental reasons for government to exist—but the police power is inherently subject to abuse. As America urbanized, metropolitan police departments were chronically beset by scandal, whether it was petty corruption, coerced confessions, or planted evidence. In the first half of the twentieth century, attempts to root out these problems through civilian oversight or internal controls had limited success. Then the pendulum swung the other way during the 1960s, when police were subjected to new procedural constraints by Supreme Court decisions. The likelihood that a felon would go to prison plummeted and the crime rate soared. By the late 1970s the pendulum had swung yet again.

Wherever the pendulum was, conscientious cops needed a way to go about their work without getting hit by bogus charges of misconduct, but citizens equally needed a way to protect themselves from cops who ran roughshod over their rights.

Both police and citizens can now have that protection in the form of cameras that record every encounter between the police and the public. They began as cameras mounted on the dashboards of highway patrol cars. A few years ago, inexpensive body cameras became available. Experience to date has been a win-win proposition. In jurisdictions using this technology, the consistent result has been that the cameras not only deter police misconduct but also deter people from falsely claiming police misconduct.[1]

In the fall of 2014, two events showcased the importance of visual evidence: the shooting death of Michael Brown in Ferguson, Missouri, and the fatal chokehold applied by a New York policeman to Eric Garner. In the Brown case, a video record would perhaps have averted the rioting (if the police officer acted with good reason) or led to prosecution (if he acted without good reason). In the Garner case, a bystander's video did exist—and the Staten Island grand jury failed to indict the police officer anyway. Some interpret this as evidence that video evidence doesn't matter. I suggest an alternative: The reaction to the Garner case was nationwide, uniting liberals and conservatives in condemnation of the failure to indict. Future grand juries and trial juries will be extremely reluctant to reach decisions that are contradicted by video evidence.

The use of video technology in law enforcement is spreading rapidly and soon will be effectively universal—good police departments want it, and bad police departments will come under too much pressure to resist buying it. We can anticipate that the lack of a visual record will eventually be treated by the courts as police malpractice.

As time goes on, it's not going to be just police who need to worry about bad behavior being recorded. So will corrupt bureaucrats, plus the larger number who misuse their authority to browbeat the people they are supposed to serve. Imagine what the defense funds could do with a video of a government official saying, "You try to fight this and we'll put you out of business." Government officials do a bad job of providing the transparency that politicians constantly promise, but technology is increasingly taking the choice out of their hands.

Public Surveillance vs. Private Surveillance

This discussion focuses on the benefits of ubiquitous video surveillance of public places and public activities. There are downsides, too—if nothing else, it is creepy to realize how much of our public activity can be caught on someone's security camera or smartphone. But public activity is just that: the things we do when we are aware that we are in a public space, which by definition means that someone might be watching. In that sense it's "our fault" if we are observed doing something embarrassing or illegal in public. The most ominous downsides of IT are associated with surveillance of private activities. The NSA and other government agencies can read our e-mail, listen to our telephone conversations, track our web surfing, and, in some cases, bug our homes or workplaces, and then store all this information indefinitely. Yes, private hackers do pose a threat to our private computers, but that's a far cry from the NSA's comprehensive daily monitoring of the nation's electronic traffic.

An additional consideration is that the great bulk of public surveillance is done by private citizens and businesses. Government has lots of traffic cameras to go with the cameras used to monitor police interactions with the public, but those resources are outweighed by the security cameras maintained by businesses plus the ability of a couple of hundred million citizens with smartphones to record whatever is happening around them. It's another example of the best and worst of times: we can celebrate the upside of public surveillance even as we worry about prospective misuse of the government's massive private surveillance.

Scraping Away Sclerosis

The most exciting potential of liberation technology is for doing what the political process cannot do: crash through the combination of regulation and collusive capitalism that stifles innovation.

From one perspective, that's what the Internet has already done. In the mid-1990s, the Internet was a patchy network of servers with clunky websites that only a computer geek could get excited about. It was not a target of regulation because there wasn't much of anything to regulate. Then, in less than a decade, the Internet was providing services that government would have loved to regulate, but they had sprung up so fast and had acquired large user bases so fast that the regulators were stymied. If the government had seen Amazon coming, for example, it would have sought to regulate it, and the big bookstore chains would have tried to enlist the regulators in giving them a competitive advantage over the upstart. But Amazon got big and popular too fast. By the time that regulators recognized what juicy targets the Internet was producing, those targets were already firmly in place and could not be regulated with impunity.

During the past decade, services made possible by information technology have undertaken a more difficult task: moving into traditional businesses that are already highly regulated and finding ways to beat the system.

GIVING PEOPLE A PLACE TO STAY. Airbnb.com was one of the first. Begun in 2008 in a loft in San Francisco, Airbnb is a way for ordinary people to rent out lodging, from a spare room to an entire house, for use as vacation housing, for travelers who are facing sold-out hotels, or for travelers who are simply tired of staying in overpriced, boring hotel rooms. Airbnb doesn't actually own a single room. It just brings together hosts and lodgers. Airbnb uses two-way feedback—ratings of lodgings by guests and ratings of lodgers by hosts—to make the system work. As of the fall of 2014, Airbnb reported more than 800,000 listings in 190 countries and had arranged lodging for more than 25 million guests.[2]

Inevitably, many jurisdictions are trying to bring Airbnb under their regulatory and taxation regimes. How these struggles will eventually play out is up in the air as I write. But this much is obvious: the regulatory state is having to play catchup.

GIVING PEOPLE A RIDE. An even more aggressive attempt to bypass the regulatory state involves real-time ridesharing, also known as "dynamic carpooling," which has taken on the taxi industry.

Taxis are highly regulated. That doesn't mean that a taxi is clean, that the trunk isn't filled with the driver's junk, or that the driver knows how to get to your destination. But in many cities, it does mean that it's hard to find even a dirty taxi with an incompetent driver, because the taxi owners and city council have colluded to limit the number of taxis on the streets.

Ridesharing is made possible by the Internet and smartphones. For readers who haven't already experienced one of the ridesharing services, I'll use Uber, the biggest one, to describe how it works. You download the Uber app to your smartphone and register, providing your credit card information. When you need to get somewhere, you open the Uber app. A map appears that shows your location, the locations of nearby Uber cars, and how long it will take the nearest one to get to you. You press the Request button, and the car comes to pick you up (you can watch its progress on the screen). You hop in, the car takes you where you want to go, and you get out (payment is handled invisibly). Just as Airbnb doesn't own a single room, Uber doesn't own a single vehicle, and it uses ratings by customers and drivers of each other as an internal regulatory mechanism.

Ridesharing services get rid of all the things that make ordinary taxis a pain. They are so convenient that many people have already decided they don't need to own cars themselves—it's just as convenient and no more expensive to go everywhere through rideshare.

Uber and its main competitors, Lyft and Sidecar, are still works in progress. Not all of Uber's drivers are paragons, and not all of its cars meet Uber's standards. Its problems get immediate media exposure because of the buzz it has created.[3] As I write, a counterattack is under way by the taxi industry.[4]

But the counterattack faces a couple of unprecedented problems. Uber doesn't apply to the municipal government for permission and struggle for months to get approval. It just moves into a city and begins operations. By the time the city council and the taxi industry can coordinate their counterattack, lots of customers have already come to love Uber. Those customers are liberals, conservatives, and everything in between. They don't see Uber as an ideological issue.[5] City councils that try to shut down Uber have encountered unprecedented public opposition.

Second, shutting down Uber is not easy—Uber often continues to operate despite injunctions to stop. Since Uber cars are unmarked, police have a hard time identifying the civilly disobedient people who insist on taking customers to destinations that they want to get to (and, one suspects, police don't see a ride in an Uber car as high on their list of transgressions that need police intervention). When fines are levied, Uber has been known to pay the fines for their drivers (just as the defense funds would do for their clients).

Third, Uber has deep pockets (as I write, valuations of Uber range up to $15 billion) and its managers have thought through their strategy. City governments that go after Uber are not dealing with a business that can be cowed by city hall. On the contrary, a city hall that tangles with Uber has to worry about how much grief it is going to bring down upon itself, in the same way that I want regulatory agencies to worry about creating problems for themselves if they litigate against defense fund clients.[6]

Companies like Airbnb and Uber are eerily analogous realizations of the kind of strategy I propose for the defense funds, with citizens of most political views agreeing that the current state of affairs is ridiculous, jointly engaging in civil disobedience where necessary, backstopped by a well-funded, private entity to do battle with the regulatory state. These extensions of the general technique into the economy, made possible by liberation technology, have potential we cannot possibly gauge. Twenty years ago, who would have been able to envision Airbnb and Uber?

The Systemic Incompetence of Visible Government

The federal government can easily hide much of its incompetence from the average citizen, who has no reason to be aware of what goes on fifteen management layers down in a federal bureaucracy. There's the occasional news story about the $400 toilet seat or the $700,000 government contract to study methane gas emissions from cows, but the federal government is mostly invisible to the average citizen. Not so with state, county, and municipal government. Much of the potential for sweeping change will arise from a broadly shared perception in certain parts of the country that government is incompetent, driven by what is happening in state capitals and city halls.

It's part of what Walter Russell Mead calls "the collapse of the blue model." At the end of World War II, the United States was in a uniquely advantageous position. The war had devastated our economic competitors and enriched us. American industries could operate without worrying about foreign competition. White-collar and blue-collar jobs were stable. Tax revenues were ample for the demands of the time. Living standards were rising, vacations were getting longer, state-supported universities were inexpensive. "Life would just go on getting better," Mead writes. "The broad outlines of our society would stay the same. The advanced industrial democracies had in fact reached the 'end of history': this is what 'developed' human society looked like and there would be no more radical changes because the picture had fully developed."[7]

But it couldn't last. Businesses that lack competition become just as sclerotic as governments. The pre-breakup AT&T did a good job of providing phone service, but it had no incentives to develop new technologies that might displace it, and no need to do so—it was cocooned in government regulations that safeguarded its monopolistic position. Lacking foreign competition, the Big Three automakers could make billions of dollars selling cars that spent far too much time in the repair shop. After a few decades of operating this way, large segments of the American economy were vulnerable to aggressive competition, and in the 1970s they began getting it. Companies across America experienced the shock of creative destruction. Unions became something that a competitive company couldn't afford. Workforces were slashed when necessary; the days of lifetime job security with the same firm were over. So was the guaranteed pension—employers would contribute to a retirement fund, but it was up to the employee to take care of it.

Government was the only sector of the economy shielded from that creative destruction. Alone among American institutions, it continued to operate according to the blue model. Even as the private sector discovered it could not afford unionization, the public sector unionized. Even as the private sector realized that defined-benefit pensions could bankrupt them, the public sector locked in ever more generous ones. Even as job insecurity became routine in the private sector, the public sector continued to make it almost impossible to fire anyone.

Over the past decade, budget crises at the state level have shown how unsustainable the governmental part of the blue model is. For example, as recently as 2001, the assets and liabilities of state pension systems were about equal. As of 2012, state-run retirement systems had a $915 billion shortfall. The most recent data show that shortfall continuing to grow, long after the economy has emerged from the worst of the Great Recession.[8] The gap is not spread equally around the country, but instead is concentrated in the bluest states—most conspicuously New York, Illinois, and California—which by now have funding deficits that will require either major tax increases or a default on the promised pensions.[9]

Blue cities are in just as much trouble as blue states. From the beginning of 2010 through the middle of 2014, thirty-eight municipalities around the country filed for bankruptcy. The most well-publicized examples are San Bernardino, Stockton, and Vallejo in California, and, of course, Detroit. But filing for bankruptcy doesn't necessarily allow for institutional revitalization. Vallejo emerged from bankruptcy in a way that left it on the hook for its pension and union obligations. The result is that it still costs $230,000 for Vallejo to employ one police officer for one year.[10]

American workers are coming to recognize that the historic trade-off people made when they began a career in government has been altered. It used to be that a government job provided lower pay but greater job security. Now, in unionized government jobs except for the top levels, pay has matched or surpassed that of comparable jobs in the private sector, while job security is nearly absolute. In 2013, the average total compensation for state and local government employees was $42.51 per hour, 45 percent more than the equivalent figure for private employees.[11] Unionized police in most jurisdictions can make good salaries, then retire after twenty years and collect a generous pension even though the retiree, still in his early forties, has taken a full-time job in the private sector. Unionized teachers almost everywhere have negotiated packages of salaries, guaranteed days off, and pensions that few private schools can match.[12]

The Internet is making these cozy arrangements visible. For example, Californians can go to TransparentCalifornia.com, which gives the income for every public employee in the state. One can search on people named "Murray," for example, and discover that in 2011 a Murray who was a Los Angeles firefighter made $273,773 in salary, overtime, and benefits; a Murray captain in the Ventura Sheriff's Department made $267,525; and a Murray deputy county administrator in Sonoma made $231,094. But it's not just the extreme cases that make the point. Another Murray in Sonoma County has the job title of accounting technician—based on the job description, a clerk.[13] Her pay and benefits came to $78,156.

The resources monopolized by generous personnel policies drain resources from the provision of essential government services. Cities with budgets that have ballooned over the last few decades don't fix potholes or collect garbage nearly as well as they did in the 1950s. The same law-enforcement system that has such generous retirement packages for police may not have enough patrol cars. In the same school system where teachers with seniority make close to six figures, students may not have enough textbooks.

Government is visibly shoddy in all sorts of ways. Contractors who work for government know that the standards are different from those of the private sector, and use the same dismissive cliché: "Good enough for government work." How do you know you're in a government office building instead a corporate one? Look at the computers. The people using them may make more money and have better benefits than their counterparts in the private sector, but the computers themselves are a couple of generations out of date. The janitors make great money and benefits compared to janitors in the private sector, but the walls haven't been repainted for years and some of the ceiling lights are burned out. How do you know that you're dealing with the government instead of with a commercial enterprise? Because, in an age when you can order just about any consumer item twenty-four hours a day, seven days a week, get it the next day, and return it with no questions asked if you don't like it, your business with the government is still likely to have to be transacted during a restricted number of hours, perhaps a limited number of days, and in person. Too often, you have to go back three times to get the thing resolved. As Mead sums it up:

> There are several ugly truths that the country (and especially the states whose governments are bigger and bluer than the rest) will be facing in the next ten years.
>
> First, voters simply will not be taxed to cover the costs of blue government. Voters with insecure job tenure and, at best, defined-contribution rather than defined-benefit pensions will simply not pay higher taxes so that bureaucrats can enjoy lifetime tenure and secure pensions.
>
> Second, voters will not accept the shoddy services that blue government provides. Government is going to have to respond to growing "consumer" demand for more user-friendly, customer-oriented approaches. The arrogant lifetime bureaucrat at the Department of

Motor Vehicles is going to have to turn into the Starbucks barista offering service with a smile.

Third, government must reconcile itself to its declining ability to regulate a post-blue economy with regulatory models and instincts rooted in the past. The collapse of a social model is a complicated, drawn out and often painful affair. The blue model has been declining for thirty years already, and it is not yet finished with its decline and fall. But decline and fall it will, and as the remaining supports of the system erode, the slow decline and decay is increasingly likely to bring on a crash.[14]

Mead referred to "voters," not "Republican voters," with good reason. It's not just conservatives who are grumbling about how their tax money is used. Failure to fix potholes is not a partisan complaint.

The Alienation of the People Who Pay the Tab for Government

The potential for sweeping change is also going to be fed by the looming fiscal crunch at the federal level. In its 2014 projections for the budget and economy, the Congressional Budget Office (CBO) projected that from 2013 to 2024, federal outlays would increase from $3.5 trillion to $6.0 trillion—using unrounded numbers, a 74 percent increase in spending in constant dollars.[15] That additional $2.5 trillion is an amount equal to the size of the entire budget as recently as 2002. It is a particularly stupendous number when you consider that this additional $2.5 trillion will be used to service a population that will have grown by just 9 percent since 2013.[16]

Where is the government going to get the money? Based on current laws (the basis on which the CBO is required to make its projections), the government will have to borrow a lot of it. The CBO projected that the federal budget deficit, which spiked to $1.4 trillion in 2009, would fall to a "low" of $478 billion in 2015 and then begin rising, passing $1 trillion in 2022 and continuing upward.[17]

Meanwhile, economic growth is expected to generate an additional $2.2 trillion in revenues. But a shrinking proportion of the population will generate that increased wealth. Two factors contribute to the shrinkage. First, the population is aging. The leading edge of the baby-boom generation turned sixty in 2006, beginning an eighteen-year bulge in the percentage of Americans leaving the workforce and starting to collect Social Security and Medicare benefits. Second, working-age Americans are dropping out of the labor force. An increasing proportion of working-age Americans are being defined as physically disabled, thereby qualifying for lifetime disability payments and free health care. Still other working-age people are simply leaving the labor force, to be supported by spouses, relatives, girlfriends, boyfriends, or welfare. The figure below uses actual labor force participation rates for 1960 to 2013 and the CBO's projections for 2014 to 2024 to show the implications of these trends.

The revenue-generation burden on people in the labor force has been growing steeply in the 21st century and is about to get worse.

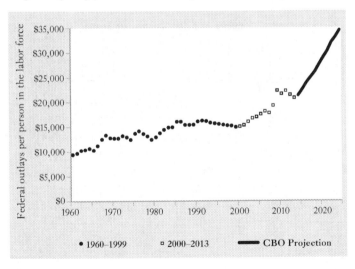

Source: For 1960–2013, Bureau of Labor Statistics and OMB. For 2014–2024, CBO. Outlays are expressed in 2010 dollars.

The graph shows the ratio of total federal outlays to the number of people in the labor force. In 1960, the revenue-generation burden was a little less than $10,000 per person. From 1960 through 1985, the burden grew to a little more than $16,000.[18] From 1986 through 1999, the ratio dropped. Then the new century brought a substantial increase, from a little less than $15,000 in 1999 to almost $21,000 in 2013 (and an even higher spike during the Great Recession). But not even that rising burden matches what we can expect during the next decade. Based on the CBO's projections, we can expect the burden to reach nearly $34,500 in 2024.

Now consider what a disproportionate amount of that burden must be carried by the top few deciles of that labor force. The IRS annually breaks down income-tax payments by income group based on adjusted gross income (AGI), showing the percentage of taxes paid by returns with AGIs in the top 1, 5, 10, 25, and 50 percent of returns. The following numbers refer to 2011, the most recent available data as I write:

- The filers in the top 1 percent of AGI paid 35 percent of all income taxes.
- The top 10 percent paid 56 percent of all income taxes.
- The top quartile paid 86 percent of all income taxes.

People who are not in the top quartile of earnings may view these numbers with equanimity ("Those rich guys can afford it"). Probably a majority of them would vote in favor of higher taxes for the rich. But only a tiny minority of the people within the top quartile are "rich" in the sense of mansions, private jets, or yachts. Sixty percent of the people in the top quartile are in the eleventh to twenty-fifth percentiles, with AGIs ranging from $70,492 to $120,136. To them, the idea that they are "rich" is crazy. A middle-aged couple in that income range is likely to have a couple of children, live in a modest house that carries a large mortgage, and drive a Honda. They're trying to save for their children's college educations and have little if any discretionary income.

Another 36 percent of those in the top quartile were in the second through tenth percentiles, with AGIs of $120,136 to $388,905. You will have a hard time convincing most of them that they are rich. At the bottom of the range, they live like those in the eleventh to twenty-fifth percentiles. At the top of that range, they are affluent, but their lifestyles are those of the upper middle class, not of the wealthy (especially if they live in an expensive city). No private jet. A Lexus, not a Rolls. A nice home, not a mansion.

The fabled 1 percent, with AGIs of $388,905 or more, does indeed include the rich who live a visibly rich lifestyle. But they are a fraction of the people in the 1 percent. Less than 1 percent of the 1 percent made more than a million dollars in 2011.[19] The hedge-fund managers and the IT billionaires who live in a different universe from the rest of us are somewhere near the top 1 percent of the top 1 percent of the top 1 percent.

Meanwhile, half of those in the top 1 percent of income as of 2011 had total incomes between $368,000 and $443,000. They are doing quite well. If they live outside the most expensive cities in the country, they can afford a lifestyle that is obviously affluent. But that's just half of the top 1 percent.

My point is that almost all of the people in the top quartile who supply 86 percent of the federal government's income-tax revenue are not billionaires or even obviously rich, but corporate managers, owners of small businesses, attorneys, physicians, and other professionals who typically work long hours, often six or seven days a week, have been doing so from the outset of their careers, and are often married to a spouse who does exactly the same thing. They have earned their success.

Now take another look at that graph of the steeply increasing demand upon people in the labor force to pay for the growth in the federal government that the next decade will bring. The CBO divided revenue into four streams—income taxes, social-insurance taxes (Social Security and Medicare), corporate taxes, and "other." Income taxes and social-insurance taxes account for 82 percent of the total. The top quartile of earners are responsible for shouldering around three-quarters of that 82 percent—and they will be responsible for shouldering about the same proportion of the increased $2.5 trillion in spending that the CBO projects for 2024.[20]

The IRS reports on the percentage of income taxes paid by different income groups get a lot of publicity. They are a common topic of conversation among people in the top quartile of income, and an impassioned topic of conversation among the people in the top decile. When they read about politicians demanding that the rich pay their "fair share," there is a lot of anger—not so much about the size of their tax bills, per se, as about what they perceive as an injustice: they see themselves as hardworking citizens who provide a disproportionate amount of the government revenues that makes it possible for those politicians to keep spending so many trillions so inefficiently. The alienation crosses party lines.

The Alienation of Big Business

Big business has an abysmal track record with respect to supporting limited government, but we shouldn't be surprised. The function of corporations is to make a profit, not to defend free markets. Unless the owner or CEO has a personal commitment to limited government, managers of corporations have generally been willing to use the legislative process to acquire tax breaks or competitive advantages without worrying about the abstract role of government.[21] Most of them have learned to live with government regulation as well. Since the regulation of specific industries began with the railroads back in the nineteenth century, the most influential corporations have been adept in capturing the regulatory process so that it favors them and makes life difficult for those who would try to enter their markets. When economy-wide regulation took off in the 1960s and 1970s, big business made the best of it, as recounted in chapter 4. Big corporations have become deeply entwined in the iron triangle of regulators, politicians, and special interests that makes lobbying such a lucrative enterprise in Washington. Occasionally, the willingness of corporations to connive in aggressively anticompetitive laws has vindicated Ayn Rand's most savage portraits of businesspeople colluding with government.

Underlying most of the collusive capitalism has been the less blameworthy mind-set described in chapter 5: "Like it or not, this is the world in which we've got to compete." Many business executives openly despise the process. They may not be Madisonians, but they typically take pride in what they do and seek to provide value for money with a good product or service. They don't like being treated as cash cows for campaign contributions, but if that's what it takes to stay in the game, they do it. Recently, however, executives have been treated not as cash cows for campaign contributions but as cash cows for supplementing government budgets through the criminalization of business.

The vulnerability of corporations and their executives to criminal prosecution for their business activities goes back to the early twentieth century, but those violations usually involved crimes by ordinary definitions. The 1940s qualitatively broadened their vulnerability to criminal prosecution through the introduction of the responsible corporate officer (RCO) doctrine discussed in chapter 3, whereby a corporate official could be criminally charged for what amounted to a management error with no awareness on his part of wrongdoing. Subsequently, that was broadened to include management errors of omission as well as errors of commission. Then in the 1980s, Rudy Giuliani made his political reputation as New York City's district attorney with highly publicized "perp walks" in which Wall Street executives were taken in handcuffs from their offices to police cars, arrested on charges of financial wrongdoing.

In the last few decades, this criminalization of American business has taken a new turn. As recently as 2002, the total annual criminal fines levied on corporations was less than $100 million. Only once between 1994 and 2002 did total fines exceed $1 billion, and then mostly because of a single large fine paid by Pfizer. Then in 2007, total fines reached $2.5 billion. In 2011 they surpassed $4 billion.[22]

The size of individual fines also went up. In 1994, the average was under half a million dollars. In 2010, the average hit almost $16 millon. In 2013, a new record was set following the BP oil spill: $1.26 billion.[23]

Then things went crazy. In just the first eight months of 2014, *The Economist* was able to identify settlements with major banks and corporations that had produced something in the neighborhood of $100 billion in fines. A single fine imposed on a French firm called BNP Paribas for breaches of American sanctions against Sudan and Iran came to $9 billion.[24]

What's going on? One possibility is that corporations have become incredibly more evil over the past few decades (and especially in the past few years), or that the Department of Justice has become incredibly more efficient at uncovering evildoing. Legal scholar Brandon Garrett makes that case, in more elegant terms and with many specific examples, in his book *Too Big to Jail*.[25] Another possibility is that we are watching shakedowns. As *The Economist* described it, "The formula is simple: find a large company that may (or may not) have done something wrong; threaten its managers with commercial ruin, preferably with criminal charges; force them to use their shareholders' money to pay an enormous fine to drop the charges in a secret settlement (so nobody can check the details). Then repeat with another large company."[26]

These settlements are known as *deferred-prosecution agreements*. Deferred-prosecution agreements had never been used before 1992. Only 17 occurred from 1993 through 2003. From 2004 to 2014, 278 such agreements were entered into. Now they are ubiquitous. Here's how Garrett approvingly describes their purpose: "Prosecutors now try to rehabilitate a company by helping it to put systems in place to detect and prevent crime among its employees and, more broadly, to foster a culture of ethics and integrity inside the company."[27] If the corporation accedes to these conditions and pays the fine, the government agrees not to bring a criminal prosecution. Among other things, the agreement usually involves embedding government enforcers within the firm.

What is rehabilitative from Garrett's point of view looks to others like the apotheosis of the regulatory state: use complex regulatory regimes to threaten years of unbearable legal hassle and expense, effectively coerce the deferred-prosecution agreement, and thereby insert government oversight into the interior of the organization and bring in hundreds of millions, or billions, of dollars of revenue.[28]

So far, corporate America has seldom fought back. It's the shareholders' money that pays the fines, and settling in secret enables executives to avoid career-ending publicity and perhaps jail time. In addition, there is a pragmatic risk/reward calculation to be made on behalf of the shareholders. Is it better to pay a billion now and get on with business, or engage in a multiyear legal battle that will cost at least hundreds of millions and may end up costing an even bigger fine? Or cost the corporation its existence? The experience of Arthur Andersen, the accounting firm, is cautionary. It fought an obstruction of justice charge in court, was convicted by the jury, appealed, and won a reversal from a unanimous Supreme Court. But the initial conviction destroyed the firm, and vindication came too late.[29] Knuckling under for the big shakedowns follows the same logic that leads corporations to reach out-of-court settlements with employees who allege racial or gender discrimination. Even if a charge is frivolous, it's cheaper to pay out of court than go to court and win.

If the government has been behaving with integrity in this process, and exposure of the sealed settlements would reveal that the companies have behaved badly enough to warrant their multibillion-dollar settlements, then corporations have no choice but to start behaving better, and that's as it should be. But if it is the government that has been behaving badly, selectively choosing what regulations to enforce against whom so as to yield a large cash windfall, corporate America will have to start asking itself whether it can afford to coexist profitably with the regulatory state.

Part of corporate America is already eager to rebel—many CEOs are already angry with the regulatory state on principle. But you don't have to hold Madisonian principles to be angered by government acting like the Mafia. Shakedowns are ugly. If that is in fact what has been going on, the time is ripening for a broad swath of CEOs to start treating government as "them," an entity to be resisted.

It will not be an across-the-board shift. Collusive capitalism has become essential to the defense, pharmaceutical, health-care, agribusiness, and financial industries, and their incentives to go along to get along will probably be too powerful to resist.[30] But that leaves large numbers of companies that are less dependent on government contracts and less enmeshed in the regulatory web. The most promising leader of a revolt against the regulatory state is the IT industry. It is still far less regulated than other industries, and the corporate cultures of places like Google, Apple, and Facebook are independent, even libertarian.

Here's where the activities of the defense funds come into play. If the defense funds have been operating for some years and have successfully challenged the government's enforcement of illegitimate regulations, large corporations will take notice. At some point, some of them will start defending themselves. If large components of corporate America decide to join the fight against intrusive government, it could be a game-changing event.

Feisty States and Cities

When Jimmy Carter left office, federalism seemed to be as dead as the enumerated powers. The original dual federalism that prevailed until the constitutional revolution of 1937–1942, in which the states still had reasonably well-understood areas of independent authority, gave way to "cooperative" federalism. Under cooperative federalism, the federal government had nearly unlimited power to override a state's policies. At the same time, large cash grants increasingly drifted downward from Washington to the states—accompanied, of course, by instruction about how those funds might be used.[31]

Then Ronald Reagan came to office with a pledge to devolve authority to the states. He was able to accomplish some of that with executive orders, increased use of block grants, and other devices that loosened the strings attached to federal aid, but his most effective ally was William Rehnquist, whom Reagan elevated from justice to chief justice of the Supreme Court in 1986. Rehnquist was the guiding force behind a series of decisions during his twenty-year tenure as chief justice that led to what has been called "the new federalism."[32] It was not a return to the pre-1930s division of power. Its real effects on the states' independence were minor, and mostly involved greater state participation in processes that remained ultimately under the control of the feds. But most legal scholars agree with Kathleen Sullivan's assessment that the "Rehnquist Court's federalism revival was theoretically deep even if practically limited."[33] The Roberts Court has continued that revival to some degree.

During the last decade, these modest increments in federalism have been augmented by what can best be described as increased feistiness on the part of the states. It is reflected in their approach to regulation. Both OSHA and the EPA permit state agencies to conduct enforcement activities, and about half of the states have availed themselves of that option. A study of 1.6 million OSHA audits from 1990 through 2010 found differences between the outcomes from inspections conducted directly by the feds and those conducted by state employees. State inspectors were more sensitive to local economic conditions, reducing the number of violations as unemployment increased. They also issued smaller fines than the federal inspectors, a procedure, the authors concluded, that "likely results in fewer hearings and challenges on the part of firms, removing a layer from the bureaucracy of enforcement and the costly employment of legal professionals and regulatory consultants on the part of sanctioned firms."[34]

A progressive website in favor of strict enforcement found similar differences between state and federal inspectors in EPA actions. The author complained that many states have "shifted resources toward compliance assistance programs" and have even gone so far as to create "customer service centers." Many states impose smaller penalties than the EPA itself assessed in similar circumstances, and "do not follow EPA guidance for responding to violations with 'timely and appropriate' enforcement actions." The list of the states' sins go on, concluding with the worst of

all: "Almost one-half of the states have enacted environmental audit privilege or immunity laws that preclude penalties for violations voluntarily
disclosed and corrected by regulated entities as a result of environmental
audits."[35] Shocking.

Apart from subtly competing with federal regulatory agencies, the
states have also been engaged in various forms of independent action that
seem plainly unconstitutional. The Supremacy Clause states that federal
laws "shall be the supreme law of the land; and the judges in every state
shall be bound thereby." In that light, it is remarkable that, as I write,
twenty-one states and the District of Columbia have passed laws legal-
izing marijuana in some form despite the Controlled Substances Act of
1970, which makes the production, distribution, or use of marijuana illegal. Most of these decriminalize the possession of small amounts of
marijuana or legalize marijuana for medical use. Two states, Colorado
and Washington, have legalized marijuana for recreational use. On August 29, 2013, the Department of Justice announced that it would defer
its right to challenge these state laws, contingent on the states establishing "strict regulatory regimes that protect the eight federal [enforcement]
interests" that are the Department of Justice's highest priority.[36] Or to put
it another way, the Department of Justice has affirmed that the federal
government can challenge those laws, which are plainly unconstitutional,
but, for the moment, never mind.

The marijuana laws are just one example of a broader phenomenon.
From the end of the Civil War through the 1960s, the traditional justification for federalism was overshadowed by a "states' rights" movement
that was identified with the South and its efforts to preserve a racially
segregated society. But in recent decades, as political scientists Christopher Banks and John Blakeman write, liberals have discovered the merits
of federalism:

> Some progressives and others observe that the growth in federal
> power has been matched by efforts in the states to legislate in social
> policy areas that traditionally have been ignored or scorned by fed-
> eral officials, especially in times of conservative control. These ini-
> tiatives, which encompass advancing gay and lesbian rights, banking
> regulation, health care, environmental control and international law
> principles, have coalesced to form "blue state federalism."[37]

Conservatives in general and Madisonians in particular have always been advocates of muscular federalism. That the left is joining in that advocacy, albeit for different reasons, gives reason to expect that the state marijuana laws are just the thin edge of the wedge. The federal government does not rely on voluntary compliance with its laws only from individuals. It also must rely on the voluntary compliance of state and municipal governments. In the past, liberal administrations in Washington have been comfortable enforcing their will on conservative states and municipalities. The marijuana case demonstrates how reluctant a liberal administration is to do the same thing with liberal states and municipalities. It is a precedent begging to be exploited.

A Dispirited Adversary

This brings us to the state of the federal bureaucracy. Bureaucrats have to endure popular abuse that is often over the top. "In America," as political scientist Peter Schuck has observed, "bureaucracy is often used as an epithet, evoking ubiquitous red tape, rigidity, soullessness, waste, unreasonableness, impenetrability, and Kafkaesque cruelty and arbitrariness."[38] Since it will soon appear that I am piling on, let me begin with some caveats.

Students of bureaucracy have consistently found that government workers who are engaged in tasks that carry with them a strong sense of mission—such as the military, police, firefighters, paramedics, and air-traffic controllers—are as likely as anyone in the private sector to perform at a high level of excellence. Some bureaucrats in the regulatory agencies with especially sensitive responsibilities—those charged with ensuring the safe handling of nuclear-weapons material, for example—presumably have a similarly strong sense of mission. To that, let me add what should be obvious: As individuals, bureaucrats are as nice, honest, loving to their children, and helpful to their neighbors as any other group of people—or such is the impression of someone who has counted many government employees as friends and acquaintances during four decades of life in the Washington area.

None of this is inconsistent with the larger truth: When the pedestrian tasks of government are involved, the rules by which government bureaucracies are run foster poor performance and low morale. I will limit the discussion to the way federal bureaucracies are structured and administered, but they apply generically to state and municipal bureaucracies as well. For readers who want the details, Paul Light's *A Government Ill Executed* is a highly regarded source, and Peter Schuck's chapter on bureaucracy in *Why Government Fails So Often* is an excellent synthesis of the recent literature. James Q. Wilson's *Bureaucracy*, first published in 1989, remains the indispensable basic text.

LEADERSHIP. The top jobs are filled by people selected by the president, often for reasons having nothing to do with their technical or administrative skills. That's a recipe for ineffectual management, especially when the incoming appointees have not had experience in Washington or are not familiar with the institution's history. Even when the newly confirmed administrators are experienced and competent, career civil-service employees all know ahead of time that the new guys are not going to be around for long.[39] The median tenure of political appointees is 2.5 years, with a quarter of them serving fewer than 18 months.[40] Many senior jobs go unfilled for long periods of time, sometimes entire presidential terms. In recent history, the Bureau of Alcohol, Tobacco, Firearms, and Explosives did not have a senate-confirmed director for six years.[41]

HIERARCHY. The typical bureaucracy in the federal government is an efficiency expert's nightmare. In the private sector, vibrant businesses are managerially streamlined, with only a few management layers and easy lines of communication between decision-makers and personnel on the front line. Vibrant or not, few corporations have more than six management layers. The median for cabinet departments in the federal government is twenty-two layers.[42] The functional distinctions among these layers are excruciatingly vague, with sixty-four executive titles open for occupancy.[43] Yes, there really are people whose job title is "deputy associate deputy administrator" and "chief of staff to the associate deputy assistant secretary." These paralyzingly numerous layers of management help explain why getting a decision on anything takes forever, and why bright ideas generated by federal employees are unlikely to get through all the approvals that are required to make a change. It also helps explain why just about everything in most federal offices is behind the times, whether we're talking about design, organization, or equipment. Even getting routine office supplies is often a hassle.

COMPENSATION. In the federal government, as in state and local governments, positions below senior management have excellent salaries and benefits compared to similar jobs in the private sector.[44] But in 2014 the federal salary scale topped out at $130,810 for the highest step of the highest grade in the General Schedule and at $181,500 for the Senior Executive Service—levels far below the compensation that a senior corporate manager gets.[45] The result: Talented managers seldom want to go into government in the first place, talented managers who do go into government get hired away by the private sector, and untalented government managers stay with the government career ladder and end up occupying many of the senior career slots.

JOB TENURE. One of the most crippling defects of the federal bureaucracy is that people are so hard to get rid of. In the private and public sectors alike, many hiring decisions are mistakes. Workers who are incompetent, lazy, or devious not only impair the productivity of the organization by failing to do their jobs well, they also create resentment and low morale among their coworkers. Besides that, people who know they can't be fired are not nearly as responsive to a supervisor's direction as workers who can be fired.

The private sector has two resources for culling incompetent workers: layoffs when business is bad or a reorganization has eliminated positions, and firing for cause. The government hardly ever lays off anybody, and firing someone for cause requires such an investment of time and effort (the process takes one to two years) that the entire federal government fired just 0.55 percent of its workers in 2010.[46] Unless government's hiring procedures are an order of magnitude more precise than the private sector's—an absurd assumption—it is inevitable that government bureaucracies are filled with people who would long since have been pushed out the door for incompetence if they worked in the private sector.

COMPETENCE ON THE JOB. Nobody really knows just how bad the situation is. The private sector has bottom lines that tell companies how well their organizations are doing as a whole. Usually there are also measures of productivity for specific jobs. Few jobs within the federal bureaucracy have such measures. There are, of course, supervisors' performance ratings of their subordinates—and they are meaningless. This was brought to public attention in 2014 when a scandal at the Veterans'

Administration broke. A congressional hearing into the many and serious failures of the VA, including a cover-up of those failures by senior management, revealed that *all* of the 470 senior executives at the VA had received annual ratings of "fully successful" or higher.[47] Of course, that also meant that none had received either of the two lowest ratings, "minimally satisfactory" or "unsatisfactory." A spokesperson for the VA defended the ratings by pointing out that in the entire federal government, only fifteen senior executives had received either of the two lowest ratings in the most recent year.

HOW HARD THEY WORK. The public's widespread belief that government workers show up late and go home early has some basis in fact. An analysis of time-use data collected by Census Bureau indicates that over the course of year, the average government employee works 152 fewer hours than employees in the private sector—equivalent to 3.8 forty-hour work weeks.[48]

MORALE. Paul Light conducted a survey of morale among federal and private-sector employees. The results once again support the stereotypes. Light found that federal employees liked their benefits and job security, and not much else. They were much less satisfied than private-sector employees with their opportunities to develop new skills and accomplish something worthwhile. They were dissatisfied with the resources they were given to do their jobs well. They gave poor ratings to the competence of their colleagues and supervisors. They rated their organizations unfavorably when it came to spending money wisely, helping people, acting fairly, and being worthy of trust.[49]

It is bad that government has these problems because it means government often performs its legitimate functions poorly and inefficiently. It is propitious because these problems make the federal government an easily discouraged adversary in cases of low-level civil disobedience.

That statement is not true for prominent cases. Surely the Department of Justice puts its best talent into key antitrust cases, the EPA does so when it takes action against the biggest polluters, and the FBI does so when it's going after the best-organized crime syndicates.

But most of the open-ended possibilities for rebuilding liberty will not involve landmark cases that the federal government can focus on—there need be no Gettysburgs or Yorktowns, just hundreds of hit-and-run guerrilla actions. The situation facing the defense funds will be an instructive model for subsequent steps to roll back the reach of government.

The defense funds are going to be defending not huge corporations but many individuals and small businesses—cases that won't be contested by a task force of attorneys but by one or two people far down in the chain of command. Some of those may end up being landmark cases, as *Sackett* became, but, like *Sackett*, they will start out as small, inconspicuous ones.

In other words, the contest between the defense funds and the government is going to be a mismatch between people who typically feel strongly that they are being arbitrarily and capriciously harassed by the government, represented by attorneys who believe strongly in the justice of their cause, fighting against government bureaucrats of middling talent and little motivation to work extra unpaid hours, for whom contesting a case against an aggressive defendant looks like a lot of hard work for no reward. They will know that a defendant won't even have to pay the fine if the government wins the case.

"A lot of hard work for no reward" brings us to the ways in which the defense funds can convert the dysfunctions of the legal system and turn them into weapons. For the defense funds, the point of litigating a case is not necessarily to win it in court. The defense fund has accomplished its goal if the regulatory agency subsequently begins backing off cases whenever it hears that a defense fund has gotten involved. It's not that the agency fears the possibility of losing. It fears the amount of work it will take to litigate the case.

These observations about the nature of the bureaucracy and of the legal system apply specifically to the work of the defense funds. But they also have another implication. Maybe, just maybe, when the other enabling forces come together, the potential for change is far broader than anything that the defense funds accomplish directly. And that in turn brings us to a speculative look at the future.

CHAPTER 14

ONCE THE CURTAIN HAS BEEN
PULLED ASIDE

*In which I conclude by presenting hopeful but not un-
realistic scenarios of what can happen when enough
people are saying of government-engendered problems,
"This is ridiculous."*

RONALD REAGAN CAME to the presidency in 1981 having declared that his strategy regarding the Cold War was "We win,
they lose." It was seen as a foolish and dangerous position by
everyone from academic Sovietologists to Henry Kissinger and Richard
Nixon. Presidents since the end of World War II had pledged themselves
to no more than containing communism and, latterly, reaching détente
with the Soviet Union. None had said anything remotely like "We win,
they lose."

Ten years later, the Soviet Union ceased to exist. When Western
scholars subsequently got access to the Soviet government's internal documents, it turned out that the Soviet Union in 1981 was already a hollow
shell, with a sick economy and political institutions that set new standards of sclerosis. What had Reagan added to these difficulties? Scholars
are still trying to determine the complete answer to that question, but it
is already clear that Reagan poked a shaky Soviet system in some vulnerable places—by arming the mujahideen in Afghanistan with Stinger mis-
siles; starting a technological arms race that the Soviet leadership knew
it could not match (Star Wars was especially unnerving); and assault-
ing the Soviet Union's pride rhetorically, from his "Evil Empire" speech

(surprisingly dismaying to the Soviets, we have since learned) to his "Mr. Gorbachev, tear down this wall" speech in Berlin.

For these and other reasons, the image of the Soviet Union changed, without and within. Before Reagan, the Soviet Union had been seen as one of the world's two superpowers, and many thought it was the ascendant one. During Reagan's time in office, the curtain was pulled aside, and the Soviet Union was exposed for what it was: a Third World country with nuclear weapons. The Soviets blundered into halfhearted, haphazard reforms, and an incompetent, divided, and dispirited *nomenklatura* finished the job without further assistance from the West.

What Reagan accomplished is analogous to what I want the defense funds to do: not pull down the US government (that seems excessive), but pull aside the curtain on one component of that government, the regulatory state, and expose the Wizard of Oz within.

Doing so might ultimately accomplish much more than plaguing the regulatory state. It could also change the zeitgeist. This is where the parallels with the Cold War are most apt. The Soviets took for granted that the arrow of history went only one way—they had added client states regularly since the end of World War II, and the West had never taken one back. Similarly, progressives have lived in a world where government constantly expands and conservatives can only slow its growth. If a significant portion of the *Code of Federal Regulations* were to become de facto unenforceable—if it can be seen that the reach of government can actually shrink, not just be slowed—all sorts of previously unthinkable things become possible. That's why I have offered the preceding discussions of the rediversification of America in chapter 12 and of the promising conditions for change in chapter 13, to give a sense of how propitious the moment is. But propitious for what? How are all these positive forces going to work their magic? What happens next?

Two Hundred Years from Now

Sometimes predicting the broad shape of the distant future can be a fruitful way of backing into implications for what might have to happen in the interim. Specifically, let's think about the overriding implications of growing wealth and advancing technology over the long term—two centuries, let's say.

Economic historians have established that per-capita wealth was effectively flat for societies throughout the world from the beginning of the Christian era until the seventeenth century. Then, starting in England and the Netherlands, subsequently spreading across western Europe, per-capita wealth began to rise and has continued rising ever since.[1] The same thing happened in the United States, starting behind Europe but growing at an even faster pace thereafter. The earliest systematic calculation of America's national wealth goes back 125 years, to 1889. Here's what the growth in per-capita national wealth has looked like since then:

American wealth per capita has increased secularly since records have been kept.

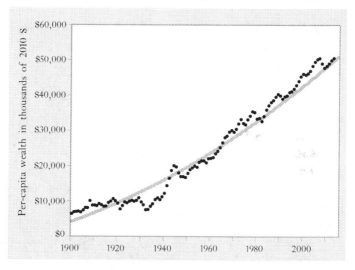

Source: US Bureau of the Census (1975), Table F1–5, Bureau of Economic Analysis, www.bea.gov. Based on GNP from 1889 to 1928, GDP from 1929 to 2013.[2]

Per-capita wealth has grown with remarkably close fidelity to the fitted trendline superimposed on the yearly data for 125 years. There have been anomalies—the Great Depression of the 1930s and the rebound during World War II and, more recently, the prosperity of the 1990s and early 2000s—but other times that have been perceived as boom years or fallow periods have been close to the overall trend.[3] The consistency of growth gives reason to hope that it will take public policy of Soviet stupidity to bring that growth to a halt over the long haul—which is not to say that it won't happen, but that it will require policymakers to ignore everything economists have learned about how wealth is created.

Let's hope for the best, and assume that two centuries from now the upward trend has continued. It's probably unrealistic to expect a continuation of the nonlinear trendline in the figure on page 249. But suppose that we grow linearly at the rate that has characterized the economy since the end of World War II. That would produce per-capita GDP in 2215 of almost $160,000 in 2010 dollars. Any subset of more than twenty years in the postwar era produces a projection greater than $150,000 per person. Today's per-capita GDP is about one-third of that. What couldn't we do today if we had three times the wealth?

It's not just wealth that we can expect to transform the range of the possible. The information technologies that have revolutionized daily life over the last three decades will look primitive compared to those of two hundred years from now. We will fully understand the human genome, and along with it deep truths about how human beings flourish that can guide public policy. For that matter, humankind will long since have acquired the ability to modify its own genome. The natural outcome of this new knowledge will be to enhance human capabilities and empower the individual in fabulous ways. It is, of course, possible that some nightmarish political dystopia will have triumphed, but that is not the most plausible scenario.

National wealth that dwarfs today's, and technology that gives the individual access to total information and the capacity to apply that information to everyday life: *Under those conditions, it is unimaginable that Americans will still think the best way to live is to be governed by armies of bureaucrats enforcing thousands of minutely prescriptive rules.* Somehow, the American polity will have evolved toward more efficient ways of working and living together. In the language I have used throughout this book, America will do a better job of leaving people free to live their lives as they see fit as long as they accord the same freedom to everyone else.

We aren't able to predict exactly how the miracle will have happened, but we may reasonably predict that it *will* have happened two centuries from now. There will be too much money and too many technological resources to make today's leviathan government necessary. Think in terms of the problems that gave rise to the EPA, OSHA, Dodd-Frank, and the Affordable Care Act, and how few of them are likely to survive until 2215. Of course new problems will also appear, but greater wealth and technology really do reduce the net number of purely technical difficulties. Compare 1815 and 2015 in terms of the technical difficulties of preparing a family meal, traveling from New York to Boston, curing a headache, or running a safe and environmentally friendly foundry.

Getting from Here to There

That optimistic view leaves open the question of how the evolution away from today's intrusive state can get started now. My generic explanation is simple, again inspired by Stein's law, "If something can't go on forever, it will stop." I propose that people don't naturally continue doing stupid things forever. A great deal of progress in our current situation requires little more than that we stop doing stupid things. That, in turn, requires that reasonable people with a wide range of political views agree regarding a given state of affairs, "This is ridiculous."

A Government of the Factions, by the Factions, and for the Factions

This book has described many problems of which reasonable people will already say "This is ridiculous." It is ridiculous for a nation to have a tax code four million words long. Ridiculous to have bureaucracies with twenty-two management layers. Ridiculous to take ten years to decide court cases.

The same may be said of many of the public-policy problems that vex us. For example: Some schools serving disadvantaged children are disorderly and sometimes dangerous, even in cities where per-student expenditures on schools are high. That's ridiculous. What percentage of parents would voluntarily send their children to such a school? One percent? Half of one percent? A tenth? It's not that the problem is unsolvable. Human beings have known how to operate orderly schools for millennia. Disorderly students are first punished and, if they don't mend their ways, expelled.

Therein lies the reason that we have the problem. People can't agree on what is to be done with the troublemakers. But there are known solutions—not perfect ones, but solutions that achieve the overriding goal of allowing students who want to learn to do so. And so I repeat: When some schools have a problem that hardly any parent, including the most progressive, would tolerate in a school that their own children attended, and when there are known solutions, it is ridiculous that any child must attend a disorderly and unsafe school. We need only muster the will to make them orderly and safe. And so progress should be possible. But it isn't.

Consider the case of the tax deduction for mortgage interest. It is regressive. That's not disputable. Richer people tend to have more expensive houses and, since the tax break exists, it is usually to their advantage to carry big mortgages. To be specific, about a third of the total mortgage tax deductions goes to households in the top 5 percent of income.[4] People can argue from principle for progressive taxes or flat taxes, but no political philosophy tries to make a principled case for a regressive tax. And so it should be possible to get rid of the mortgage interest deduction. But it isn't.

Or consider a more abstruse example of something that's ridiculous. It's ridiculous that the cost of routine health care has not been falling for decades.[5] By *routine health care* I mean treatment of the garden-variety ailments and accidents that account for almost all of our visits to a physician's office: things like a sinus infection, strep throat, a gash that needs closing, a broken bone, a rash, childhood diseases, a bad sprain, or GI distress. The real costs of dealing with such problems has typically been going down. That the costs being charged for dealing with them have gone up at all, let alone soared, should be a scandal.

The biggest reduction in costs has been produced by antibiotics, which have consigned many painful, expensive, and sometimes fatal ailments to medical history. But the reduction in costs has occurred in almost everything that physicians do. Wounds that used to require stitching often can be closed with adhesives. Blood tests that used to require labor-intensive analysis are now done automatically by machines.

Ulcers that used to require surgery are now controlled through over-the-counter pills.

It's not just garden-variety ailments that are now cheaper to fix. Cost per outcome has been dropping for many medical technologies. Laparoscopic surgery is an example: The cost of laparoscopic instruments is greater than the cost of a scalpel and retractors for traditional surgery, but the patient goes home much sooner, saving hospitalization costs. Those savings occur with every operation, while the cost of the laparoscopic instruments is amortized over many operations.

Even the labor costs of health care should be falling, because productivity per employee has been rising. Remote monitoring of symptoms means that it takes fewer nurses to keep track of more patients. Improvements in technologies for everything from hospital beds to food preparation increase the productivity of support staff. If other forces weren't getting in the way, the cost of keeping a person in a hospital bed for a day would be going down.

That the charges for routine health care have soared has nothing to do with the underlying real costs but with the medical cartel, malpractice insurance, regulations, and other ways in which the health-care industry is segregated from ordinary market forces that would produce lower costs. In light of the reality that most costs of routine health care have been dropping but the prices we actually pay for such health care have been soaring, progress should be possible. But it isn't.

Every one of the ridiculous things in these examples has a constituency that is able to block a sensible, affordable fix for it—not because the fix wouldn't work but because for some reason, sometimes a complicated reason, implementing the fix would not be in the self-interest of teachers, physicians, health-insurance companies, or the politicians' own political survival. Currently, their interests must be satisfied before any fix becomes possible.

We have reached precisely that state of government that the founders most feared: one in which factions have taken over—*factions* as Madison defined the word in *Federalist #10*: "a number of citizens . . . who are united and actuated by some common impulse of passion, or of interest, adverse to the rights of other citizens, or to the permanent and aggregate interests of the community." The five chapters of Part I may be read as an extended description of Madison's nightmare come true. We now have a government of the factions, by the factions, and for the factions. Or, if you prefer the modern term, government of special interests, by special interests, and for special interests.

Breaking the Logjam

Now imagine a time in the future when somehow the grip of special interests has been loosened. What needs to have happened? First, when a problem was sufficiently ridiculous, people of different ideologies must have learned to put aside their differences long enough to collaborate. For that learning process to have taken place, they must have been put in situations where they have gotten used to being on the same side. To have gotten used to being on the same side, they must have had a common adversary that brought them together. That's where the activities of the defense funds come in.

The defense funds will be defending everyone who is being harassed by the regulatory state, and its beneficiaries will include many liberals.[6] Liberals and conservatives will often find themselves in agreement that certain regulations are ridiculous. And in that cumulative experience, over a matter of years, will come recognition of a truth: To be a liberal doesn't require that one think that *everything* the government does is justified. It is possible to oppose the government on a specific issue without ceasing to be a liberal. Similarly, conservatives will have a cumulative experience of being on the same side of a dispute as liberals are.

Citizens from different places on the political spectrum will have a cumulative common experience of treating the regulatory state as an adversary, becoming accustomed to the fact that elements of the federal government have become "them," not "us"; that the regulators are not our elected representatives but our unelected minders. Once it becomes normal for liberals as well as conservatives to react to stupid regulations with "This is ridiculous," the way will have been opened for larger changes. Systematic civil disobedience is the blunt instrument from outside the system that will mobilize forces for change independently of the system's sclerosis.

I want to emphasize that I am not envisioning a time when liberals decide that conservatives were right after all. On the contrary, the key is that both liberals and conservatives (and we Madisonians) understand that a common cause against stupid government regulations exists outside the normal left-right policy continuum.

This vision sounds idealistic only because of the extreme political polarization of our era. Historically, the American norm was for politicians to say terrible things about one another for public consumption while enjoying cordial personal relationships behind the scenes, quietly recognizing common ground, and cutting deals. Among the public at large, political differences among friends were just that—differences of political preferences, not a Manichean divide between the forces of light and the forces of darkness. If done properly, the defense funds' work will be equally welcome to liberals and conservatives who are having problems with the government, and the Manichean divide will have been blurred at least a little.

There is an analogy to be drawn between the defense funds and the American Civil Liberties Union (ACLU). From its founding in the 1920s until it gradually succumbed to political correctness after the 1970s, the ACLU transcended politics in a similar way. Its purpose was to defend constitutional rights, especially free speech, against all challenges, and in that effort its clients included Communists, Jehovah's Witnesses, the Ku Klux Klan, and anyone else who was being silenced. There was a liberal cast to the ACLU's image, just as the defense funds will have an antiprogressive cast (since they will be locked in combat with the regulatory state), but the ACLU was not considered partisan in the usual sense of that term, nor will the defense funds be considered partisan. If you've got the government on your back for no good reason, the defense funds will be on your side no matter what your politics may be.

That's the environment in which the logjam can begin to break up—in which the factors that make this a propitious moment, described in the preceding chapters, come into play. People who have strong ideological convictions can begin to say, in effect, "I know some of my political friends will get mad at me for saying it, but this is ridiculous."

But for the logjam to break, there need to be signs that both ends of the political spectrum are participating, and this puts a special burden on people on the right. Most public policies that have evolved into the obviously ridiculous were originated by the left. If liberals think that giving an inch on the ridiculous things is going to be a process where they do all the compromising while the right sits tight, we're going to remain in our respective trenches, barbed wire coiled around our positions, machine guns sighted in. There has to be evidence of good faith on both sides. We need a pact that says, "Here are some policies that we are all willing to put in the 'this is ridiculous' category. Some of them are allied to issues we favor; others are allied to issues that you favor. We'll fix the ridiculous things while agreeing to disagree on the allied issues."

How might the logjam be broken in practice? As always, I have no confidence in my specific predictions, but let me offer three ridiculous states of affairs as examples. One requires liberals to give ground. Another requires conservatives to give ground. The third requires liberals to disavow progressives and Madisonians to disavow social conservatives.

It's ridiculous that towns and cities can't afford to provide basic services.

Many towns and cities around America are doing fine. They have enough police and firefighters, potholes get fixed, the garbage is collected regularly, and all these good things are done within a balanced budget. Meanwhile, as the discussion of the collapse of the blue model noted in chapter 12, other towns and cities are going bankrupt. Many that are not bankrupt are providing inferior basic services.

The explanation is seldom that tax revenues are not large enough. More commonly, two kinds of overspending have occurred. First, the city government has installed discretionary programs over the years, often with start-up grants from the federal government. Now they find they can't afford them anymore, but the programs have factional support that keeps the city council from ending them until the heat from the electorate becomes unbearable. Often, only the prospect of imminent bankruptcy can generate that heat.

Second, personnel costs in these cities have gone through the roof. The reason personnel costs have gone through the roof is because of contracts negotiated between a public employees' union that wanted more money and benefits, and municipal politicians who were elected with the support of the very union that was making the demands.[7]

That's ridiculous. For union-management negotiations to work, management must have a strong incentive to resist excessive demands. A mayor and city council don't. Even when they are not beholden to the employees' unions for political support, they don't have anything approaching the same incentive to fight union demands that motivates the CEO and executives of a private company—elected officials can always grant concessions in unobtrusive ways (for example, pension and overtime benefits) that don't create political problems for them. Even someone as unimpeachably liberal as Franklin Roosevelt and someone as unimpeachably pro-union as George Meany thought that unionization of government workers was ridiculous.[8]

It would go a long way toward breaking the logjam from the left if liberals started joining with conservatives in recognizing that public employee unions are inherently inappropriate. The collapse of the blue model is going to help push them in that direction. Liberals who do so wouldn't have to alter their support for unions in the private sector or any of their other political beliefs. They just have to want to provide their fellow citizens with affordable police and fire protection, well-maintained streets, prompt garbage pickup, and other basic city services. There's nothing illiberal about any of that. They don't have to strip public employees of the job security that has traditionally led some people to find government jobs attractive. They just have to return to an older model of city governance that many other cities around the country have continued to practice successfully. It could happen.

In a country as rich as America, it is ridiculous that anyone lacks the means to live a decent life.

The potential for breaking the logjam from the right is for conservatives to accept that large income transfers are a reality of advanced societies, to stop complaining about them, and to begin actively trying to improve the way they are accomplished.

It's worth spelling out how ridiculous the present state of affairs is. It's not that the United States is too stingy with its income transfers. In 2012, the United States transferred more than $2 trillion to individuals to provide for retirement, health care, and the alleviation of poverty, yet we still have millions of people without comfortable retirements, without adequate health care, and in poverty. Only a government could spend so much money so ineffectually. Eliminating cash poverty altogether without adding a dime to the budget would be technically easy right now.

The devil is in the details, of course, and this is not the place to deal with them. I want to make three simpler points about why Madisonians should be as pragmatic about welfare as liberals should be pragmatic about public employees' unions.

First, it's time for us to let go of some good arguments that it's the liberals' fault we're in this mess. Two things can be true at the same time:

- The perverse incentives of the welfare state have created dependency and human suffering. If we could go back and change history, we would have a healthier, happier society.
- We can't go back and change history.

Second, changes in the labor market have changed the moral arguments in favor of redistribution for the working population. At the top end of the economy, to have a high level of cognitive ability has become far more valuable over the course of the last half century. This is most obvious in the IT and financial worlds, but it applies to virtually all professions and managerial jobs. Meanwhile, the economic value of many blue-collar and midlevel white-collar jobs has stagnated or dropped, not because of policy or market failures but because so many jobs can be done as well, and cheaper, by machines. The number of such jobs continues to grow, now reaching well into white-collar jobs. We can argue about how much we can change our fortunes in life through industriousness and perseverance, but IQ is pure luck of the draw. Faced with a situation in which national wealth keeps growing but a substantial portion of the population is doomed to stagnant wages through no fault of their own, we need to figure out ways to augment the income of working people who are doing everything right.

Third, even though income transfers always have negative incentives, the magnitude of those problems can vary widely depending on how the transfers are administered. In a previous book (*In Our Hands*), I argued that a basic guaranteed income can be structured not only so that the negative incentives are minimized but so that positive incentives for the revitalization of civil society are introduced. Others, notably Congressman Paul Ryan, have introduced other approaches for making income transfers a positive as well as a problematic element of public policy.[9]

For all these reasons, it is time for conservatives to make some of their political friends mad at them and acknowledge that, in a country as rich as America, it is ridiculous that anyone lacks the means for a decent life. As evidence of good faith, it would go a long way toward helping to break the logjam. And, as Henry Kissinger said in another context, it has the added advantage of being true.

In a nation as diverse as America, it is ridiculous to impose one-size-fits-all national solutions for policies that involve morally complex cultural differences.

So far, I have tried to use examples of "it is ridiculous . . ." that can withstand challenges (at least to my own satisfaction). This one cannot. The alternative position, that it is our duty to search for the One Best Way on any policy issue that involves a moral principle, and to hold all Americans to it, is defensible. If one makes that argument with regard to something like slavery, I agree with it. But which moral issues fall into the category of ones on which all civilized people should agree?

I would argue that not one of the hot-button issues that have had social liberals and social conservatives screaming at one another for decades falls into that category. Not abortion, not gay rights, not any of the others. All of them involve bundles of competing moral dimensions that reasonable and virtuous people will weight differently, leading them both to different conclusions and to different kinds of lives.

We have been treating those issues as a culture war, as if the only solution is for one side to win and the other side to lose. But why? The only people who need to feel that way are the absolutists for whom one side is in sole possession of truth, the other side's position has no legitimacy, and any tolerance of diversity is morally wrong. The polls indicate that the great majority of the American people are not so absolutist. Why not instead celebrate diversity, celebrate our increased ability to choose places where we can live life as we see fit, and start to treat the locality as the proper unit of aggregation for working out peace terms in the culture war? It can't be done officially, but to a substantial degree it can be done de facto.

The ground rules are simple. No one may deny to others the freedom to live their lives as they see fit, and that means strict enforcement of laws against the acts by which people have denied that freedom to others in the past, from physical violence to throwing garbage on people's lawns and everything in between. But—to take an example that has recently been in the news—if a photographer is personally opposed to gay marriage, forcing that photographer to work a gay wedding is unnecessary. Here's where the de facto part comes in. What I'm proposing is not a campaign to repeal antidiscrimination laws but the restoration of a frame of mind that once again leads people to say of others' choices, "It's a free country."

Restoring this de facto freedom of choice will require some introspection within both the left and the right.

On the left, it is time for a distinction to be made between liberals and progressives. As matters stand, the two terms are used interchangeably, but in fact they refer to two streams of thought that emerged from the Progressive Era at the beginning of the twentieth century.

To recapitulate from the first three chapters, progressive intellectuals were passionate advocates of rule by disinterested experts led by a strong unifying leader. They were in favor of using the state to mold social institutions in the interests of the collective. They thought that individualism and the Constitution were both outmoded.

That core impulse to mold all of American society in the One Best Way still animates progressives today. It is primarily found among those who are described as the hard left. They do not constitute a large proportion of Democratic voters. But there is no denying their totalitarian streak. In many universities, where the progressives are most dominant, they have nearly shut down intellectual debate on many issues, making certain that the faculty and even visiting speakers pass progressive litmus tests.

But the Progressive Era also consisted of a "good government" movement that went in a different direction, fighting political machines in the cities and advocating for more complete democracy. The Seventeenth Amendment mandating the direct election of senators was a product of that aspect of the Progressive Era, as were state laws—California's, for example—allowing ballot initiatives that pass binding laws without the approval of the legislature. This stream of thought produced a political legacy that corresponds to the liberalism of the much larger proportion of Democrats who are usually described as part of the moderate left. Liberals (that's what I want to call them) were at the forefront of the civil rights movement, and also of the broader civil liberties movement that defended free speech in all circumstances.[10]

I, along with other Madisonians, disagree with the liberals' policy agenda. They think that an activist federal government is a force for good and approve of the growing welfare state. But most of them are personally tolerant and are willing to engage in civil discourse. They still believe that the individual should not be sacrificed to the collective and that people who achieve success should be praised for what they have built. I'm not happy that liberals like the idea of a "living Constitution," but they still believe in the separation of powers, checks and balances, and the president's duty to execute the laws faithfully. Liberals can be brought to support freedom of choice on complex moral issues. Progressives cannot.

On the right, we have a similar split between what the press usually describes as "conservatives" and "social conservatives." It's more nuanced than that. Many people who are in favor of limited government and free markets describe themselves as conservatives because they also hold conservative views on marriage, abortion, pornography, drug use, and other social issues. But many of these conservatives do not want the federal government to legislate on these issues. These conservatives fit my definition of Madisonians. The social conservatives who are the right's version of the progressives are those who want to enact their social agenda nationwide.

Progressives and social conservatives are minorities of their respective sides of the political divide, but they drive the political polarization. Here's my proposition: Liberals have to begin distinguishing themselves from progressives, and Madisonians have to begin distinguishing themselves from social conservatives, openly and explicitly rejecting the aspects of the progressive and social conservative agendas that seek to impose their respective worldviews on the entire nation. If that were to happen, not only would freedom of choice on complex moral issues have a chance to evolve, but the rediversification of America would make it virtually inevitable. The return of that freedom of choice would in itself constitute a major revival of the American project.

In Conclusion

As I close these speculations about the prospects for rebuilding American liberty, I am conscious of three quite different reactions, each reasonable, that readers might have.

The first, of course, is that I am wrong in my diagnosis of America's problems and wrong in my prescriptions for their solution. To that, I can only say: Fair enough; you've heard me out.

The second reaction is that I'm far too optimistic about how much effect the defense funds could have. It's unlikely that they will ever operate at anything approaching the scope I have described. Even if they did, it's unlikely that they would have the transformative effects I envision— Goliath would brush them off without even noticing. To that, my reply is: Attacking the regulatory state through the legal system is the only option for rebuilding liberty. You are not going to stop the growth of government through the political process, let alone reverse it. It can't be done, for the reasons I described in chapters 4 and 5. Systematic civil disobedience may be a long shot, but it is, in fact, a shot. *It could work.* The bureaucracies of the federal government really are sclerotic. Their thousands of edicts really can't be enforced without our voluntary compliance. Withholding that compliance really could have transforming effects on the political landscape.

The third reaction concerns something that I too have worried about: I'm oblivious to the dangers of success. By definition, a successful program of systematic civil disobedience would further erode the legitimacy of the federal government. Is that something we can afford to risk? Political polarization is at unprecedented levels, with large portions of the electorate convinced that the other side is not only mistaken in its political views but evil. The nation is already riven by a new kind of class divide, with a lower class and an upper class that are culturally separated in unprecedented ways. America's ethnic mix is in the process of a historic change. In this situation, shouldn't we be seeking reconciliation and unity, not encouraging America's balkanization? Perhaps Sam Rayburn and Lyndon Johnson were right: we should indeed seek to become one America, with no East, no West, no North, no South.

Part of my response is that we don't have the option of restoring the consensus that seemed to characterize the 1950s. We have already come apart. We must deal with that reality. More fundamentally, America was not meant to be one America. It was intended to accommodate diversity. I like David Gelernter's way of putting it: "'The founders designed a vast garment for America that hugs where it should hug and stretches where it should stretch; each state creates its own society, and the Constitution stitches them all together into a comfortable, sensible union suit."[11] Restoring that design is not something we should see ourselves as forced to do by circumstances, but something that we urgently want to do. Eroding the legitimacy of the federal government as it now exists is essential to avoid an America that is defined geographically as it is now but is no longer spiritually America.

The disappearance of the authentic America would be an immeasurable loss. America isn't the only great place to live. I can think of a dozen countries, just among the ones I know, where I could have made a satisfying life for myself. The loss of the way of life of any one of them would make the world culturally poorer.

But that truth should not obscure another one: America is unique not because of the kinds of cultural particularities that make every country different from every other country. If America becomes like the advanced social democracies of Europe, as it threatens to do, it would mean the loss of a unique way of life grounded in individual freedom.

No other country throughout the history of the world began its existence with a charter focused on limiting the power of government and maximizing the freedom of its individual citizens. Even after we set the example, no other new country subsequently has followed it. Neither has any old country modified its charter to become more like ours. The United States of America from 1789 to the 1930s is the sole example of truly limited government anywhere, at any time. Under that aegis, we also happened to go from a few million colonists along the East Coast of North America to the richest and most powerful nation on Earth. We became a magnet for people around the world who wanted to share in the opportunities afforded by American freedom. But these achievements were ancillary to the most important of all:

America's unique charter produced a unique culture. American exceptionalism is not an idea that we invented to glorify ourselves but a reality recognized around the world at the time of the founding and for well over a century thereafter.[12] America's unique culture—its civic religion, as I have called it—made for a unique people. Some of our characteristics are not to everyone's taste, but I love them all. Our openness. Our passion to get ahead. Our passion to see what's over the next hill. Our egalitarianism. Our over-the-top patriotism. Our neighborliness. Our feistiness. Our pride. Our generosity. All wrapped in our individualism.

Those American qualities are fading, once-bright colors left too long under an alien sun. The words from Alexis de Tocqueville that I used as an epigraph for *By the People* increasingly describe us today. The government now "covers the surface of society with a network of small, complicated rules, minute and uniform." As Tocqueville predicted, we have experienced not tyranny but a state that "compresses, enervates, extinguishes, and stupefies a people."[13]

Systematic civil disobedience offers a chance to revive those colors. Perhaps not to the primary intensity they once had, but enough that we are once again different from everyone else, uniquely American. If that process diminishes the majesty of the American government, I don't care. Our government is not supposed to be majestic. Neither does the government command our allegiance independently of its own allegiance to its proper role. The federal government was created with one overriding duty: to allow us to live freely as we see fit, as long as we accord the same right to everyone else. It has betrayed that duty.

America can cease to be the wealthiest nation on Earth and remain America. It can cease to be the most powerful nation on Earth and remain America. It cannot cease to be the land of the free and remain America. I am not frightened by the prospective loss of America's grandeur. I am frightened by how close we are to losing America's soul.

Acknowledgments

———

$\mathbf{B}$*y the People* is mostly about the law, and I am not a lawyer. I am philosophically comfortable intruding into an alien domain—just as war is too important to be left to generals, the law is too important to be left to lawyers—but I came to this project aware that just reading a lot of books about the law wouldn't save me from grievous errors. I needed the help of people who have the professional training and experience I lack.

I began by going to Chip Mellor, president of the Institute for Justice, to tell him my idea for the book and ask whether it made any sense. He was intrigued by my idea, which he summarized on that first visit as "putting sugar into the government's gas tank," and agreed to help. Subsequently, he and the Institute for Justice's staff were invaluable in getting me started. I had the good fortune of already knowing others who are leading academic experts in the topics I was taking up, plus one eminent practitioner, a judge emeritus on a federal circuit court of appeals. As usual in such endeavors, people who were already colleagues were able to point me to others whom I did not know but who were generous in their response to my requests for them to review drafts.

Before I list the names of these people who were so much help to me, imagine that this standard caveat is in a headline-size font, all caps: The errors that remain are mine alone. For example, brilliant constitutional scholars reviewed chapter 1. They made many suggestions, many of which I incorporated into the text. But they also suggested alterations to my narrative that I reluctantly ignored so that the chapter could be kept of manageable length, knowing that I could tell the truth about the constitutional revolution but didn't have space for the whole truth. At points when I erred, leaving out complications that should have been included, it was my call. The same choices among options had to be made for all of the chapters, and they were all my calls. It should also be kept in mind that none of the people listed below saw more than parts of the manuscript—in some cases, they saw only a few pages.

With that in mind, I want to express my gratitude, in alphabetical order, to Randy Barnett, Dana Berliner, Clint Bolick, Scott Bullock, Matthew Christiansen, Greg Conko, Christopher DeMuth, Richard Epstein, Sean Farhang, Michael Greve, Philip Howard, Robert Kaiser,

William Maurer, Chip Mellor, Michael Milbin, Clark Neily, Walter Olson, Norman Ornstein, George Priest, Jonathan Rauch, Jeff Rowes, Timothy Sandefur, Paul Sherman, Michael Strain, Stan Veuger, Peter Wehner, Adam White, Stephen Williams, and Joseph Yalch.

My editor at Crown Forum, Roger Scholl, had no choice but to read the whole thing. Thanks to Roger for his enthusiasm about this odd project, and for an editorial eye that materially improved both my thinking and my writing. Rachelle Mandik meticulously copyedited the manuscript, and Barbara Sturman came up with a striking book design for it.

Thanks to Caroline Kitchens, who took a variety of tasks off my back at AEI. Amanda Urban, to whom *By the People* is dedicated, completed her third decade watching sedulously over the book-writing part of my career. Thanks to Carrol and Tom Noorman and the rest of the crew for providing the seclusion I needed when I was writing some particularly difficult parts of the book.

The acknowledgments section of almost every book I have written since 1990 has included a word of thanks to my professional home, the American Enterprise Institute. This is a good occasion to be more explicit and emphatic. During nineteen years under the leadership of Chris DeMuth and then six years under that of Arthur Brooks, AEI has been my safe haven. We live in an era when social-science departments on college campuses have become notoriously unwelcoming to people who look like they might not share the received wisdom. AEI has given me given freedom to write on whatever topic I choose, presenting whatever conclusions I think justified by the evidence. When my work has drawn the kind of criticism that has caused other institutions to throw personnel (including eminent personnel) overboard, AEI's executives and trustees have not even flinched. I am honored to be part of such a splendid institution.

As I worked on *By the People*, my wife and chief editor, Catherine Cox, watched with growing apprehension. "No more mister nice guy," I would say ominously, and then disappear back into my lair. When it was all over, and she had applied her red ink to the final chapters, she told me that I had been frightening her for nothing. That she could read her husband calling for massive civil disobedience, which, if successful, might destabilize the polity, and call it "nothing," says something about what thirty-two years of my company have done to her sensibilities. She agrees, but says she loves me anyway, which is all that matters.

Notes

M any of the books I cite in *By the People* were e-book editions, few of which let the reader know the page numbers of the print version. Most of the technical articles, magazine articles, reports, and databases I cite were found on the Internet. In both cases, standards for citations are still evolving. I have followed the Chicago style with a few simplifying adaptations. For e-books, I give the chapter from which my material was drawn, and the figure or table number when appropriate. For sources taken from the Internet, I give the website's name and the URL for the home page. I do not give the specific web page because websites change their indexes frequently. Nor do I include the date when I accessed the website; if the page no longer exists when you read the book, knowing that it did at some particular date in the past does not seem helpful. For the many Supreme Court decisions cited in Parts I and II, I give the standard identifying information. The full text of all the decisions may be found on a single website, Justia (www.justia.com).

The full citations of articles in newspapers, magazines, and websites are given in the notes. The bibliography is reserved for books, journal articles, and other scholarly works.

Prologue: The Paradox

1. The text gives the version that came to be treated as the definition of modern Republicanism and that Eisenhower did not disown. It is actually condensed from this passage in Eisenhower's remarks at a Lincoln Day Box Supper on February 5, 1954: "So that here we have, really, the compound, the overall philosophy of Lincoln: in all those things which deal with people, be liberal, be human. In all those things which deal with the people's money or their economy, or their form of government, be conservative—and don't be afraid to use the word" (www.presidency.ucsb.edu).

2. Arthur Krock (1960), "In the Nation," *New York Times*, February 28.

3. Charles Frankel (1960), "A Liberal Is a Liberal Is a Liberal—," *New York Times*, February 28.

4. Two classic conservative works published in 1953, Russell Kirk's *The Conservative Mind* and Robert Nisbet's *The Quest for Community*, contributed to a revival of classic conservative thought, but they do not count as part of the Madisonian resurgence.

5. The most notable were the Mercatus Center (1980), Property and Environment Research Center (1980), National Center for Policy Analysis (1983), Competitive

Enterprise Institute (1984), Heartland Institute (1984), Independent Institute (1986), and Acton Institute (1990). The Hudson Institute, founded in 1961 by Herman Kahn and originally focused on international affairs, developed a strong program of free-market domestic studies after Kahn's death in 1983. I have limited this list to organizations that follow the think-tank model: a staff of full-time scholars who produce original policy studies. This list omits groups that are on the social-conservative end of the spectrum, advocacy groups, more than sixty state-level policy organizations, and other organizations promoting conservative or libertarian ideas, such as the Liberty Fund, Reason Foundation, Institute for Humane Studies, Intercollegiate Studies Institute, and Federalist Society. I discuss the organizations that litigate Madisonian legal cases in chapter 8.

6. The *Code of Federal Regulations* represents all the regulations currently in force, and must be distinguished from another statistic that is often used, the number of pages published in the *Federal Register* in a given year.

7. Murray (1984), 244.

8. Office of Management and Budget, "Historical Budget Data" (www.whitehouse .gov/omb).

9. A spreadsheet showing pages in the CFR from 1938 to 2013 is on the website for the *Federal Register*, but hard to find. The URL that worked as of December 2, 2014, was www.federalregister.gov/uploads/2014/04/OFR-STATISTICS -CHARTS-ALL1-1-1-2013.xls.

10. These counts were assembled from *Wikipedia* pages showing cabinet offices and lists compiled by the author from "Budgets of the United States Government," Government Printing Office (www.gpo.gov).

11. I conducted this exercise near the end of 2013. When I set out to check it in October 2014, I was unable to find the interactive organization chart I had used previously. I further discovered that sometime between January and October 2014, the Office of Health, Safety and Security had been moved, and was now under the Office of the Under Secretary for Management and Performance. But when I tried to access its organization chart, I was routed to a page that I was told does not exist. Rather than find a new example, I decided to leave the description in the text unchanged. Insofar as the point of that description is to convey how opaque the bureaucracy has become to outsiders, I decided that the results of my attempt to check back a year later amounted to QED. For the most recent DOE organization chart as I write, go to www.energy.gov.

12. This text is very similar to the text on page 127 of DiIulio (2014). A little explanation is in order. When the writing of *By the People* was well along, John DiIulio asked me to contribute a response to his forthcoming book, *Bring Back the Bureaucrats*. Coincidentally, his topic—the need to increase the number of federal employees and decrease the federal government's reliance on contractors—touched on several themes of *By the People*. I therefore lifted small pieces from various places in the draft of *By the People* and incorporated them into my essay for *Bring Back the Bureaucrats*. It's an odd situation. Authors often incorporate text from previously published work into a new book (I have done so with three of my own previously published pieces in *By the People*), but I've never heard of text being lifted from an unpublished manuscript and incorporated into a piece that is pub-

lished before the original source of the text appears. But that's what happened in this case.

13. *Statistical Abstract of the United States 1963*. Washington, DC: US Bureau of the Census, Table 575; Jessie and Tarleton (2014), 2.

14. DiIulio (2014), 17–18.

15. Ibid., 18.

16. Office of Management and Budget, "Historical Budget Data," www.whitehouse .gov/omb.

Chapter 1. A Broken Constitution

1. *Statistical Abstract of the United States 1928*. Washington, DC: US Bureau of the Census, Table 185.

2. *Scott v. Sandford*, 60 U.S. 393 (1856); *Slaughterhouse Cases*, 83 U.S. 36 (1872); *Plessy v. Ferguson*, 163 U.S. 537 (1896).

3. Goldberg (2007), chapter 3.

4. Goodnow (1911), 9–10.

5. Ibid., 2.

6. Epstein (2006), 3.

7. Wilson (1913), 56–57.

8. Louis D. Brandeis, "The Living Law," *Illinois Law Review* 10, 1917, quoted in Epstein (2006), 4.

9. The erosion began in 1934 with the Court's ruling in *Home Building & Loan Association v. Blaisdell* (290 U.S. 398) that a Minnesota law retroactively changing the terms of existing mortgages was constitutional. The Minnesota legislature appeared to have obviously impaired the obligation of contracts with a law that authorized the retroactive extension of the time during which mortgagers could redeem their mortgages from foreclosure. But how could anyone object to using the power of the state to help farmers trying to survive the Great Depression hang on to their farms? Hard cases make bad law. The five-justice majority rationalized its decision on various grounds, among them that the Minnesota law affected the *remedy* given by the legislature to enforce the obligations of a contract, not the obligations themselves, and that the force of the Contracts Clause must be balanced against the state's obligation to protect its citizens in an emergency situation. In his dissent, Justice Sutherland was biting in his condemnation of the decision and prescient about its consequences. The direct effect of the Minnesota legislation was bad enough, he wrote, but it was "of trivial significance compared with the far more serious and dangerous inroads upon the limitations of the Constitution which are almost certain to come."

Blaisdell was reinforced by the Court's ruling in 1935 that Congress's retroactive voiding of "gold clauses" in contracts was constitutional. As part of FDR's steps to take the United States off the gold standard and remove gold from the hands of Americans, Congress had passed a joint resolution that canceled the validity of all gold clauses. At that time, "gold clauses" were common in contracts, giving the creditor the option of receiving payment in gold. It was a hedge against inflation. To see what the congressional resolution meant, imagine that you were to give the buyer of your home a thirty-year mortgage with a floating interest rate based on the prime rate (your hedge against inflation), and the next year the government passed a law saying that floating interest rates are illegal and your mortgage will now be paid off for all thirty years at the 4 percent rate that applied when you sold your house. That's comparable to what the cancellation of the gold clauses did. In four cases that came to the Supreme Court in 1935, known as the *Gold Clause Cases*, the Supreme Court found the congressional resolution to be constitutional. The Court's rationale was that Congress was exercising an enumerated power (the power to regulate the value of money), and that gold clauses presented a threat to Congress's control of the monetary system.

10. *Schechter Poultry Corp. et al. v. United States*, 295 U.S. 495 (1935), emphasis added.

11. The standard narrative has been around since the New Deal. A well-regarded recent statement of it is Leuchtenburg (1995).

12. Cushman (1998).

13. Keynes's magnum opus, *The General Theory of Employment, Interest, and Money*, was published in 1936.

14. Most recently, a major crash had occurred in 1921, but its effects dissipated in a matter of months. See Grant (2014). The notable exception was the "Long Depression" of 1873–1879.

15. Ivan Pongracic Jr. (2007), "The Great Depression According to Milton Friedman," *The Freeman*, September 1 (www.fee.org).

16. The words also appear in the preamble—"We the people of the United States, in order to form a more perfect union, establish justice, insure domestic tranquility, provide for the common defence, promote the general welfare, and secure the blessings of liberty to ourselves and our posterity, do ordain and establish this Constitution for the United States of America"—but that use was seldom invoked as a potential loophole. In this quotation and those in the text, I conform capitalization and punctuation to contemporary usage.

17. Hamilton, Madison, and Jay (1787), #41.

18. Natelson (2003), 45–46.

19. From Madison's *Records of the Federal Convention of 1787* (Max Farrand ed., 1911), quoted in Natelson (2003), 46. Hamilton revealed those anomalous sentiments in a six-hour speech on June 18, during which he inveighed against democracy and proposed a system that, among other things, would have a president and senators that, once elected, would serve for life on "good behavior." See Chernow (2004), 231–33. In *The Federalist*, Hamilton alludes to the phrase "general welfare" only once, in #23, quoting the Articles of Confederation, section VIII, about the obligation of the states to supply support for national defense. See Hamilton, Madison, and Jay (1787), #23.

20. *Helvering v. Davis*, 301 U.S. 619, at 301 (1937). To make the quotation more readable, I have omitted the citations following the first sentence and the one following "settled by decision." The former citations were "Constitution, Art. I, section 8; *United States v. Butler*, 297 U.S. 1, 65; *Seward Machine Co. v. Davis, supra*." The latter was "*United States v. Butler, supra*." The case cited twice, *Butler*, was a harbinger. Six justices agreed in *Butler* that "the power of Congress to authorize expenditure of public moneys for public purposes is not limited by the direct grants of legislative power found in the Constitution."

21. Apparently Hamilton never supported the limits on the federal government imposed by the Constitutional Convention. As early as 1782 (on July 4, perhaps significantly), he had written that "there is something noble and magnificent in the perspective of a great federal republic . . . but there is something proportionably diminutive and contemptible in the prospect of a number of petty states, with the appearance only of union, jarring, jealous, and perverse, without any determined direction, fluctuating and unhappy at home, weak and insignificant by their dissentions, in the eyes of other nations." See Hamilton (1904), vol. 1, 286–87. In a paper written in September 1787, just days after the Constitutional Convention adjourned, he looked forward to a Washington presidency in which the national government may "triumph altogether over the state governments and reduce them into an entire subordination." See Natelson (2003), 47.

    Someone who did not know about Hamilton's position in Philadelphia couldn't possibly have imagined it by reading *The Federalist*. Only hindsight lets us see foreshadowings. In #31, Hamilton wrote, "A government ought to contain in itself every power requisite to the full accomplishment of the objects committed to its care," but without suggesting that the "objects committed to its care" went beyond those enumerated in the Constitution. He wrote in #70, "Energy in the executive is a leading character in the definition of good government," but that was followed by an extended defense of a single executive rather than a committee, and by assurances that the Constitution protected against broad presidential power. During New York's ratifying convention in Poughkeepsie, Hamilton's defense of the powers of the states and dismissal of Anti-Federalist fears about a strong central government were so eloquent that he was accused by his fellow New York delegate to the Constitutional Convention of saying one thing in Philadelphia and another in Poughkeepsie. See Chernow (2004), 266.

22. *Annals of Congress* (1834–56), James Madison, House of Representatives, June 8, 1789. The argument against a bill of rights to which Madison alludes was also made by Hamilton in *Federalist #84*.

23. For a review of the various subsequent interpretations of the Ninth Amendment, see Barnett (2004), xii and chapter 9.

24. *Lessee of Livingston v. Moore*, 32 U.S. 469 (1833), and *Scott v. Sandford*, 60 U.S. 393 (1856).

25. Thayer (1893).

26. In *Lochner*, the Court struck down a New York law that limited the number of hours bakers could work on grounds that it constituted "unreasonable, unnecessary, and arbitrary interference of the individual . . . to enter into those contracts . . . appropriate or necessary for the support of himself or his family." See *Lochner v. New York*, 198 U.S. 45 (1905). The New York law was written to protect large bakeries against smaller ones that had gained a competitive advantage by working longer hours.

27. In effect, the Presumption of Constitutionality Doctrine said to complaining citizens, "Maybe one of your rights was technically violated, but the legislature had a plausible reason for what it was trying to do. You can't prove otherwise. You have no case." Even before it was incorporated into constitutional jurisprudence, the growing popularity of the Presumption of Constitutionality Doctrine among legal

scholars represented a profoundly important shift among the legal elite, away from a view of the United States as a republic centered on the protection of individual rights and toward a view of the United States as a democracy centered on majority rule.

28. *O'Gorman & Young, Inc., v. Hartford Fire Insurance Co.*, 282 U.S. at 258 (1931).

29. The defendant, Leo Nebbia, had been convicted of selling two quarts of milk and a five-cent loaf of bread for eighteen cents, when New York's Milk Control Board had set the price of milk at nine cents a quart. Nebbia filed suit on grounds that the New York statute violated the Equal Protection Clause and Due Process Clause of the Fourteenth Amendment, and those were the grounds on which the Court ruled. But surely (a naïve reader of the Constitution would assume) his freedom to sell something he owned at a price that the customer was willing to pay easily fell under the Ninth Amendment as well. No, said the Supreme Court. For decades, the Court had approved of state regulation of rates in industries that were inclined toward monopoly power (most notoriously, the railroads operating in the west in the latter part of the nineteenth century). Justice Roberts justified the action of the Milk Control Board on grounds that rate regulation had sometimes been used in situations not involving monopoly. That much was correct, Richard Epstein acknowledges, "but in his willingness to extend rate regulation to ordinary competitive transactions, he never once articulated a limiting principle on how far state regulation could go, a point that generated much unease among the more classically liberal justices." See Epstein (in press). *Nebbia* left the barn door wide open.

30. An important intervening case was *West Coast Hotel v. Parrish*, 300 U.S. 379 (1937), in which the Court upheld the validity of the same kind of minimum-wage legislation that it had voided (thereby getting the Court in such hot water) in *Morehead v. New York ex rel. Tipaldo*, 298 U.S. 587 (1936).

31. *United States v. Carolene Products Co.*, 304 U.S. 144 at 152 (1938), emphasis added.

32. Levy and Mellor (2008), 192.

33. Barnett (2008) points out that in *Carolene Products* and other key decisions, "the New Deal Court only *disparaged* the unenumerated rights retained by the people; it did not *deny* them altogether." Barnett argues that complete denial was left to the Warren Court in its decision in *Williamson v. Lee Optical of Oklahoma, Inc.*, 348 U.S. at 487–88 (1955), when the Court ruled that a hypothetical rationale, or one concocted *ex post*, was sufficient to provide a "rational basis." See Barnett (2008), 1484–86.

34. *United States v. Carolene Products Co.*, 304 U.S. 144 (1938).

35. In the words of Footnote Four, "legislation which restricts those political processes which can ordinarily be expected to bring about the repeal of undesirable legislation." Ibid.

36. Ibid.

37. *United States v. Lopez*, 514 U.S. 585 (1995).

38. Barnett (2001).

39. In the first major case, *Gibbons v. Ogden*, 22 U.S. 1 (1824), Chief Justice Marshall asserted Congress's affirmative power to issue regulations governing interstate commerce, but the substance of the decision was to strike down a New York law

that impeded an open national transportation market. *Gibbons v. Ogden* also specified that the transportation within the interior of the state would *not* be subject to federal oversight under the Commerce Clause. Subsequent cases extended the precedent of *Ogden*, leading to a legal term, the *dormant Commerce Clause*. The Commerce Clause was supposed to ensure that interstate commerce remained open and competitive, which in turn meant voiding state-level efforts to impede open and competitive markets. At the same time, those decisions left space for states to impose regulations or conduct activities that might have indirect effects on interstate commerce, but were justified on other appropriate grounds (e.g., in *Willson v. Black-Bird Creek Marsh Co.*, 27 U.S. 245 [1829]). The New Deal Supreme Court used *Ogden* to justify *Wickard v. Filburn*, and it continues to be cited by liberal jurists, but Michael Greve's observation on such interpretations is apposite: "But while some general statements in Marshall's opinion [in *Gibbons*] may suggest such an interpretation, his opinion also rattles off an 'immense' mass of functions *not* surrendered to the federal government, including 'inspection laws, health laws of every description, as well as laws for regulating the internal commerce of a State.' *Gibbons* at 203. There, one would think, goes most of the Environmental Protection Agency, the Food and Drug Administration, and the Occupational Safety and Health Administration." Greve (1999), 153, emphasis in the original. Richard Epstein points out that *Gibbons* was followed by an unbroken line of consistent cases that rejected the relevance of indirect effects to interpretation of the Commerce Clause prior to *Wickard*. Epstein (1987), 1432–43.

The major expansion of the Commerce Clause during the nineteenth century occurred in response to the passage of the Sherman Anti-Trust Act through *United States v. E.C. Knight Co.*, 156 U.S. 1 (1895), in which the Court held that price-fixing cartels based on mergers of companies across states met the constitutional test of affecting interstate commerce. This expansion of the Commerce Clause, described as "sensible but measured" by a critic as severe as Richard Epstein, left a Commerce Clause that, in practice, still meant something intelligible to ordinary readers of Article 1, Section 8—which is to say, the Supreme Court agreed that Congress had power to regulate commerce among the several states when an issue arose that really did involve an impediment to buying, selling, and bartering, and really did involve an activity that crossed state lines. See Epstein (2006), 33.

40. In the Shreveport rate cases (1914), the Supreme Court ruled that the Interstate Commerce Commission could regulate the shipping rates of a railroad that operates within a single state if it competed with railroads that operated across states. Six years later, Congress passed the Transportation Act of 1920, authorizing comprehensive federal rate regulation over the entire railroad system, including all intrastate lines. The constitutionality of the act was sustained by the Supreme Court in *Wisconsin Railroad Commission v. Chicago, Burlington & Quincy Railroad*, 257 U.S. 563 (1922). In the Shreveport case, the Interstate Commerce Commission introduced protectionism for interstate railway carriers rather than removing an impediment to open competition. The Transportation Act of 1920 brought under federal purview large chunks of the railway system—railroads operating within a single state, even if they didn't compete with interstate rail carriers—that had previously been exempt.

41. See Berger (1996) for an explication of the jurisprudence on the Commerce Clause.
42. *National Labor Relations Board v. Jones & Laughlin Steel Corp.*, 301 U.S. 1 (1937).
43. Kozinski (1995), 5.
44. The Second Amendment decision was *District of Columbia v. Heller*, 554 U.S. 570 (2008). The First Amendment decision was *McCutcheon et al. v. Federal Election Commission*, 572 U.S. ___ (2014). The key decision regarding the Commerce Clause was *United States v. Lopez*, 514 U.S. 585 (1995), followed by *United States v. Morrison*, U.S. 598 (2000), and *Solid Waste Agency of Northern Cook Cty. v. Army Corps of Engineers*, 531 U.S. 159 (2001).
45. Segregation had been compulsory in the states that had made up the Confederacy, plus Delaware, Kentucky, Maryland, Missouri, Oklahoma, and West Virginia. Segregation had been optional in Kansas, New Mexico, Arizona, and Colorado.
46. Lawson (1994), 1236.
47. Thomas Jefferson to Edward Carrington, Paris, May 27, 1788. Thomas Jefferson Foundation (www.monticello.org).
48. Hamilton, Madison, and Jay (1787), #51.

Chapter 2. A Lawless Legal System

1. Locke (1689), book 2, chapter 18, section 202.
2. Clarke (1962), 36.
3. Howard (2014), chapter 2, "Rethinking the Rule of Law," makes many of the same points as this section of my chapter 2—sometimes so similarly that I must say explicitly that my draft was completed before I came across *The Rule of Nobody*.
4. The same problem usually applies to people who are sued by another private party, but in some cases (e.g., small-claims courts) an inexpensive option is available.
5. The relevant Latin phrase is *"Actus non facit reum nisi mens sit rea,"* which translates as "The act is not culpable unless the mind is guilty."
6. The account of federal law through the nineteenth century is drawn from Strazella (1998), 5–6. The estimates of the number of federal laws from the last third of the nineteenth century through 1990–99 is based on the data in "Chart 2, Percent of Statutory Sections Enacted by Time Period," page 9. This material is integrated with the count of actual federal crimes in 1983, 2000, and 2007, reported in Baker (2008).
7. Silverglate (2009) and Healy (2004).
8. It is also known as the "Dotterweich-Park Doctrine" after the name of two key Supreme Court cases, *United States v. Dotterweich*, 320 U.S. 277 (1943), and *United States v. Park*, 421 U.S. 658 (1975).
9. *Dotterweich*, 320 U.S. at 281.
10. *Morissette v. United States*, 342 U.S. 246, 256 (1952).
11. *United States v. Park*, 421 U.S. 658 (1975).
12. *Edward Hanousek, Jr. v. United States*, 176 F.3d 1116 (9th Cir. 1999).
13. Clarence Thomas, dissent from the denial of certiorari in *Hanousek v. United States*, January 10, 2000.
14. "Storage bins shall be provided with gaskets and locks or latches to keep the cover closed, or other equivalent devices in order to insure the dust tightness of

the cover. Covers at openings where an employee may enter the bin shall also be provided with a hasp and a lock, so located that the employee may lock the cover in the open position whenever it is necessary to enter the bin." Regulation 1910.263(d)(6)(ii), OSHA website (www.osha.gov).

15. OSHA Manuals for Physicians, Dentists, and Veterinarians (www.oshamanual .com).

16. DeLong (2004), 15.

17. Hamilton, Madison, and Jay (1787), #62. The most widely used contemporary definition of the "rule of law" was laid out by legal philosopher Lon Fuller in his 1963 Storrs Lectures at the Yale Law School. See Fuller (1964), 39. The eight characteristics of the rule of law he specified were clarity, internal consistency, practicability, generality, public promulgation, prospectiveness (new laws should not be applied retroactively), broad consistency of the law over time, and congruence between the wording of the law and the way it is administered by the officials.

18. Madison was clear-eyed about the limits of specificity in a law. See *Federalist #37*, where he writes that "no language is so copious as to supply words and phrases for every complex idea, or so correct as not to include many equivocally denoting different ideas." Hamilton, Madison, and Jay (1787), #37. But the limits are not remotely approached by laws I am complaining about.

19. Public Law 107–204, 107th Congress. Text is available at the Securities and Exchange Commission website (www.sec.gov).

20. Public Law 111–148, 111th Congress. Text is available at the Government Printing Office website (www.gpo.gov).

21. Tax Payer Advocate Service of the Internal Revenue Service, 2012 Annual Report to Congress, available at the Internal Revenue Service website (www.irs .gov). The most common word count for the King James version of the Bible on the Internet is about 790,000, though some are over 800,000.

22. Howard (2014), 36.

23. For a discussion of the problems associated with assigning awards, and an experiment demonstrating how sensitive the amount of awards can be to the way the trial is conducted, see Poser, Bornstein, and McGorty (2003).

24. For an account of the changing status of written contracts, see Olson (1991), chapter 10.

25. For an example of how tortuous the requirements in mixed-motive cases are, read the Supreme Court's decision in *Price Waterhouse v. Hopkins*, 490 U.S. 228 (1989).

26. Tim Wu (2007). "American Lawbreaking," *Slate*, October 14 (www.slate.com).

27. Quoted in Healy (2004), introduction.

28. John Carroll, quoted in Anderson (2009), 12. For a detailed account of the Milken case by a member of his defense team, see Silverglate (2009), chapter 4.

29. DeLong (2004), chapter 2.

30. Quoted in Silverglate (2009), introduction.

31. Parker (2013), 415. For a complete discussion of the ways in which corporations are deterred from supporting employees who come under federal prosecution, see Hasnas (2005).

32. DeLong (2004), chapter 2.

33. For an account of just how far government officials can go in trying to put private

citizens who refuse to cooperate out of business, read the account at the opening of the Supreme Court's opinion in *Wilkie v. Robbins*, 551 U.S. 537 (2007), in which government officials of the Bureau of Land Management tried to drive a dude-ranch owner out of business. After reading that account, proceed to Justice Souter's characterization of the behavior of the government officials. Souter concedes, "It is one thing to be threatened with the loss of grazing rights, or to be prosecuted, or to have one's lodge broken into, but something else to be subjected to this in combination over a period of six years, by a series of public officials bent on making life difficult. Agency appeals, lawsuits, and criminal defense take money, and endless battling depletes the spirit along with the purse." And yet, subsequently characterizing this as "hard bargaining" on the government's part, Souter concludes for the majority that a lower court opinion should be reversed. The plaintiff had no grounds for judicial relief. Legislation was required.

34. Paul (1987), 9.
35. Kochan (1998), 60–65.
36. Levy and Mellor (2008), 157.
37. *Hawaii Housing Authority v. Midkiff,* 467 U.S. 229 at 241 (1984), quoted in Sandefur (2006), 95.
38. Quoted in Sandefur (2006), 81.
39. *Penn Central Transportation Co. v. New York,* 438 U.S. at 123–24 (1978), quoted in Levy and Mellor (2008), 174.
40. Sandefur (2006), 79.
41. See Balko (2013); Radley Balko (2014), "And Now: The Criminalization of Parenthood," *Washington Post,* July 14; Sarah Stillman (2013), "Taken," *New Yorker,* August 12; and Michael Sallah, Robert O'Harrow Jr., and Stephen Rich (2014), "Stop and Seize," *Washington Post,* September 6.
42. See Buckley (2013), Howard (1995), Howard (2009), Howard (2014), Howard (2002), Olson (1991), and Olson (2011).
43. Olson (1991), 280.
44. Blackstone (1769), 135.
45. Olson (1991), 2–3.
46. That is the title of Canon 28, which is still part of the ABA's code, though now ignored.
47. Priest (2013), 250.
48. *Greenman v. Yuba Power Prods., Inc.,* 59 Cal 2d 57, 377 P.2d 897, 27 Cal. Rptr. 697 (1963).
49. A seminal article is Coase (1960), and the venerable basic text is Posner (2014), originally published in 1972 and now in its ninth edition.
50. For an excellent account of the state of knowledge about the complications, see Viscusi (2013).
51. Rubin and Shepherd (2007).
52. Priest (2013), 252–53.
53. Documenting these kinds of costs of tort law has been done by several of the books I listed earlier. I particularly recommend Olson (1991) and Howard (2002).
54. *Walrath v. Hanover Fire Ins. Co.,* 110 N.E. 426, 427 (N.Y. 1913), quoted in Olson (1991), 92.

55. This account of discovery is drawn from Olson (1991), chapter 5.

56. *Arnstein v. Porter*, 154 F.2d 464 (2nd Cir. 1946).

57. "In appraising the sufficiency of the complaint we follow, of course, the accepted rules that a complaint should not be dismissed for failure to state a claim unless it appears beyond doubt that the plaintiff can prove no set of facts in support of his claim which would entitle him to relief." *Conley v. Gibson*, 355 U.S. 41, 45–46 (1957).

58. *Bell Atlantic Corp. v. Twombly*, 550 U.S. 544 at 570 (2007). This new guideline was reinforced in *Ashcroft v. Iqbal*, 556 U.S. 662 (2009).

59. For a detailed discussion of the changes in discovery, see Olson (1991), chapter 6.

60. The current version of the rules for discovery (Rule 26) of the Federal Rules of Civil Procedure may be found at www.law.cornell.edu.

61. Olson (1991), 107.

62. *International Shoe Co. v. Washington*, 326 U.S. 310 (1945).

63. Olson (1991), 80.

64. Another crucial decision handed down by the New Deal Supreme Court was *Erie Railroad Co. v. Tompkins*, 304 U.S. 634 (1938). See Olson (1991), 82.

65. The incentives to work on contingency are also increased by federal law permitting multiple damages for job discrimination, discussed on page 58. The financial risks of losing a case are so great that corporations often agree to an out-of-court settlement even for the weakest cases.

66. Farhang (2010), 64.

67. Ibid., 63.

68. Prepared using the raw data from Farhang (2010), generously provided by the author. The operational definition of *private enforcement regime* was a provision either for plaintiff fee-shifting or multiple damages. Legislation that provided for both of those mechanisms is counted as having two private enforcement regimes.

69. Rate per 100,000 population, based on cases classified by the Administrative Office of the United States Courts as private/federal question/statutory cases, excluding prisoner petitions and deportation cases. See Farhang (2010), 272.

70. Farhang (2010), 10. This figure is derived from Farhang's statement that a total of 165,000 have been filed, 97 percent of which were filed by private citizens.

71. Ibid., 74, Table 3.1.

72. Ibid., 74.

73. Priest (2013), 249.

74. The Association of Trial Lawyers of America changed its name to the American Association for Justice. For a specific example of how the trial lawyers' lobby can block legislation, see Andrew Hawkins (2014), "Cuomo Won't Push Scaffold-Law Reform This Year," *Crain's New York Business*, April 25 (www.crainsnewyork.com). For the extent of influence within a state, see Chris Dickerson (2012), "Trial Lawyers Spend $20M in N.Y. Politics," *Legal Newsline Legal Journal*, December 12 (www.legalnewsline.com). For the trial lawyers' strenuous efforts in the 2014 election, see Timothy Carney (2014), "Trial Lawyer Industry Tries to Buy a Democratic Majority," *Washington Examiner*, October 24 (www.washington examiner.com).

75. Three 1986 Supreme Court cases known as the "summary judgment trilogy" made

it easier for judges to expedite litigation by issuing summary judgments. The real effects of these reforms are debated. Linda Mullenix concludes, "Simply stated, the trilogy has not resulted in federal judges granting or denying summary judgment in statistically significant ways than before the trilogy. Although the courts did experience a brief uptick in summary judgment dismissals in the immediate aftermath of the trilogy, things soon settled back to the summary judgment relative equilibrium that existed prior to the trilogy." Mullenix (2012), 561–62. For more optimistic assessments see Cook (2013) and Elliott (2004).

Three Supreme Court cases, in 1993, 1997, and 1999, have led to what is known as the *Daubert* standard, named after the initial of the three cases, *Daubert v. Merrell Dow Pharmaceuticals*, 509 U.S. 579 (1993), which requires evidence that expert testimony meets basic standards of scientific legitimacy.

Important recent cases regarding class-action suits include *Wal-Mart v. Dukes et al.*, 564 U.S. _____ (2011); *AT&T Mobility v. Concepcion*, 563 U.S. 321 (2011); *American Express Co. et al. v. Italian Colors Restaurant et al.*, No. 12-133 (2013); and *Comcast Corp. v. Behrend*, 569 U.S. _____ (2013).

Chapter 3. An Extralegal State Within the State

1. Lawson (1994), 1248–49.
2. Under *informal* rule making, which applies to the great majority of rules, the agency is supposed to reflect upon the public comments and then publish a final regulation in the *Federal Register*. The regulation goes into effect thirty days after publication, during which time interested parties can ask the agency to amend or repeal the rule. See DeLeo (2008), 53.
3. Congress can legislatively stipulate a *formal* rule-making process that requires hearings, but this happens rarely. There are occasional examples of *hybrid* rule making, which allows some aspects of a hearing (limited cross-examination, presentation of rebuttal evidence). An even rarer form of rule making is *negotiated*, in which the agency and the affected parties jointly agree on a rule. DeLeo (2008), 53–66.
4. OIRA took on its regulatory review function in the early days of the Reagan administration. In 1993, the definition of *significant* was established by President Clinton's Executive Order 12866. Under the current definition, a regulation is automatically deemed significant if it has an annual effect greater than $100 million. Other qualifying characteristics are that it is likely to have major adverse effects, create inconsistencies with actions taken by another agency, materially alter the budgetary effects of entitlements or other transfers, or raise novel legal or policy issues. See Sunstein (2013a), 1850–51. Cass Sunstein, administrator of OIRA during the Obama administration's first term, summarizes OIRA's activities during his term in office as follows: "OIRA reviewed 2,304 regulatory actions between January 21, 2009, and August 10, 2012. In that period, 320 actions, or about 14%, were approved without change; 161 actions, or about 7%, were withdrawn; and 1,758 actions, or about 76%, were approved 'consistent with change.' In assessing the importance of review, it is important to note that the words 'consistent with change' reveal that the published rule is different from the submitted rule, but do not specify the magnitude of the change. In some cases, the changes are

minor, perhaps even cosmetic; in others, they are substantial." Sunstein (2013a), 1847.

What do these percentages look like with regard to the entire body of new regulations added to the *Code of Federal Regulations?* According to the Congressional Research Service, 13,039 rules were added to the *Code of Federal Regulations* from 2009 to 2012. Prorating that number for January 21, 2009, to August 10, 2012, Sunstein's figures refer to a universe of approximately 11,583 new rules. Relative to that universe, of which 20 percent were reviewed by OIRA, 1.4 percent of them were withdrawn and the other 98.6 were approved, almost all of them with changes, consisting of an unknown mix of significant and trivial changes. This is not to say that OIRA has been ineffective. On the contrary, Sunstein's book about his time in office has a number of examples of bad regulations forestalled or changed for the better. See Sunstein (2013b). I will add that I wish Sunstein had remained at OIRA longer—if his attitudes toward regulation were more widely shared, we would have much better regulation. But after reading his account of how the review system works in Sunstein (2013a), the question is not why he left after three and a half years but how he survived psychologically unimpaired for even three and a half months.

5. Apart from these severe limitations on the restraining power of cost-benefit analyses, some regulations are statutorily exempt from cost-benefit analysis, and the requirement does not apply to independent commissions such as the FCC and the SEC.

6. Other categories not discussed in the main text are rule making in the area of military or foreign affairs; procedural rules about how an agency functions; rules concerning public property, loans, benefits, and contracts; statements about policy plans for the future; and "good-cause exceptions" based on an agency's determination that notice and comment would be impracticable, unnecessary, or contrary to public interest. See DeLeo (2008), 64.

7. Michael S. Greve (2014), "Prescription for a Banana Republic," *Library of Law and Liberty,* October 7 (www.libertylawsite).

8. Ibid.

9. *Appeal of FTC Line Business Report Litigation,* 595 F.2d at 703–704.

10. DeLeo (2008), 83.

11. *United States v. Morton Salt Co.,* 338 U.S. 632, 642–643 (1950), emphasis added.

12. Clint Bolick, personal communication, October 12, 2014.

13. *Camara v. Municipal Court,* 387 U.S. at 538 (1967).

14. For a description of the ALJ's appointment and tenure, see Barnett (2013), 804–8.

15. The discussion of the internal review process is taken from DeLeo (2008), chapter 4.

16. A concise review of this literature and the relevant court decisions may be found in Barnett (2013), 816–26.

17. The discussion of the review process is taken from DeLeo (2008), chapter 6. Section 701(a)(1) of the Administrative Procedure Act allows Congress to stipulate in the enabling legislation that no outside judicial review is possible. Congress has occasionally done so, but mostly in matters involving military affairs and intelligence agencies.

18. *Chevron v. Natural Resources Defense Council*, 467 U.S. 837 (1984).
19. *Ibid.*, 837, 842–843.
20. DeLeo (2008), 200.
21. Gillette (2000), 102.
22. Hamburger (2014).
23. Ibid., conclusion.
24. *Wayman v. Southard*, 23 U.S. 1, 43 (1825).
25. *Field v. Clark*, 143 U.S. 649 (1892).
26. Pestritto (2007), 42.
27. Fukuyama (2014).
28. Woodrow Wilson, "Notes for Lectures at the Johns Hopkins," January 26, 1891, quoted in Pestritto (2007), 41.
29. *J. W. Hampton Jr. Co. v. United States*, 276 U.S. 394, 409 (1928).
30. *Panama Refining Co. v. Ryan*, 293 U.S. 388 (1935), and *Schechter Poultry Corp. v. United States*, 295 U.S. 495 (1935).
31. In *NBC*, the Court relied especially on the precedents in *New York Central Securities Corp. v. United States*, 287 U.S. 12 (1932), and *Federal Communications Commission v. Pottsville Broadcasting Co.*, 309 U.S. 134 (1940).
32. *National Broadcasting Co., Inc. v. United States*, 319 U.S. 190 (1943).
33. *Yakus v. United States*, 321 U.S. 414, 420 (1944).
34. Levy and Mellor (2008), 73.
35. Congress has the power to veto revisions within seven months of their promulgation.
36. Pollack (2011).
37. *Chevron*, 467 U.S. 837, 842–843 (1984).
38. *Chevron* deference is now limited to agency actions that have the "force of law," excluding such things as a simple letter sent by an agency. See, for example, *Christensen v. Harris County*, 529 U.S. 576 (2000). Scalia wrote dissents for one portion of the decision in *Barnhart v. Walton*, 535 U.S. 212 (2002), while concurring in the decision as a whole, and dissented from *United States v. Mead Corp*, 533 U.S. 218 (2001), but neither of these involved arguments for limitations on *Chevron* deference.
39. *Whitman v. American Trucking Associations, Inc.*, 531 U.S. 457 (2001). In effect, Congress's amendment of the Clean Air Act was so incoherent that it gave the EPA two illegitimate choices. As described by Levy and Mellor, the EPA had to "either set the standard for nonthreshold pollutants at zero, in direct contradiction of congressional intent, or arbitrarily select a nonzero standard at which adverse health effects would still exist." See Levy and Mellor (2008), 76.
40. McCarthy (2014), 96–154. The subsequent examples are also drawn from that source. They constitute a small subset of all the items in McCarthy's list.
41. Jeremy Herb (2014), "GAO, Taliban Prisoner Swap Violated Law," *Politico*, August 21 (www.politico.com).
42. The twenty cases are detailed in Cruz (2013) and Cruz (2014). The twenty do not include unanimous Supreme Court rejections of cases for which the administration filed amicus briefs. If the Obama administration continues at the same

pace, it will accumulate about double the 9–0 defeats for George W. Bush's eight years.

43. I am referring to Court decisions regarding the president's discretionary power to implement legislation as he sees fit. The 2012 Supreme Court decision validating the Affordable Care Act (*National Federation of Independent Business et al. v. Sibelius*, 567 U.S.   [2012]) and the pending case on the legitimacy of premium subsidies for states that have not established exchanges (*King v. Burwell*, No. 14-1158, 4th Cir. [2014]) are both about the meaning of the text of the Affordable Care Act, not the executive branch's alterations of its provisions.

Chapter 4. A Systemically Corrupt Political System

1. Twain and Warner (1873).
2. See Higgs (1987), chapter 5, for a description of this period.
3. Henry B. Brown, quoted in Higgs (1987), 80.
4. Wettergreen (1988), 7.
5. Kaiser (2009), chapter 8.
6. Ibid., chapter 8. The first good data on the costs of political campaigns comes from 1974. The average cost of a House campaign was just $236,120 (this and all the rest of the numbers are in 2010 dollars). Senate campaigns, once every six years, averaged $1,935,002. We know that those numbers were necessarily much higher than they had been in the early 1960s, because television and polling costs for campaigns had been rising dramatically for a decade.
7. For example, money was sometimes taken from the corporate till and hidden with accounting tricks, or executives who made political contributions were compensated through year-end bonuses. See Mutch (1988), 166.
8. Quoted in Kaiser (2009), chapter 8.
9. Ibid., chapter 8.
10. Wettergreen (1988), 6.
11. Mann and Ornstein (2006), 52.
12. Ibid., 47–63.
13. Ornstein et al. (2013), Table 3-5.
14. Ibid., Table 3-2.
15. Kaiser (2009), chapter 8.
16. Ornstein et al. (2013), Table 3-10.
17. Legend has it that the word was coined by President Grant with reference to persons hanging around the Willard Hotel. But the *Oxford English Dictionary* shows *lobby* being used as a verb in its contemporary sense as early as 1850, referring to the lobby outside the House of Commons.
18. Ornstein et al. (2013), Table 5-2.
19. Quoted in Kaiser (2009), chapter 4.
20. Ryan Grim and Sabrina Siddiqui (2014), "Call Time for Congress Shows How Fundraising Dominates Bleak Work Life," *Huffington Post*, January 8 (www.huffingtonpost.com).
21. Kennedy (2009), 486. See Howard (2014), 132–33 for more on this.
22. Kaiser (2009), chapter 8. Before 1975, most lobbying was done out of law firms.

23. General Accounting Office (1991).

24. Kaiser (2009), chapter 21.

25. Quoted in ibid., chapter 21.

26. Lewis (2013), 64.

27. Kelly Bit (2014), "Hedge Funds Trail Stocks for Fifth Year with 7.4% Return," *Bloomberg*, January 8 (www.bloomberg.com/news).

28. Ziobrowski et al. (2004), described in Schweizer (2011), introduction.

29. Schweizer (2011), introduction.

30. Kaiser (2009), chapter 18.

31. Ibid., chapter 24.

32. Ibid., chapter 24.

33. Ibid., chapter 24.

34. Ibid., chapter 24.

35. Ibid., chapter 19.

36. Schweizer (2013), introduction.

37. Ibid., chapter 2. Schweizer used data from MapLight (www.maplight.org).

38. Quoted in ibid., chapter 2.

39. Hatch (2012), 3.

40. The criteria used by Citizens Against Government Wasted are: (1) requested by only one chamber of Congress, (2) not specifically authorized, (3) not competitively awarded, (4) not requested by the president, (5) greatly exceeds the president's budget request or the previous year's funding, (6) not the subject of congressional hearings, and (7) serves only a local or special interest (www.cagw.org).

41. Citizens Against Government Waste, "Congressional Pig Book" (www.cagw.org).

42. Kaiser (2009), chapter 24.

43. Fulmer, Knill, and Yu (2012), 1, 16.

44. Yu and Yu (2011), 1865.

45. For the full story of the creation of earmarks, see Kaiser (2009), chapter 5.

46. Congressional Research Service (2006).

47. Transparency International has created an index of corruption for 177 countries. The three I named were among the twenty most corrupt in 2013 (www.transparency.org).

48. Kaiser (2009), chapter 24.

49. For a quantitative analysis of effects on the revolving door (minor, even when confining the analysis to officially registered lobbyists), see Cain and Drutman (2014).

50. Erika Eichelberger (2013), "Washington's Vanishing Lobbyists Hide Behind the Rules," *Mother Jones*, April 9 (www.motherjones.com).

51. Lee Fang (2014), "Where Have All the Lobbyists Gone?" *The Nation*, March 10–17 (www.thenation.com).

52. Lewis (2013), 72.

53. Kaiser (2009), chapters 5–18; Mann and Ornstein (2006), chapter 3.

54. Kaiser (2009), chapter 22.

55. Quoted in ibid., chapter 19.

56. Quoted in Mann and Ornstein (2006), 5.

57. Ibid., 1–6.

58. Author's analysis of federal budgets available from Office of Management and Budget, "Historical Budget Data," whitehouse.gov/omb/budget/historicals. The categories of domestic spending included in the calculations were the following: Total general science, space, and technology; Total energy; Total natural resources and environment; Farm income stabilization; Agricultural research and services; Total transportation; Total community and regional development; Total education, training, employment, and social services; Total health (Medicare is a separate category from Total health); General retirement and disability insurance; Housing assistance; Other income security.

59. A table of pages in the *Code of Federal Regulations* from 1938 through 2013 may be downloaded from the *Federal Register* website. See note 9, prologue.

Chapter 5. Institutional Sclerosis and Advanced Democracy

1. In my view, the closest thing to one-sentence summaries of their respective mindsets are Ronald Reagan's line in his 1981 inaugural address, "In this present crisis, government is not the solution to our problem; government is the problem," and George W. Bush's line in a 2003 Labor Day speech in Richfield, Ohio, "We have a responsibility that when somebody hurts, government has got to move." Quotations found at the American Presidency Project (www.presidency.ucsb.edu).

2. For accounts of earlier attempts to end the sugar subsidy, see Rauch (1999), 130–31.

3. Ibid., 193–96. The book was originally published in 1994 as *Demosclerosis*. In describing the thought experiment, I have substituted some details of my own for Rauch's.

4. Ibid., 197.

5. Joe Weisenthal (2013), "The Four Things That Worry Jamie Dimon . . . ," *Business Insider*, February 4 (www.businessinsider.com).

6. Rauch (1999), 12.

7. Eberstadt (2012).

8. Author's analysis of Social Security, Medicaid, Medicare, AFDC, and TANF data from various editions of the *Statistical Abstract of the United States*, US Census Bureau (www.census.gov), and Klemm (2000).

9. Jessie and Tarleton (2014), 2.

10. DiIulio (2014), 17–18.

11. Ibid., 18.

12. Author's analysis of the Census Bureau's voting and registration data available at www.census.gov.

13. Author's analysis of General Social Surveys, available at www3.norc.org/GSS+Website/.

14. The GOP is facing a demographic headwind, but for the next few election cycles it is a zephyr rather than a gale. It seems impossible that the headwind is not already a gale, or even a hurricane. After all, we know from the national census that non-Latino whites (hereafter just *whites*) fell to 64 percent of the population in 2010, while Latinos continued their skyrocketing rise, now constituting 16 percent of the population, overtaking African Americans as the nation's largest minority. We know from the National Election Pool exit polls, the source used

by all the major news organizations, that Democrats captured large majorities of Latinos (averaging 64 percent of the vote), blacks (92 percent), and Asians (62 percent) in the four presidential elections from 2000 through 2012. The Census Bureau's projections tell us that America's minorities will continue to increase as a proportion of the population, with whites becoming a minority of all Americans in the early 2040s.

And yet, when these numbers are plugged into the standard arithmetic for predicting voting outcomes, the expected increase in the Democratic vote in 2016 is not 5, 6, or 7 percentage points. Nor even 1 or 2 percentage points. The demographic changes I just described may be expected to produce an increase in the Democratic presidential vote of just three-tenths of 1 percentage point.

That counterintuitive result is possible because of another set of numbers that goes into the arithmetic, also produced by the Census Bureau in periodic special surveys for the November Current Population survey: voter turnout. In the presidential elections from 2000 through 2008 (the 2012 figures aren't available as I write), the percentage of Americans eighteen years and older who actually voted averaged 57 percent. But those percentages varied widely by ethnic group. Among whites, the average turnout was 64 percent. Among blacks, 57 percent. Among Latinos and Asians, just 29 percent.

That's why the headwind is so feeble in the near term. Between 2012 and 2016, the Census Bureau estimates that the population of voting-age Latinos will increase by 3.9 million people, compared to an increase of just 1.8 million whites. But because of their much lower turnout, the expected increase in Latino voters is 9,513 fewer—yes, *fewer*—than the expected increase in white voters. The only reason that the Democrats can expect even a microscopic 0.3 percentage-point increase in the 2016 vote is because of an increase in the black voting-age population.

In the long term, the GOP will indeed face a gale. Much of the explanation for the low turnout of Latinos and Asians is that many are recent immigrants, are not yet citizens, and hence are not eligible to vote. Among citizens, turnout in presidential elections is already around 47 percent for Latinos and 45 percent for Asians. As time goes on, it is plausible that the percentage of Latinos and Asians who are citizens will increase, and that the propensity of Latinos and Asians to vote will eventually be about the same as the propensity of other Americans. To be specific, suppose I assume that the overall turnout rate for Latinos and Asians will linearly converge on the African American turnout rate of 57 percent, reaching that point by 2040. Leaving the other parameters unchanged, the expected Democratic vote for president will rise from 51 percent in 2012 to 55 percent in 2024 and to 64 percent by 2040. The original version of this discussion appeared on the AEI public policy blog on February 8, 2013, and includes links to the sources. Charles Murray (2013), "The GOP's Electoral Collapse Is Postponed," *AEIdeas*, February 8 (www.aei-ideas.org).

Chapter 6. On the Choice of Civil Disobedience

1. I am drawing from Weber (1918) and more generally from Fabienne (2014).
2. Quoted in Lipset (1996), 18.

3. Locke (1689).
4. Grund (1837), vol. 1, 265.
5. Ibid., 293.
6. Tocqueville (1838), vol. 2, part 2, chapter 8.
7. In any discussion of limited government, you are sure to hear from the left that the federal government began to expand from the beginning, with Thomas Jefferson's approval of the Louisiana Purchase and Abraham Lincoln's approval of federal participation in the building of the transcontinental railroad as prime exhibits. In reality, the departures from strict constitutional limits were remarkable for both their rarity and the gravity with which they were debated. The famous debates about whether the federal government should fund internal improvements are a case in point. As early as Jefferson's administration, a limited federal role in aiding the National Road was authorized under special conditions that satisfied Jefferson of its constitutionality. Congress justified and Jefferson approved the National Road for two reasons. First, Congress did have the explicit power to establish and maintain post roads, and there was no existing road to the newly settled lands of the west that could be used for that purpose; second, a contractual arrangement for funding the road meant that the federal government would not be out of pocket. The new state of Ohio had entered into an agreement with the federal government whereby Ohio would not tax the proceeds from the sale of federal land for five years, in return for the federal government spending one-twentieth of the proceeds on the National Road. In the early 1830s, the costs of extensions to the federal road were returned to the states through which it went. Even so, Jefferson wanted a constitutional amendment adding authority for certain internal improvements as a new enumerated power. Madison, Monroe, Jackson, Polk, Pierce, and Buchanan—two Jeffersonian Republicans and four Jacksonian Democrats—also went on record, often using strong language, as saying that internal improvements were unconstitutional, though some small projects slipped through. The chief offender against the prohibition on funds for internal improvement was James Monroe (an Anti-Federalist during the ratification debate), who, despite his strong statement about the unconstitutionality of such expenditures in his first annual message to Congress, signed several bills in the last two years of his administration that provided modest sums to survey harbor obstructions and the routes of proposed roads and canals. See Eastman (2001), 82–83. For different interpretations of the importance of these exceptions, see Greve (2012), chapter 7, and Epstein (2014), 197–98. The only president who disagreed was John Quincy Adams, defeated after one term by Andrew Jackson in part because of the unpopularity of augmenting federal power. It should be noted that even when the Constitution provided for a federal role, pre–Civil War Congresses were sometimes slow to exercise their authority. Despite the Constitution's explicit authorization of federal national bankruptcy laws, for example, only two such bills were passed from 1790 until the Civil War, and both of those were repealed within a few years of their passage. When the federal government intervened in state affairs, it was usually to assert the primacy of individual rights over state incursions on those rights. For example, the Constitution forbade states from weakening the obligations of private contracts, and the Supreme Court's decisions

on that topic uniformly used an expansive definition of *contract*, invalidating state laws that even came close to crossing the constitutional prohibition.

8. Grover Cleveland's message to Congress vetoing the Texas Seed Bill, February 16, 1887, available at the Mises Institute website, www.mises.org.

9. Bryce (1903), 536–37.

10. In a poll conducted in August 2014, 11 percent of the respondents described themselves as libertarian and also knew what "libertarian" means. See Kiley (2014). Many who think of themselves as conservatives will also be persuaded by the Madisonian case for lost legitimacy, but coming up with any specific number must be an estimate. I base my 20 percent upper-bound estimate on May 2014 polls by AP/GfK (GfK is a leading market research agency) and NBC/Wall Street Journal finding, respectively, that 20 and 24 percent of respondents self-identified as supporters of the Tea Party movement. See also Bowman and Marsico (2014).

11. "Public Trust in Government, 1958–2013." 2014. Pew Research Center for the People & the Press, November 13 (www.people-press.org). "CNN Poll: Trust in Government at All-Time Low," *Political Ticker Blog*, August 8, 2014 (www.politicalticker.blogs.cnn.com).

12. While there are no data for breaking out how blacks in the late 1950s and early 1960s answered the question about trusting the federal government, there is reason to infer that their percentages would not have been much different from those of white Americans. African Americans, acutely conscious of the failure of America to live up to its ideals, saw the federal government as their protection against oppression at the state and local levels.

13. This discussion of the three compacts draws from Charles Murray (1997), "Americans Remain Wary of Washington," *Wall Street Journal*, December 23.

14. The phrase appears in Jefferson's draft of the Virginia Act for Establishing Religious Freedom.

15. Howard (2014), 139.

Chapter 7. The Ground Rules for Civil Disobedience

1. This example was made famous by Kohlberg (1981).

2. For more complete discussions of *public goods*, see Epstein (1985), 166–69, or Murray (1997), 11–17.

3. This logic justifies the use of tax dollars to fund education but does not require the government to run the school system.

4. *Korematsu v. United States*, 323 U.S. 214 (1944).

5. For an overview of the abuses of property rights, see Sandefur (2006).

6. Some of the abuses associated with wetlands arise from absurd interpretations of the Rivers and Harbors Appropriations Act of 1899 (33 United States Code Part 403).

7. Carpenter, Knepper, and Ross (2012) describe the proliferation of occupational licensing. See also Sandefur (2010).

8. Guerin and DelPo (2013).

9. Administrative Procedure Act, 5 U.S.C. § 706(a)(2).

10. The farm exemption does not apply if the farm has employee housing.

Chapter 8. Help for Ordinary Americans

1. From the FAQ page at the OSHA website, www.osha.gov.
2. Jung and Makowsky (2014), 3.
3. *OSHA Inspections* (2002), 3–4 (www.osha.gov).
4. For the complete list of civil and criminal enforcement actions, search for "Enforcement Annual Results Numbers at a Glance for Fiscal Year (FY) 2013" at the EPA website, www2.epa.gov.
5. Federalist Society website, www.fed-soc.org.
6. Institute for Justice website, www.ij.org; Goldwater Institute website, www .goldwaterinstitute.org; Pacific Legal Foundation website, www.pacificlegal.org.

Chapter 9. Treating Government as an Insurable Hazard

1. These activities are all described on the American Dental Association website, www.ada.org.
2. Census Bureau, "2011 County Business Patterns Data," www.censtats.census.gov.
3. The seminal disquisition on the role of approbation in enabling limited government is Smith (1759).
4. Restatement (Second) of Contracts, §178 (1981). "Restatements of the Law," of which the Restatement (Second) of Contracts is one, are developed by the American Law Institute and are used by lawyers and judges as the most authoritative statement of the principles of common law.

Chapter 10. From Systematic Civil Disobedience to a "No Harm, No Foul" Regulatory Regime

1. David W. Brown (2011), "In Praise of Bad Steve," *The Atlantic*, October 6.
2. There is a huge literature on this issue. For an overview, see Sunstein (2009).
3. Five of the justices—Hugo Black, Stanley Reed, Felix Frankfurter, William Douglas, and Robert Jackson—were on the Court in both 1942 and 1954. Of the four who were not on the Court in 1942, two were Democrats nominated by Truman (Tom Clark and Sherman Minton) and two were Republicans, one nominated by Truman (Harold Burton) and the other nominated by Dwight Eisenhower (Earl Warren). The four not on the Court in 1954 were two Republicans nominated by Coolidge (Harlan Stone) and Hoover (Owen Roberts), and two Democrats (Frank Murphy and James Byrnes) nominated by FDR. Of the four new members of the Court in 1954, Minton and Burton were generally conservative (Minton, conspicuously liberal as a senator, voted much more conservatively when he reached the Supreme Court), and Clark had a mixed record. Only Warren was reliably liberal. Overall, the 1954 Court does not look like a noticeably more liberal Court than the one that decided *Wickard* in 1942.
4. Section 706 of the Administrative Procedure Act of 1946 reads as follows:

> To the extent necessary to decision and when presented, the reviewing court shall decide all relevant questions of law, interpret constitutional and statutory provisions, and determine the meaning or applicability of the terms of an agency action. The reviewing court shall—

(1) compel agency action unlawfully withheld or unreasonably delayed; and

(2) hold unlawful and set aside agency action, findings, and conclusions found to be—

(A) arbitrary, capricious, an abuse of discretion, or otherwise not in accordance with law;

(B) contrary to constitutional right, power, privilege, or immunity;

(C) in excess of statutory jurisdiction, authority, or limitations, or short of statutory right;

(D) without observance of procedure required by law;

(E) unsupported by substantial evidence in a case subject to sections 556 and 557 of this title or otherwise reviewed on the record of an agency hearing provided by statute; or

(F) unwarranted by the facts to the extent that the facts are subject to trial de novo by the reviewing court.

In making the foregoing determinations, the court shall review the whole record or those parts of it cited by a party, and due account shall be taken of the rule of prejudicial error.

5. *Citizens to Preserve Overton Park v. Volpe*, 401 U.S. 402 (1971). The cases cited by the Court in support of this interpretation were *McBee v. Bomar*, 296 F.2d 235, 237 (6th Cir. 1961); *In re: Josephson*, 218 F.2d 174, 182 (1st Cir. 1954); *Western Addition Community Organization v. Weaver*, 294 F.Supp. 433 (ND Cal. 1968); and *Wong Wing Hang v. Immigration and Naturalization Serv.*, 360 F.2d 715, 719 (2nd Cir. 1966).

6. *Overton*, 401 U.S. 402 (1971), emphasis added. The Court revisited "arbitrary and capricious" in *Motor Vehicle Mfrs. Assn. v. State Farm Mut.*, 463 U.S. 29 (1983), in which it held that the National Highway Traffic Safety Administration's rescission of the regulatory requirement for automatic seat belts was arbitrary and capricious. To me as a nonlawyer, it seems laughable that out of all the ways in which the regulatory state has behaved arbitrarily and capriciously, the one thing that the Supreme Court ruled was arbitrary and capricious was a regulatory agency's decision to get rid of a regulation mandating one of the most foolish ideas for automotive safety ever concocted, the automatic seat belt. But I'm not a lawyer.

7. My thanks to Amy Korenvaes for suggesting that reality TV would be a terrific way to publicize the defense funds' work, and for coming up with the title.

8. Howard (1995), 11–14. Howard's book was published in 1995, so the details of the regulations I cite may have changed since then, but the tone of Howard's account will sound grimly familiar to factory managers today.

9. 5 U.S.C. 706(2)(A).

10. This is a common feature of regulatory inspections. Braithwaite and Braithwaite (1995), 320, document that inspectors of nursing homes focus on ten to twenty regulations, but each inspector focuses on a different set. Cited in Howard (2014), 36.

11. The ways in which safety regulations backfire is the subject of a large literature. One of the most famous problems is the moral hazard introduced by safety equipment. Knowing (or thinking) they are protected from accident, people tend to engage in riskier behavior. You may have noticed this in yourself if you own two cars with different cornering abilities—you round the same corner at different

speeds depending on which car you're driving. When elaborate safety regulations are in place, people also get sloppier about planning for unlikely scenarios. The Kemeny Commission's investigation of the Three Mile Island nuclear accident found that elaborate safety regulations had displaced the operators' knowledge about the workings of the individual systems under their control, preventing them from knowing how to deal with combinations of small equipment failures that could have averted the accident. In still other cases, safety equipment that would be useful in one kind of accident makes matters worse in other kinds of accidents. The worst of the damage in the *Deepwater Horizon* oil spill in 2010 would probably have been avoided if the crew hadn't directed the spewing mud and gas into a "safety" device that, in the prevailing circumstances, enveloped the rig in explosive gas. See Howard (2014), chapter 2, for a discussion of these and other cases.

12. Many libertarian readers are thinking to themselves that any company that has poisonous substances around with no labeling and no restricted access is leaving itself open to a gigantic lawsuit if an accident occurs, and everyone knows that. You could get rid of OSHA's regulation altogether and the safety statistics wouldn't change. I agree with that logic. Except for issues such as the environment, which involve genuine externalities, just about everything the regulatory state does could be done more efficiently through a properly designed tort system. I am convinced of that, but I am discussing realistic options for rolling back the regulatory state, and getting rid of the regulatory state altogether isn't one of them.

13. Google "images for Sacketts' home lot" for ground-level photographs and use Google Earth to see a bird's-eye view of 1604 Kalispell Bay Road, Priest River, ID 83856.

14. The Sacketts won their case, but, incredibly, the EPA is still pursuing the Sacketts as I write (October 2014).

Chapter 11. A Necessary Crisis

1. Storage drums need reconditioning to cleanse them of whatever they previously contained—liquids such as paints, resins, tars, solvents, oils, acids, and adhesives—and to restore the drums' shape and integrity.

2. This brief narrative is taken from the decision issued in 1985 by the United States District Court of New Hampshire, 630 F.Supp 1361 (1985).

3. The First Circuit affirmed the district court's decision with two minor exceptions. 900 F.2d 419.

4. Breyer (1993), chapter 1.

5. Ibid.

6. Even water and sewage services can be objects of controversy. People in small towns who want to avoid development rationally fight against offers by the county or state to finance water and sewage systems, because requiring land to support individual wells and septic fields makes large housing developments uneconomic.

7. This account of the Forest Service draws from a longer discussion in Fukuyama (2014).

8. Murray (2008) documents this assertion for both K–12 and higher education.

9. I date the beginning of quantitative policy science to the massive study of the

relationship of schools and family background to academic achievement mandated by Congress in the aftermath of the 1964 Civil Rights Act and directed by sociologist James Coleman in 1965–66, which employed the first major multivariate quantitative analysis (using regression analysis). The statistical theory of regression analysis had been known for decades, but until the advent of sufficiently advanced computers and software, multivariate analyses with several variables and adequate samples were impractical—the computational requirements were too great.

10. I'm assuming that it's 2020 and the 174,545 pages in the *Code of Federal Regulations* as of 2012 have continued to increase at the 4,143-page-per-year average established during President Obama's first four years.

11. Stein (1998), 32.

Chapter 12. The Return of Diversified America

1. Lyndon Johnson, December 9, 1964, remarks at a reception for new Democrats in Congress (www.presidency.ucsb.edu).

2. Fischer (1989).

3. Ibid., 227.

4. Ibid., 703.

5. Ibid., 680.

6. This account draws from Barone (2013), chapter 3.

7. Before the Irish arrived, Catholics were a significant presence only in parts of Maryland.

8. Barone (2013), 127.

9. I do not mention Chinese and Japanese immigration because it was so isolated to parts of the West Coast (and Hawaii, after the United States acquired Hawaii in 1898), and the numbers were so small. From the first census data in 1850 through 1960, the Chinese and Japanese never amounted to more than 0.2 percent and 0.3 percent of the population, respectively. Author's analysis of decennial census data from Social Explorer (www.socialexplorer.com).

10. World War I did not have nearly as much effect as World War II. Only 2.7 million American young men were drafted to serve, less than a sixth of the number drafted in World War II, and the effort lasted just a year and a half. See Bruscino (2010), 6.

11. The National World War II Museum, "By the Numbers," www.nationalww2 museum.org.

12. Murray (1984), chapters 1–3.

13. I present that case in Murray (2012), Part I.

14. I'm referring to Dunbar's number, based on the work of British anthropologist Robin Dunbar. See Dunbar (1992).

15. Why do I refer to "churches" instead of using a more inclusive term? Because I'm talking about religion as a source of social capital, and in the United States that means Christianity. In the General Social Surveys taken from 2000 to 2012, 94 percent of people who expressed a religious preference were Christian. Only in the largest cities are synagogues a significant source of social capital. Mosques are significant in only a handful of ethnic neighborhoods. Author's analysis, General Social Survey, combined for 2000–2012.

16. Putnam (2000).

17. For a graphic description of one such distressed rural area (Harlan County, Kentucky), see Bishop (2008), 136–41.

18. Big cities comprise the 62 cities with more than 500,000 people. Satellites to major urban areas comprise the 1,112 cities or towns of any size that are in a contiguously urbanized area containing a city with at least 500,000 people. Most of these are suburbs. Small cities comprise the 1,464 stand-alone cities (i.e., not satellites to a nearby big city) of 25,000 to 499,999. Rural and small-city America refers to rural areas and to the 24,411 towns of fewer than 25,000 people that are not satellites to a large city.

    The classifications are based on the 2010 census, the category of a place in the 917 Core Based Statistical Areas defined by the Census Bureau, and city populations. In reaching my definition of a "Greater X" for the fifty largest cities, you may be wondering if I checked the location of every town in America that was in an MSA with a city of 500,000 persons or more. I did not. Empirically, there is a high degree of consistency between population density and whether a place in an MSA with a big city is a satellite or a standalone, and a useful cutoff point is 2,000 persons per square mile. Even a little more than that, and places have a high probability of being a satellite; even a little lower than that, and places are almost always standalone towns or cities. I have no theory for 2,000. It just works out that way. After assuring myself of the high reliability of this indictor, I visually checked all towns that were in the 1,800–2,200 person range, plus the towns that were larger than 50,000 persons regardless of density.

19. I think that people in even the largest cities need a lot less oversight than they're getting, but I acknowledge that this reflects my libertarian bias. When it comes to cities of 500,000 and smaller, the empirical case for my position becomes quite strong; it's weaker for the largest cities.

20. Author's analysis of decennial census data from Social Explorer (www.social explorer.com).

21. "Minorities Expected to Be Majority in 2050," CNN, August 13, 2008, www.cnn .com.

22. Author's analysis of 2010 census data from socialexplorer.com.

23. In this discussion, the most relevant issue is political power in a city. I therefore use the official city population, not the more accurate representation of contiguous urban population used in the discussion of size of place.

24. Jens Krogstad and Mark Lopez (2014), "Hispanic Nativity Shift: U.S. Births Drive Population Growth as Immigration Stalls," Pew Research Hispanic Trends Project, April 29 (www.pewhispanic.org).

25. Barone (2013), 254–56.

26. The nineteen cities outside the former Confederacy with more than 100,000 African Americans in 2010 were, in descending order of their black populations, New York City, Los Angeles, Detroit, Philadelphia, Baltimore, Chicago, St. Louis, Cleveland, Washington, Newark, Cincinnati, Indianapolis, Las Vegas, Columbus, Minneapolis, Sacramento, Seattle, San Francisco, and Milwaukee.

27. Originally, the area known colloquially as Silicon Valley followed the Santa Clara Valley south of San Francisco, and was bounded roughly by San Jose on the south

and Redwood City on the north. That area is still home to the most famous IT firms—Apple, Google, Intel, Cisco, and Oracle among them—but growth has now effectively extended Silicon Valley around the southern edge of San Francisco Bay to Fremont and Milpitas, southwest past San Jose, and northward to Burlingame. Silicon Valley thus defined has 1.7 million people.

28. Bishop (2008).

29. Most of the noncompetitive counties were in the South, where voters had a chance to vote for the first presidential candidate from the Deep South since 1808 (Charles Pinckney of South Carolina, who ran unsuccessfully against Thomas Jefferson in 1804 and James Madison in 1808). Andrew Jackson was born on the border of North and South Carolina, but lived as an adult in Tennessee. Subsequent Southern presidential candidates came from the mid-South.

30. Bishop (2008), 10, Table 1.1.

31. Alan Murray (2014), "The Divided States of America," *Wall Street Journal,* June 12.

32. Ibid. For a quantitative measure of partisan conflict that goes back to 1891, see Azzimonti (2014).

33. Murray (2012).

34. Herrnstein and Murray (1994), chapter 1; Murray (2012), chapter 2.

35. Florida (2012), Appendix.

Chapter 13. The Best of Times

1. Randall Stross (2013), "Wearing a Badge, and a Video Camera," *New York Times,* April 6.

2. Airbnb, "About Us," www.airbnb.com.

3. Some examples: Olivia Nuzzi (2014), "Uber's Biggest Problem Isn't Surge Pricing. What If It's Sexual Harassment by Drivers?," *The Daily Beast,* March 28 (www.thedailybeast.com); Jeff Bercovici (2014), "Uber's Ratings Terrorize Drivers and Trick Riders. Why Not Fix Them," *Forbes,* August 14 (www.forbes.com). For a good summary of the issues swirling around Uber and the taxi companies, see Emily Badger (2014), "Taxi Medallions Have Been the Best Investment in America for Years. Now Uber May Be Changing That," *Washington Post,* November 27 (www.washingtonpost.com).

4. Luz Lazo (2014), "Cab Companies Unite Against Uber and Other Ride-Share Services," *Washington Post,* August 10.

5. Hard-core progressives do see Uber as an ideological issue—and rightly so, because Uber challenges the foundations of the regulatory state. For an impassioned denunciation of Uber and the threat it poses, see Andrew Leonard (2014), "Why Uber Must Be Stopped," *Salon,* August 31 (www.salon.com).

6. For a description of Uber's resources in fighting city hall, see Rosalind Helderman (2014), "Uber Pressures Regulators by Mobilizing Riders and Hiring Vast Lobbying Network," *Washington Post,* December 13.

7. Walter Russell Mead (2010), "American Challenges: The Blue Model Breaks Down," *The American Interest,* January 28 (www.the-american-interest.com).

8. Public Sector Retirement Systems (2014), "The Fiscal Health of State Pension

Plans Funding Gap Continues to Grow," Pew Charitable Trusts, April 8 (www .pewtrusts.org).

9. For an extended analysis of California's pension mess, see Steve Malanga, "The Pension Fund That Ate California," *City Journal*, Winter (www.city -journal.org).

10. Ibid.

11. Bureau of Labor Statistics (2013), Employer Costs for Employee Compensation—September. Washington, DC: Department of Labor.

12. Richwine and Biggs (2011).

13. From the official job description of accounting technicians in California. California Department of Human Resources (www.calhr.ca.gov).

14. Mead, "American Challenges."

15. Congressional Budget Office (2014), *The Budget and Economic Outlook, 2014–2024*, February 4 (www.cbo.gov), table 1-2. I assumed that the CBO was using 2013 dollars. I could not find an explicit statement to that effect, but neither was any other year mentioned, and 2013 dollars were the most recent available when the study was published.

16. The federal budget is commonly expressed as a percentage of GDP. In those terms, federal outlays amounted to 20.8 percent of GDP in 2013 and are projected to be 22.4 percent in 2024. That's relevant to the sustainability of the budget. But why should it be that larger GDP requires larger absolute expenditures? The cost of the military depends on the threats we face, not the size of its GDP. Income transfers (which comprise by far the greatest proportion of the budget) depend on the number of people who qualify for them, not the size of GDP. The education budget depends on the number of students, not the size of GDP. To treat absolute increases in the federal budget as normal just because GDP has gone up strikes me as nonsensical.

17. CBO (2014), *The Budget and Economic Outlook, 2014–2024*, February 4 (www.cbo .gov).

18. The apparent drop in the last half of the 1970s is illusory, created by the high inflation rate during that period—the federal budget grew, but the purchasing power of the budget fell.

19. Author's analysis of the American Community Survey for 2011, accessed through Social Explorer, www.social.explorer.com.

20. CBO (2014), *The Budget and Economic Outlook, 2014–2024*, February 4 (www.cbo .gov).

21. The heads of certain corporations have been passionate and principled defenders not only of free enterprise but also of the most abstract principles of limited government, and they have operated their business in accordance with those principles. Some of these individuals were instrumental in the founding of the think tanks of the right recounted in the prologue.

22. Garrett (2014), chapter 1, fig. 1.1.

23. Ibid., appendix, fig. A.1 and following page.

24. "The Criminalization of American Business," *Economist*, August 30, 2014.

25. Garrett (2014).

26. "The Criminalization of American Business."
27. Garrett (2014), chapter 1.
28. Copland (2010) and Copland and Gorodetski (2014), both available at www .manhattan-institute.org, are excellent companion reading for Garrett (2014).
29. For a detailed account of the Arthur Andersen case, see Silverglate (2009), chapter 5.
30. See Lewis (2013) for a roundup of the industries that are most compromised by their reliance on government cooperation and favors.
31. Banks and Blakeman (2012), chapter 2.
32. Ibid., chapter 3.
33. Quoted in ibid., chapter 3.
34. Jung and Makowsky (2014), 14.
35. Center for Progressive Reform, "Environmental Enforcement" (www.progressive reform.org).
36. Office of Public Affairs (2013), "Justice Department Announces Update to Marijuana Enforcement Policy," Department of Justice, August 13 (www.justice.gov).
37. Banks and Blakeman (2012), chapter 2.
38. Schuck (2014), 307.
39. Heclo (1977), 237.
40. Dull (2009), 436–37.
41. Schuck (2014), 315.
42. This is a median for the number of managerial levels (in parentheses) in the cabinet departments reported by Light (2008), 59, 61, as of 2004: Defense (30), Transportation (25), Agriculture, Interior, Treasury (24), Commerce (22), Homeland Security (21), Education (19), Veterans Affairs (18), HUD (15), State (10). Light does not provide figures for HHS or Energy.
43. Light (2008), 59.
44. Congressional Budget Office (2014), *Comparing the Compensation of Federal and Private-Sector Employees.* Washington, DC: Congressional Budget Office (www.cbo .gov); Andrew Biggs and Jason Richwine (2012), "The Truth About Federal Salary Numbers," *Washington Post*, November 18.
45. Office of Personnel Management, Salary Table No. 2014-ES and Salary Table 2014-GS (www.opm.gov).
46. Schuck (2014), 321.
47. Richard A. Oppel (2014), "Every Senior V.A. Executive Was Rated 'Fully Successful' or Better over 4 Years," *New York Times,* June 20.
48. Andrew Biggs and Jason Richwine (2012), "The Underworked Public Employee," *Wall Street Journal,* December 4.
49. Light (2008), chapters 4 and 5 for discussion of surveys of federal employees and prospective federal employees. The text draws from Schuck (2014), 321.

Chapter 14. Once the Curtain Has Been Pulled Aside

1. A spreadsheet with the latest estimates of historical per-capita GDP may be downloaded from the Maddison Project (www.ggdc.net). The project is named after Angus Maddison, a pioneer in long-term historical economic statistics.
2. The two measures are only fractionally different. In 1929, the first year in which

GDP was calculated, per capita GNP was $10,797 (2010 dollars) while per capita GDP was $10,954.

3. I presented a version of this graph ending in 2004 and a similar argument in Murray (2006), 126.

4. Matthew O'Brien (2012), "Why the Mortgage Interest Deduction Is Terrible," *The Atlantic*, October 21 (www.theatlantic.com).

5. The following argument draws directly from Murray (2006), 38–40.

6. In retirement, liberal senator George McGovern, the Democratic presidential nominee in 1972, bought and operated an inn that went bankrupt in large part because of the costs of dealing with senseless regulations. He wrote in the *Wall Street Journal* that he wished that "during the years I was in public office, I had firsthand experience about the difficulties business people face every day. That knowledge would have made me a better U.S. Senator and a more understanding presidential contender." See George McGovern (1992), "A Politician's Dream Is a Businessman's Nightmare," *Wall Street Journal*, June 1.

7. For a detailed account of the process, see DiSalvo (2011).

8. Ibid., 11.

9. Ryan (2014).

10. This line of argument draws from Charles Murray (2014), "The Trouble Isn't Liberals. It's Progressives," *Wall Street Journal*, July 1.

11. David Gelernter (2006), "Back to Federalism: The Proper Remedy for Polarization," *The Weekly Standard*, April 10 (www.weeklystandard.com).

12. For my own account of American exceptionalism, see Murray (2013).

13. Tocqueville (1838), 380.

Bibliography

Anderson, William L. 2009. "Federal Crimes and the Destruction of Law." *Regulation* (Winter): 10–15.

Annals of Congress. The Debates and Proceedings in the Congress of the United States. 42 vols. Washington, DC: Gales & Seaton, 1834–56.

Baker, John S. 2008. "Revisiting the Explosive Growth of Federal Crimes." In *Legal Memorandum #26*. Washington, DC: Heritage Foundation.

Balko, Radley. 2013. *Rise of the Warrior Cop: The Militarization of America's Police Forces.* New York: PublicAffairs.

Banks, Christopher P., and John C. Blakeman. 2012. *The U.S. Supreme Court and New Federalism: From the Rehnquist to the Roberts Court.* Lanham, MD: Rowman & Littlefield Publishers.

Barnett, Kent. 2013. "Resolving the ALJ Quandary." *Vanderbilt Law Review* 66 (3): 797–865.

Barnett, Randy E. 2001. "The Original Meaning of the Commerce Clause." *University of Chicago Law Review* 68 (1): 101–47.

———. 2004. *Restoring the Lost Constitution: The Presumption of Liberty.* Princeton: Princeton University Press.

———. 2008. "Scrutiny Land." *Michigan Law Review* 106: 1479–1500.

Barone, Michael. 2013. *Shaping Our Nation: How Surges of Migration Transformed America and Its Politics.* New York: Crown Forum.

Berger, Raoul. 1996. "Judicial Manipulation of the Commerce Clause." *Texas Law Review* 74 (4): 696–717.

Bishop, Bill. 2008. *The Big Sort: Why the Clustering of Like-Minded America Is Tearing Us Apart.* Boston: Houghton Mifflin.

Blackstone, William. 1769. *Commentaries on the Laws of England.* Vol. 4. Oxford: Clarendon Press.

Bowman, Karlyn, and Jennifer Marsico. 2014. *The Tea Party Movement: The Latest.* Washington, DC: American Enterprise Institute.

Braithwaite, John, and Valerie Braithwaite. 1995. "The Politics of Legalism: Rules Versus Standards in Nursing-Home Regulations." *Social & Legal Studies* 4 (3): 307–41.

Breyer, Stephen. 1993. *Breaking the Vicious Circle: Toward Effective Risk Regulation.* Cambridge, MA: Harvard University Press.

Brooks, David. 2000. *Bobos in Paradise: The New Upper Class and How They Got There.* New York: Simon & Schuster.

Brown, David W. 2011. "In Praise of Bad Steve." *The Atlantic*, October 6.

Bruscino, Thomas A. 2010. *A Nation Forged in War: How World War II Taught Americans to Get Along*. Nashville: University of Tennessee Press.

Bryce, James. 1903. *The American Commonwealth*. 3rd ed. Vol. 2. New York: Macmillan.

Buckley, F. H., ed. 2013. *The American Illness: Essays on the Rule of Law*. New Haven: Yale University Press.

Buckley, William F., Jr. 1951. *God and Man at Yale: The Superstitions of Academic Freedom*. Chicago: Regnery.

Cain, Bruce E., and Lee Drutman. 2014. "Congressional Staff and the Revolving Door: The Impact of Regulatory Change." *Election Law Journal* 14 (1): 27–44.

Carpenter, Dick M., Lisa Knepper, and John K. Ross. 2012. *License to Work: A National Study of Burdens from Occupational Licensing*. Arlington, VA: Institute for Justice.

Chernow, Ron. 2004. *Alexander Hamilton*. New York: Penguin.

Clarke, Arthur C. 1962. *Profiles of the Future: An Inquiry Into the Limits of the Possible*. 1973 ed. New York: Henry Holt & Co.

Coase, Ronald H. 1960. "The Problem of Social Cost." *Journal of Law and Economics* 3 (1): 1–44.

Congressional Research Service. 2006. Earmarks in Appropriation Acts: FY1994, FY1996, FY1998, FY2000, FY2002, FY2004, FY2005. Washington, DC: Congressional Research Service.

Cook, Andrew C. 2013. *Tort Reform Update: Recently Enacted Legislative Reforms and State Court Challenges*. Washington, DC: Federalist Society.

Copland, James. 2010. "Regulation by Prosecution: The Problems with Treating Corporations as Criminals." New York: Manhattan Institute.

Copland, James, and Isaac Gorodetski. 2014. "The Shadow Lengthens: The Continuing Threat of Regulation by Prosecution." New York: Manhattan Institute.

Cruz, Ted. 2013. *The Legal Limit Report No. 1: The Obama Administration's Attempts to Expand Federal Power*. Washington, DC: United States Senate.

———. 2014. *The Legal Limit Report No. 5: The Obama Administration's Attempts to Expand Federal Power*. Washington, DC: United States Senate.

Cushman, Barry. 1998. *Rethinking the New Deal Court: The Structure of a Constitutional Revolution*. New York: Oxford University Press.

DeLeo, John D. Jr. 2008. *Administrative Law*. Clifton Park, NY: Delmar Cengage.

DeLong, James V. 2004. "The New 'Criminal' Classes: Legal Sanctions and Business Managers." In *Go Directly to Jail: The Criminalization of Almost Everything*, edited by Gene Healy, 9–44. Washington, DC: Cato Institute.

DiIulio, John J. Jr. 2014. *Bring Back the Bureaucrats*. West Conshohocken, PA: Templeton Press.

DiSalvo, Daniel. 2011. *Government Unions and the Bankrupting of America*. New York: Encounter.

Dull, Matthew, and Patrick S. Roberts. 2009. "Continuity, Competence, and the Succession of Senate-Confirmed Agency Appointees, 1989–2009." *Presidential Studies Quarterly* 39:432–53.

Dunbar, Robin. 1992. "Neocortex Size as a Constraint on Group Size in Primates." *Journal of Human Evolution* 22 (6): 469–93.

Eastman, John C. 2001. "Restoring the 'General' to the General Welfare Clause." *Chapman Law Review* 4: 63–87.

Eberstadt, Nicholas. 2012. *A Nation of Takers: America's Entitlement Epidemic.* West Conshohocken, PA: Templeton Press.

Elliott, Cary. 2004. *The Effects of Tort Reform: Evidence from the States.* Washington, DC: Congressional Budget Office.

Epstein, Richard A. 1985. *Takings: Private Property and the Power of Eminent Domain.* Cambridge, MA: Harvard University Press.

———. 1987. "The Proper Scope of the Commerce Power." *Virginia Law Review* 73 (8): 1387–1455.

———. 2006. *How Progressives Rewrote the Constitution.* Washington, DC: Cato Institute.

———. 2014. *The Classical Liberal Constitution: The Uncertain Quest for Limited Government.* Cambridge, MA: Harvard University Press.

———. In press. "The Progressives' Deadly Embrace of Cartels: A Close Look at Labor and Agricultural Markets 1890–1940." In *The Progressives' Century: Democratic Reform and Constitutional Government in the United States,* edited by Bruce Ackerman, Stephen Engel, and Stephen Skowronek.

Fabienne, Peter. 2014. "Political Legitimacy." In *The Stanford Encyclopedia of Philosophy,* edited by Edward N. Zalta. http://plato.stanford.edu.

Farhang, Sean. 2010. *The Litigation State: Public Regulation and Private Lawsuits in the United States.* Princeton: Princeton University Press.

Farrand, Max, ed. 1911. *The Records of the Federal Convention of 1787.* New Haven: Yale University Press.

Fischer, David Hackett. 1989. *Albion's Seed: Four British Folkways in America.* New York: Oxford University Press.

Florida, Richard. 2012. *The Rise of the Creative Class, Revisited.* Tenth Anniversary ed. New York: Basic Books.

Friedman, Milton. 1962. *Capitalism and Freedom.* Chicago: University of Chicago Press.

Friedman, Milton, and Anna J. Schwartz. 1963. *A Monetary History of the United States, 1867–1960.* Cambridge, MA: National Bureau of Economic Research.

Fukuyama, Francis. 2014. "America in Decay: The Sources of Political Dysfunction." *Foreign Affairs* (September/October). www.foreignaffairs.com.

Fuller, Lon L. 1964. *The Morality of Law: Storrs Lectures on Jurisprudence, Yale Law School, 1963.* New Haven: Yale University Press.

Fulmer, Sarah, April M. Knill, and Xiaoyun Yu. 2012. "Political Contributions and the Severity of Government Enforcement." Paper presented at the American Finance Association annual meeting, San Diego, March 1.

Garrett, Brandon L. 2014. *Too Big to Jail: How Prosecutors Compromise with Corporations.* Cambridge, MA: Belknap Press.

General Accounting Office. 1991. *Federal Lobbying: Federal Regulation of Lobbying Act of 1946 Is Ineffective.* Washington, DC: General Accounting Office.

Gillette, W. Michael. 2000. "Administrative Law Judges, Judicial Independence, and Judicial Review: *Qui custodiet ipsos custodes?*" *Journal of the National Association of Administrative Law Judges* (Spring): 95–117.

Goldberg, Jonah. 2007. *Liberal Fascism: The Secret History of the American Left from Mussolini to the Politics of Meaning.* New York: Doubleday.

Goldwater, Barry. 1960. *The Conscience of a Conservative.* Shepherdsville, KY: Victor Pub. Co.

Goodnow, Frank J. 1911. *Social Reform and the Constitution.* New York: Macmillan.

Grant, James. 2014. *The Forgotten Depression: 1921: The Crash That Cured Itself.* New York: Simon & Schuster.

Greve, Michael S. 1999. *Real Federalism: Why It Matters, How It Could Happen.* Washington, DC: AEI Press.

———. 2012. *The Upside-Down Constitution.* Cambridge, MA: Harvard University Press.

Grund, Francis J. 1837. *The Americans in Their Moral, Social, and Political Relations.* Vol. 1. London: Longman, Rees, Orme, Brown, Green, & Longman.

Guerin, Lisa, and Amy DelPo. 2013. *The Essential Guide to Federal Employment Laws.* 4th ed. Berkeley, CA: Nolo.

Hamburger, Philip. 2014. *Is Administrative Law Unlawful?* Chicago: University of Chicago Press.

Hamilton, Alexander. 1904. "The Continentalist No. VI." In *The Works of Alexander Hamilton*, edited by Henry Cabot Lodge. New York: G. P. Putnam's Sons.

Hamilton, Alexander, James Madison, and John Jay. 1787. *The Federalist Papers.* Project Gutenberg. www.gutenberg.org.

Hasnas, John. 2005. *Trapped: When Acting Ethically Is Against the Law.* Washington, DC: Cato Institute.

Hatch, Orrin. January 31, 2012. *Hearing Before the Committee on Finance by United States Senate.* Washington, DC: Government Printing Office.

Hayek, Friedrich A. 1944. *The Road to Serfdom.* 1972 ed. Chicago: University of Chicago Press.

Healy, Gene, ed. 2004. *Go Directly to Jail: The Criminalization of Almost Everything.* Washington, DC: Cato Institute.

Heclo, Hugh. 1977. *A Government of Strangers.* Washington, DC: Brookings Institution Press.

Herrnstein, Richard J., and Charles Murray. 1994. *The Bell Curve: Intelligence and Class Structure in American Life.* New York: Fress Press.

Higgs, Robert. 1987. *Crisis and Leviathan: Critical Episodes in the Growth of American Government.* New York: Oxford University Press.

Howard, Philip K. 1995. *The Death of Common Sense: How Law Is Suffocating America.* New York: Random House.

———. 2002. *The Collapse of the Common Good: How America's Lawsuit Culture Undermines Our Freedom.* New York: Ballantine.

———. 2009. *Life Without Lawyers: Liberating Americans from Too Much Law.* New York: W. W. Norton.

———. 2014. *The Rule of Nobody: Saving America from Dead Laws and Broken Government.* New York: W. W. Norton.

Huntington, Samuel P. 2004. *Who Are We? The Challenges to America's National Identity.* New York: Simon & Schuster.

Jessie, Lisa, and Mary Tarleton. 2014. *2012 Census of Governments: Employment Summary Report*. Washington, DC: US Bureau of the Census.

Jung, Juergen, and Michael D. Makowsky. 2014. "The Determinants of Federal and State Enforcement of Workplace Safety Regulations: OSHA Inspections 1990–2010." *Journal of Regulatory Economics* 45: 1–33.

Kaiser, Robert G. 2009. *So Damn Much Money: The Triumph of Lobbying and the Corrosion of American Government*. New York: Alfred A. Knopf.

Kennedy, Ted. 2009. *True Compass: A Memoir*. New York: Twelve.

Keynes, John Maynard. 1936. *The General Theory of Employment, Interest and Money*. New York: Harcourt Brace.

Kiley, Jocelyn. 2014. "In Search of Libertarians." Pew Research Center FactTank, August 25. www.pewresearch.org.

Kirk, Russell. 1953. *The Conservative Mind: From Burke to Santayana*. Chicago: Regnery.

Klemm, John D. 2000. "Medicaid Spending: A Brief History." *Health Care Financing Review* 22 (1): 105–12.

Kochan, Donald J. 1998. "'Public Use' and the Independent Judiciary: Condemnation in an Interest-Group Perspective." *Texas Review of Law & Politics* 3 (1): 1–190.

Kohlberg, Lawrence. 1981. *The Philosophy of Moral Development: Moral Stages and the Idea of Justice*: Vol. 1, *Essays on Moral Development*. San Francisco: Harper and Row.

Kozinski, Alex. 1995. "Introduction to Volume 19." *Harvard Journal of Law and Public Policy* 19: 1–8.

Lawson, Gary. 1994. "The Rise and Rise of the Administrative State." *Harvard Law Review* 107 (6): 1231–54.

Leuchtenburg, William E. 1995. *The Supreme Court Reborn: The Constitutional Revolution in the Age of Roosevelt*. New York: Oxford University Press.

Levy, Robert A., and William H. Mellor. 2008. *The Dirty Dozen: How Twelve Supreme Court Cases Radically Expanded Government and Eroded Freedom*. 2009 ed. Washington, DC: Cato Institute.

Lewis, Hunter. 2013. *Crony Capitalism in America: 2008–2012*. Edinburg, VA: AC2.

Light, Paul 2008. *A Government Ill Executed: The Decline of the Federal Service and How to Revive It*. Cambridge, MA: Harvard University Press.

Lipset, Seymour Martin. 1996. *American Exceptionalism: A Double-Edged Sword*. New York: W. W. Norton & Company.

Locke, John. 1689. *Two Treatises of Government*. 1960 ed. Cambridge, UK: Cambridge University Press.

Mann, Thomas E., and Norman J. Ornstein. 2006. *The Broken Branch: How Congress Is Failing America and How to Get It Back on Track*. New York: Oxford University Press.

McCarthy, Andrew. 2014. *Faithless Execution: Building the Political Case for Obama's Impeachment*. New York: Encounter Books.

Mullenix, Linda S. 2012. "The 25th Anniversary of the Summary Judgment Trilogy: Much Ado About Very Little." *Loyola University Chicago Law Journal* 43: 561–91.

Murray, Charles. 1984. *Losing Ground: American Social Policy 1950–1980*. New York: Basic Books.

————. 1997. *What It Means to Be a Libertarian: A Personal Interpretation.* New York: Broadway Books.

————. 2006. *In Our Hands: A Plan to Replace the Welfare State.* Washington: AEI Press.

————. 2008. *Real Education: Four Simple Truths for Bringing America's Schools Back to Reality.* New York: Crown Forum.

————. 2012. *Coming Apart: The State of White America, 1960–2012.* New York: Crown Forum

————. 2013. *American Exceptionalism.* Washington, DC: AEI Press.

Mutch, Robert E. 1988. *Campaigns, Congress, and Courts: The Making of Federal Campaign Finance Law.* New York: Praeger.

Natelson, Robert G. 2003. "The General Welfare Clause and the Public Trust: An Essay in Original Understanding." *University of Kansas Law Review* 52: 1–54.

Nisbet, Robert. 1953. *The Quest for Community: A Study in the Ethics of Order and Freedom.* New York: Oxford University Press.

Nozick, Robert. 1974. *Anarchy, State, and Utopia.* New York: Basic Books.

Olson, Walter K. 1991. *The Litigation Explosion: What Happened When America Unleashed the Lawsuit.* New York: Dutton.

————. 2011. *The Rule of Lawyers: How the New Litigation Elite Threatens America's Rule of Law.* New York: Truman Talley Books.

Ornstein, Norman J., Thomas E. Mann, Michael J. Malbin, and Andrew Rugg. 2013. *Vital Statistics on Congress.* Washington, DC: American Enterprise Institute, Brookings Institute, Campaign Finance Institute. www.brookings.edu/vitalstats.

Parker, Jeffrey S. 2013. "Corporate Crime, Overcriminalization, and the Failure of American Public Morality." In *The American Illness: Essays on the Rule of Law,* edited by F. H. Buckley, 407–33. New Haven: Yale University Press.

Paul, Ellen F. 1987. *Property Rights and Eminent Domain.* New Brunswick, NJ: Transaction Publishers.

Pestritto, Ronald J. 2007. "The Progressive Origins of the Administrative State: Wilson, Goodnow, and Landis." *Social Philosophy & Policy* 24 (1): 16–54.

Pollack, Michael C. 2011. "*Chevron*'s Regrets: The Persistent Vitality of the Nondelegation Doctrine." *NYU Law Review* 86: 316–50.

Poser, Susan, Brian H. Bornstein, and Erinn Klernan McGorty. 2003. "Measuring Damages for Lost Enjoyment of Life: The View from the Bench and the Jury Box." *Law and Human Behavior* 27 (1): 53–68.

Posner, Richard A. 2014. *The Economic Analysis of Law.* 9th ed. New York: Wolters Kluwer Law & Business.

Priest, George. 2013. "The Expansion of Modern U.S. Tort Law and Its Excesses." In *The American Illness: Essays on the Rule of Law,* edited by F. H. Buckley, 249–69. New Haven: Yale University Press.

Putnam, Robert D. 2000. *Bowling Alone: The Collapse and Revival of American Community.* New York: Simon & Schuster.

Rand, Ayn. 1957. *Atlas Shrugged.* New York: Random House.

Rauch, Jonathan. 1999. *Government's End: Why Washington Stopped Working.* New York: Public Affairs.

Richwine, Jason, and Andrew Biggs. 2011. *Assessing the Compensation of Public School Teachers*. Washington, DC: Heritage Foundation.

Rubin, P. H., and J. Shepherd. 2007. "Tort Reform and Accidental Deaths." *Journal of Law and Economics* 50: 221–38.

Ryan, Paul. 2014. *The Way Forward: Renewing the American Idea*. New York: Hachette Book Group.

Sandefur, Timothy. 2006. *Cornerstone of Liberty: Property Rights in 21st-Century America*. Washington, DC: Cato Institute.

———. 2010. *The Right to Earn a Living: Economic Freedom and the Law*. Washington, DC: Cato Institute.

Schuck, Peter. 2014. *Why Government Fails So Often: And How It Can Do Better*. Princeton: Princeton University Press.

Schweizer, Peter. 2011. *Throw Them All Out: How Politicians and Their Friends Get Rich Off Insider Stock Tips, Land Deals, and Cronyism that Would Send the Rest of Us to Prison*. Boston: Houghton Mifflin Harcourt.

———. 2013. *Extortion: How Politicians Extract Your Money, Buy Votes, and Line Their Own Pockets*. Boston: Houghton Mifflin Harcourt.

Silverglate, Harvey A. 2009. *Three Felonies a Day: How the Feds Target the Innocent*. New York: Encounter.

Smith, Adam. 1759. *The Theory of Moral Sentiments*. 1979 ed. Oxford: Oxford University Press.

Stein, Herbert. 1998. *What I Think: Essays on Economics, Politics, and Life*. Washington, DC: AEI Press.

Strazella, James A. 1998. *The Federalization of Criminal Law*. Washington, DC: American Bar Association.

Sunstein, Cass R. 2009. *A Constitution of Many Minds: Why the Founding Document Doesn't Mean What It Meant Before*. Princeton: Princeton University Press.

———. 2013a. "The Office of Information and Regulatory Affairs: Myths and Realities." *Harvard Law Review* 126: 1838–878.

———. 2013b. *Simpler: The Future of Government*. New York: Simon & Schuster.

Thayer, James B. 1893. *The Origin and Scope of the American Doctrine of Constitutional Law*. Boston: Little, Brown.

Tocqueville, Alexis de. 1838. *Democracy in America*. Translated by Henry Reeve. 1904 ed. New York: Adlard & Saunders.

Trilling, Lionel. 1950. *The Liberal Imagination: Essays on Literature and Society*. New York: Viking Press.

Twain, Mark, and Charles Dudley Warner. 1873. *The Gilded Age: A Tale of Today*. Hartford, CT: American Publishing Co.

US Bureau of the Census. 1975. *Historical Statistics of the United States, Colonial Times to 1970*. 2 vols. Washington, DC: US Bureau of the Census.

Viscusi, W. Kip. 2013. "Does Product Liability Law Make Us Safer?" In *The American Illness: Essays on the Rule of Law*, edited by F. H. Buckley, Part 3. New Haven: Yale University Press.

Weber, Max. 1918. "Politics as a Vocation." In *From Max Weber: Essays in Sociology*, edited by C. Wright Mills, 77–128. London: Routledge.

Wettergreen, John Adams. 1988. *The Regulatory Revolution and the New Bureaucratic State.* Washington, DC: Heritage Foundation.

Wilson, Woodrow. 1913. "What Is Progress?" Project Gutenberg. www.gutenberg.org.

Yu, Frank, and Xiaoyun Yu. 2011. "Corporate Lobbying and Fraud Detection." *Journal of Financial and Quantitative Analysis* 46: 1865–891.

Ziobrowski, Alan J., et al. 2004. "Abnormal Returns from the Common Stock Investments of the U.S. Senate." *Journal of Financial and Quantitative Analysis* 39 (4): 661–76.

Index

Page numbers in *italics* refer to charts.

Printed in the United States
by Baker & Taylor Publisher Services